WOOLWICH

THROUGH TIME

Kristina Bedford

AMBERLEY PUBLISHING

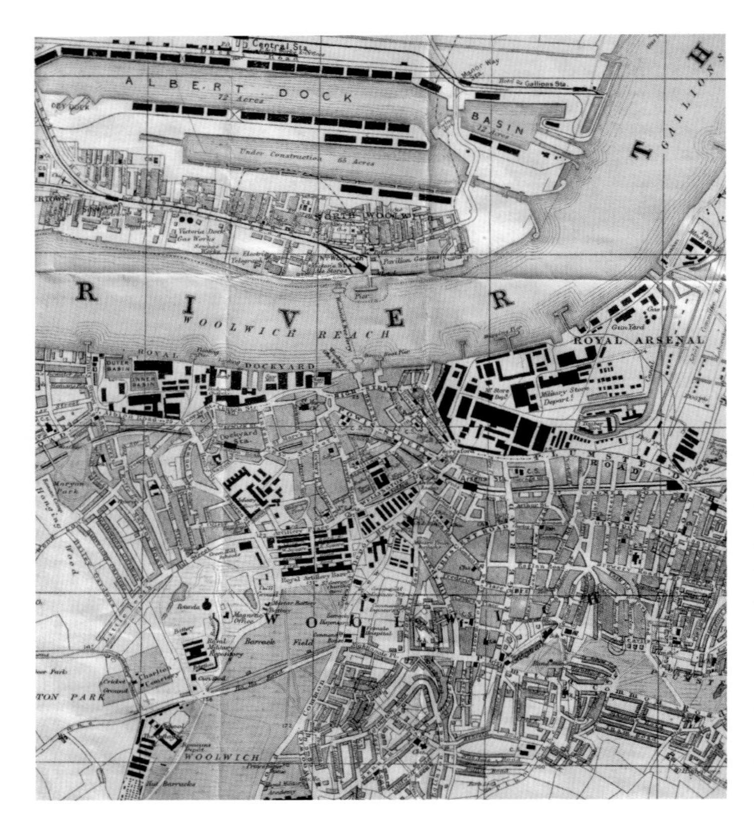

Detailed Map of Woolwich
This segment reproduced from G. W. Bacon & Co.'s *Large Scale Plan of Woolwich, Including Plumstead, Eltham, Blackheath, Bromley, and Chislehurst* (no date, *c.* 1920) demonstrates the military identity of Woolwich, south of the Thames in Kent, with North Woolwich in Essex predominantly defined by its docks.

For Ken, ever and always, and for the residents and workers of Woolwich who stopped to share stories and memories, concerned to preserve their village at a time of radical change.

What is the city but the people?
True,
The people are the city.

(William Shakespeare, *Coriolanus*, Act III, scene i)

First published 2014

Amberley Publishing
The Hill, Stroud, Gloucestershire, GL5 4EP
www.amberley-books.com

ISBN 978 1 4456 1599 8 (print)
ISBN 978 1 4456 1608 7 (ebook)

British Library Cataloguing in Publication Data.
A catalogue record for this book is available from the British Library.

Typesetting by Amberley Publishing.
Printed in Great Britain.

Introduction

Woolwich lies 9 miles from London, within the Hundred of Blackheath, recorded in Domesday as Grenviz (Greenwich) Hundred, straddling both banks of the Thames. Historically in the county of Kent to the south and Essex to the north, from 1900 it was counted with Eltham and Plumstead as the Borough of Woolwich, before it was subsumed into the Greater London Area in 1965 as part of the Borough of Greenwich. The ancient parish boundaries of North Woolwich touch Barking and Barking Creek, while the significantly larger area south of the river adjoins Charlton and Eltham to the west and Plumstead to the east. Although decreed to fall within the Royal Manor of Eltham, it was considered a manor in itself, gifted as such by King Henry II in around 1160 to the church of St John the Baptist.

Woolwich appears in the Domesday Book as 'hvlviz', but its Old English equivalent of 'Wull-wic', meaning 'town where wool was exported', is more recognisable to the modern eye. Within the Half-Lathe of Sutton, 63 acres pertaining to Woolwich were then held by Haimo, the sheriff, under Odo, Bishop of Bayeux, Earl of Kent and half-brother to William the Conqueror, who had granted him the lands, including the detached section on the north bank. Until 1066, the acreage was held under Edward the Confessor by William the Falconer. By 1086 it housed eleven bordars (smallholders), paying 41*d*, with the whole worth £3. When Odo fell from favour in around 1090, his estates in Eltham and their appurtenances in Woolwich were confiscated by the Crown. Following its ecclesiastic grant, the Manor of Woolwich passed through a series of laymen's hands, including: Gilbert de Marisco, who took his name from his estate in the marshes, early in the reign of King Edward I (1272–1307); Sabina de Windlesore in 1324; and Sir John de Pulteney in 1327, who also held an estate of some 100 acres in the north marshes, the parcel of the Manor of Poplar, formerly belonging to the Abbey of St Mary de Grace near the

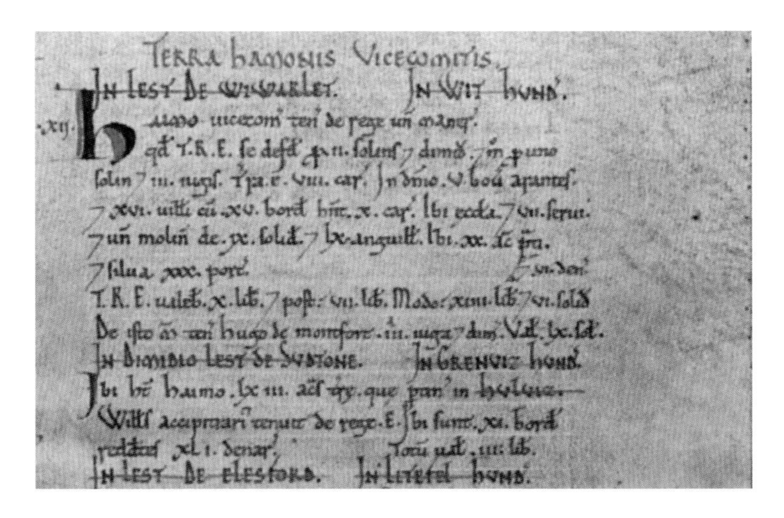

Woolwich's Entry in Great Domesday
Woolwich, Kent Folio: 14r Great Domesday Book, *The National Archives, ref. E 31/2/1/451.*

Tower of London. In 1328, the Earl of Hereford granted Sir John his interest in the same estate as the Manor of Southall in Woolwich. Sir John died seised of the estate in 1349. His son and heir William died childless in 40 Edward III (1366–67), having granted his Manor of Southall in trust to John, Bishop of Worcester, and others, four years earlier. John Revel, in pursuance of another trust granted by Sir William de Pulteney, quitclaimed the Manor to Sir Nicolas Lovain, Aubrey de Vere, and others, in 48 Edward III (1374–75). Held by William Chichele in around 1400, it was inherited by his son John, who in turn dowered it at the marriage of his eldest daughter Agnes to John Tattershall; according to an Inquisition dated 25 Henry VI (1446/47), the Manor of Woolwiche then consisted of two messuages, three tofts, 342 acres of arable, meadow, marsh, woodland, and 30s rent in Woolwiche.

Woolwich had a dockyard by 1512, when the ship *Henry Grace à Dieu*, also known as 'The Great Harry', was built there. In 1546, Sir Edward Boughton, who held the Manor of Southall, conveyed to King Henry VIII two parcels of land named Bowton's Docks and two parcels named Our Lady-hill and Sand-hill, with the docklands continuing to increase over time. The gunwharf is likewise of an early date; originally sited where the market place evolved, it moved to Woolwich Warren to provide a gun depot for the Naval ordnance, a brass cannon foundry, a laboratory for making gunpowder and cartridges for both Army and Navy, and a repository for machinery used by both services. The Warren was also the first home of the Royal Artillery, before construction of the barracks began in 1774, and the Royal Military Academy, popularly known as 'The Shop' because of its workshop quarters that relocated in 1806. The Warren developed into the sprawling Royal Arsenal factory complex, which extended over 1,300 acres by the First World War, prompting the redevelopment of rural Eltham to supply urban housing for its influx of workers. Currently in the midst of redevelopment, with the high-rises springing from the old Arsenal grounds behind market stalls greatly reduced in numbers, Woolwich is here captured at a moment of profound transition – and heightened security, following the assassination of drummer Lee Rigby at Artillery Place on 22 May 2013. Today's Woolwich will be profoundly different tomorrow, with reviewing the past through time an essential, as well as agreeable, pastime.

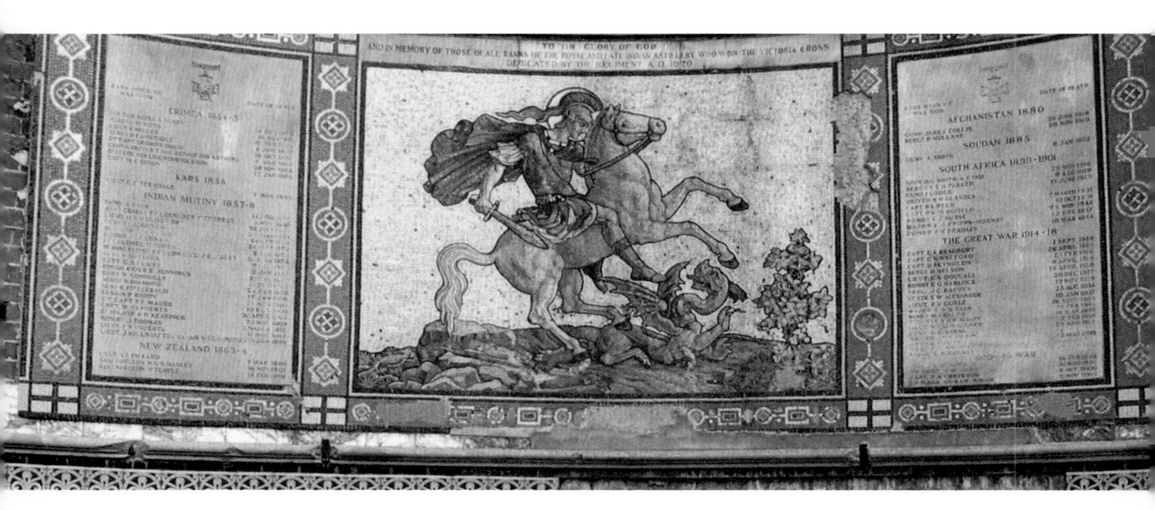

St George's Royal Garrison Church Mosaic, 16 September 2007
Pictured during London Open House, two months after the last Artillery Regiment left the barracks.

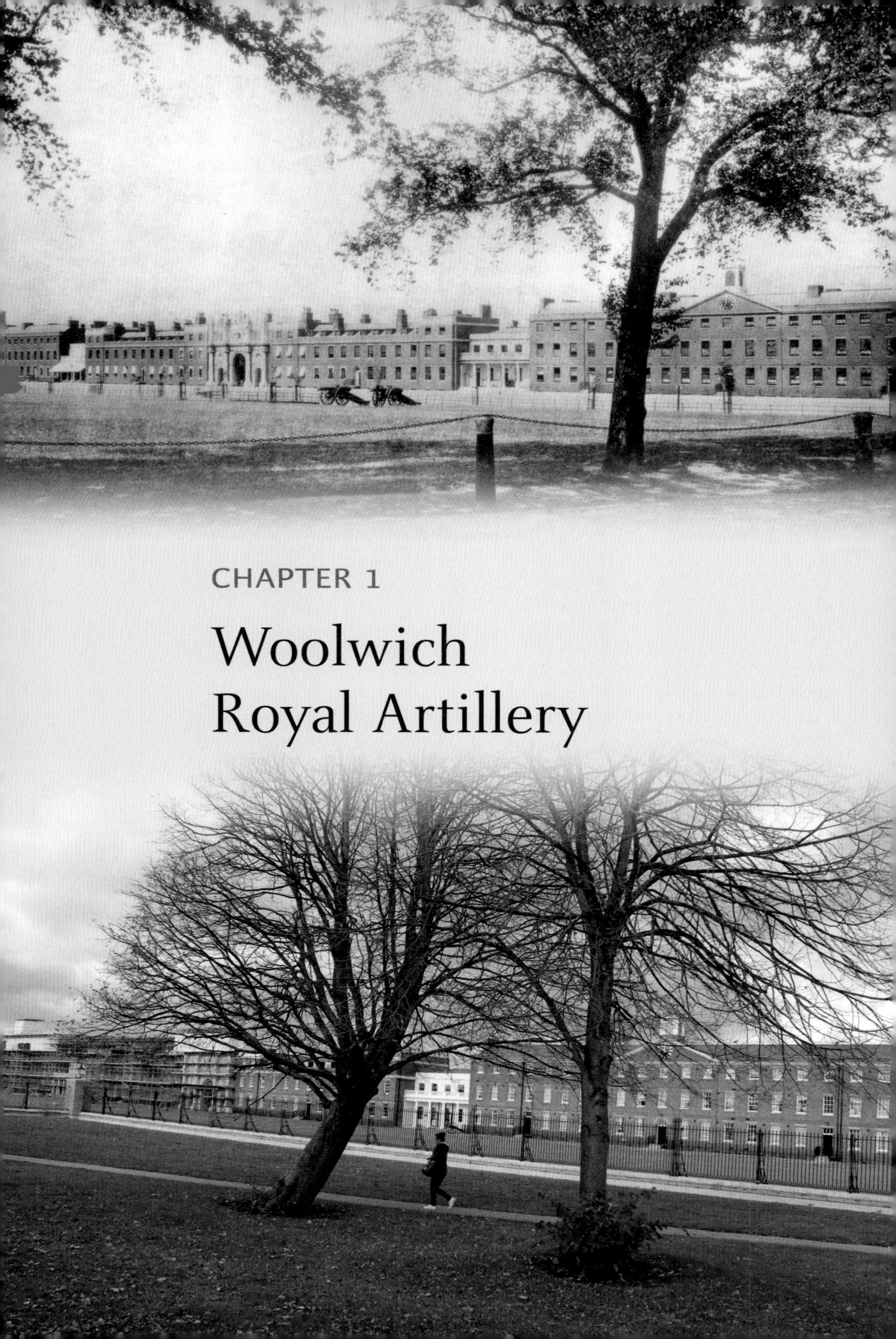

CHAPTER 1

Woolwich Royal Artillery

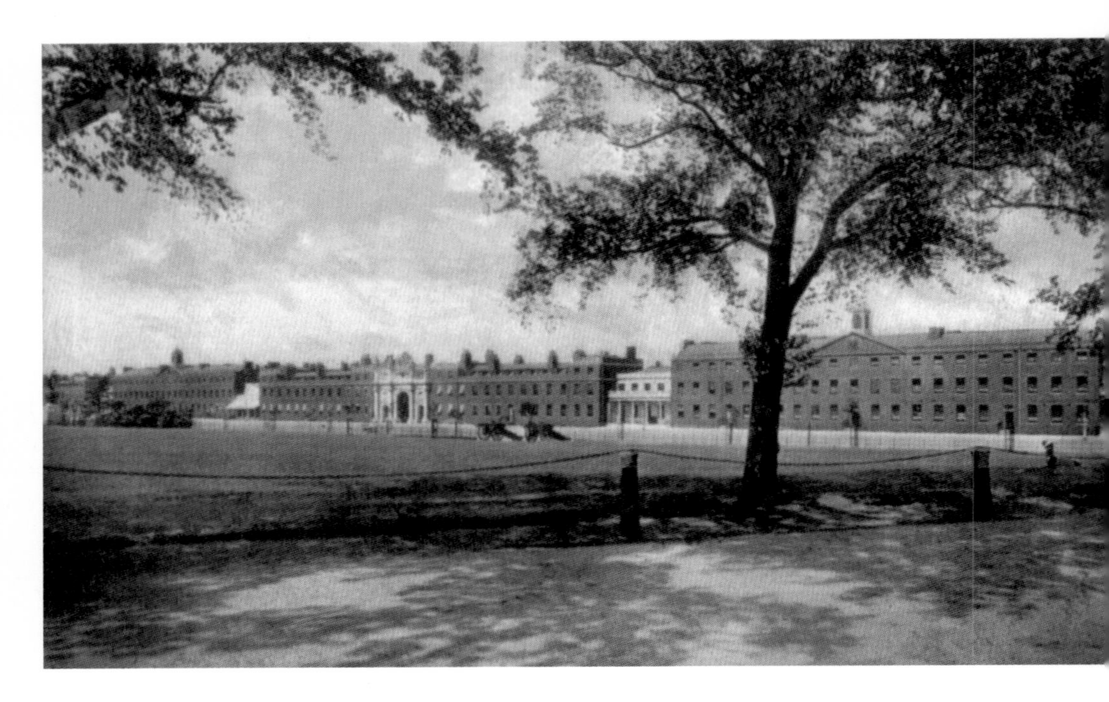

Royal Artillery Barracks, Woolwich, 1905

Commonly known as the 'Gunners', the Royal Artillery was formed at Woolwich by Royal Warrant of King George I in 1716. Having used Woolwich Common for testing ordnance during the 1720s, and for artillery practice in 1773, the Board of Ordnance acquired land, including the northernmost section of the common that same year, to provide a site for the the barracks, which were built between 1776 and 1802. This elegant neoclassical edifice boasts the longest continuous façade in the UK, being a fifth of a mile long.

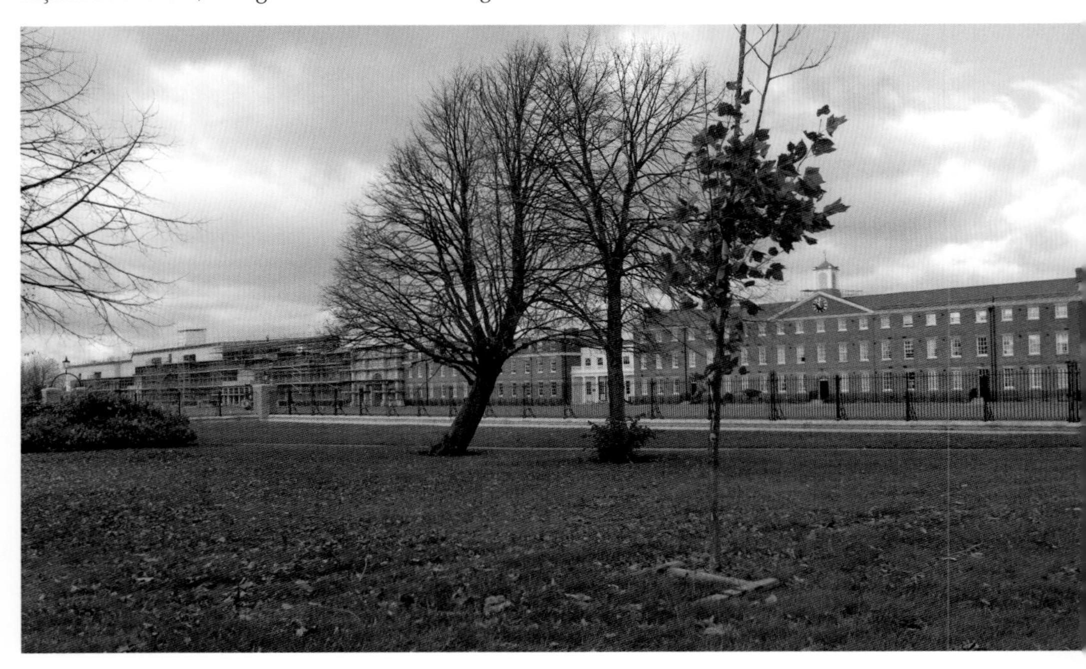

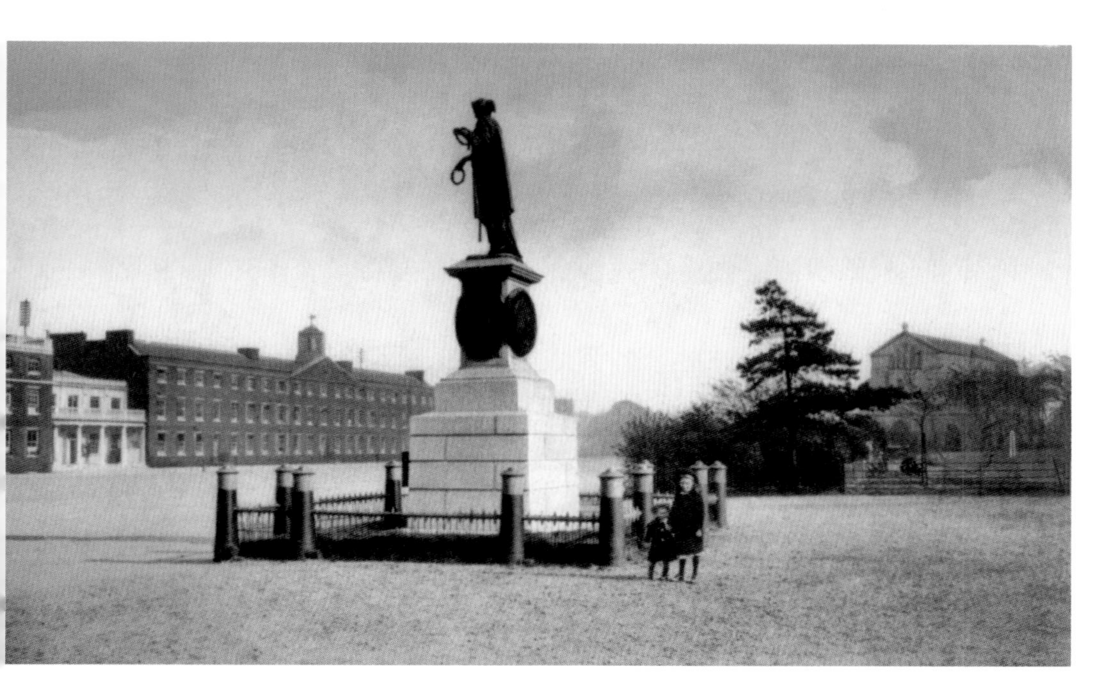

Crimean Memorial, Woolwich

Still holding a central position on the widened parade ground, although situated further south since 2008, the Royal Regiment of Artillery's Crimean memorial dominates the landscape. Sculptor John Bell made the statue in 1861, originally intending her to stand directly in front of the central arch, facing south, with trophies and guns lining the parade, which would have obstructed drill. Despite Bell's objections, she was therefore positioned on the parade's southern edge, facing north toward Woolwich Barracks, in January 1862.

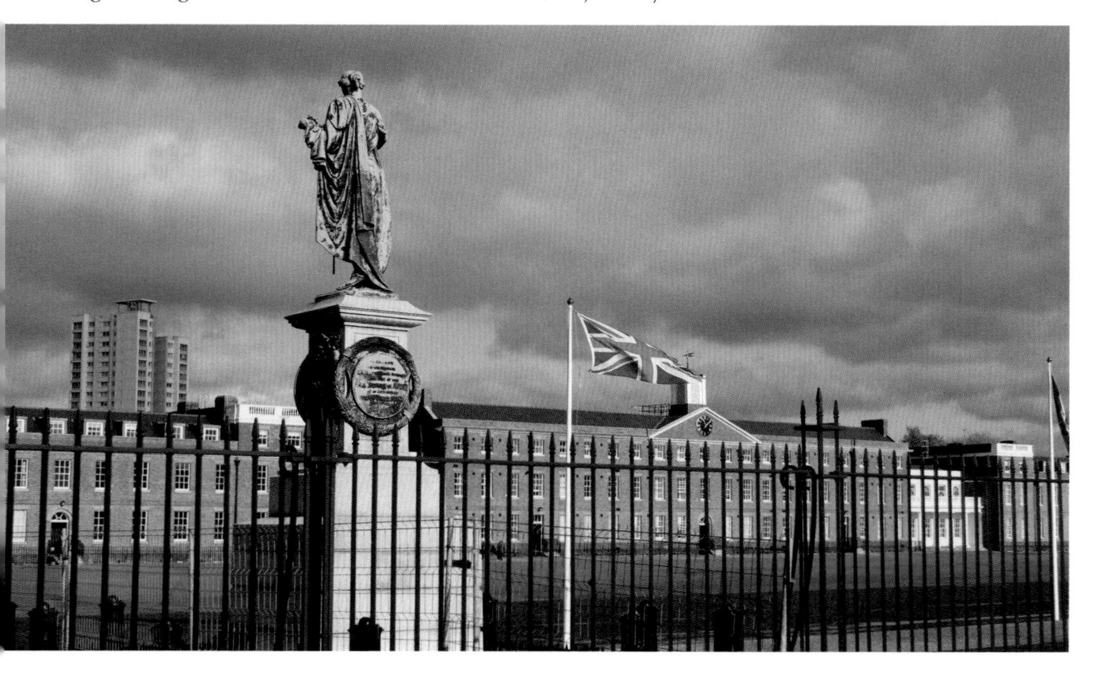

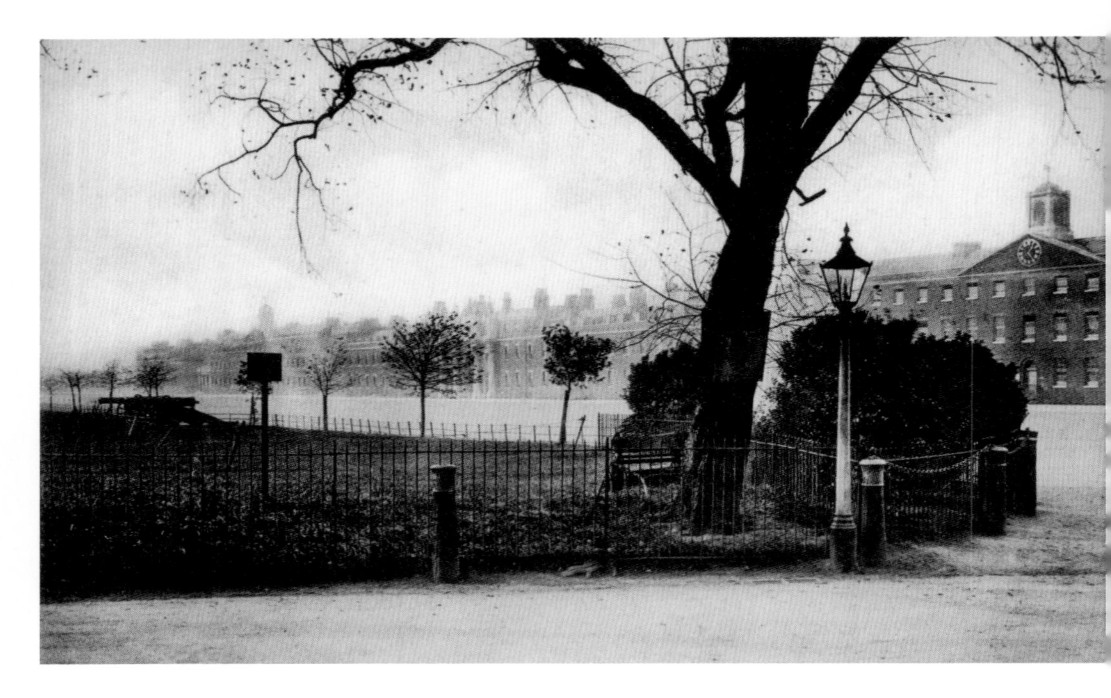

Royal Artillery Barracks, Woolwich

The Crimean memorial represents Honour – a nearly 10-foot-tall bronze figure, cast from Russian cannon, captured in 1855 at Sebastopol – distributing laurel wreaths. She stands on a substantial granite plinth, bearing bronze wreathed inscriptions and cartouches with regimental arms, inside an enclosure containing twelve cannon-bollards. For reasons lost to time, she is familiarly known to personnel as Barbara. The cannon, with other historic guns, accompanied the Royal Artillery to Larkhill, Wiltshire, in 2007. Iron railings now separate the memorial and the parade from Barrack Field.

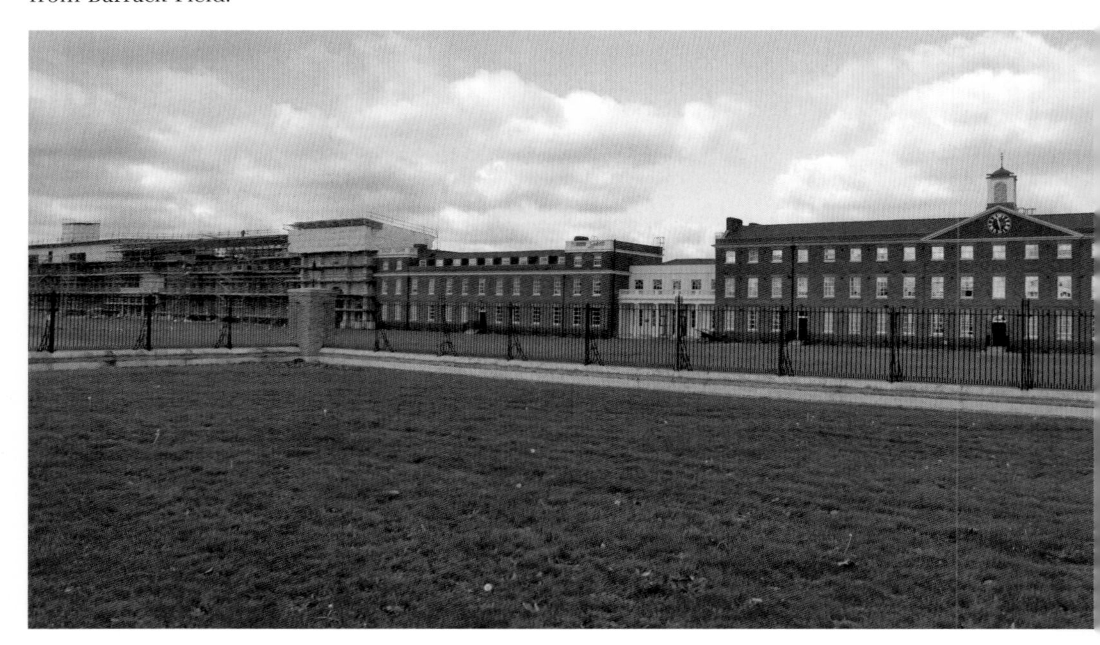

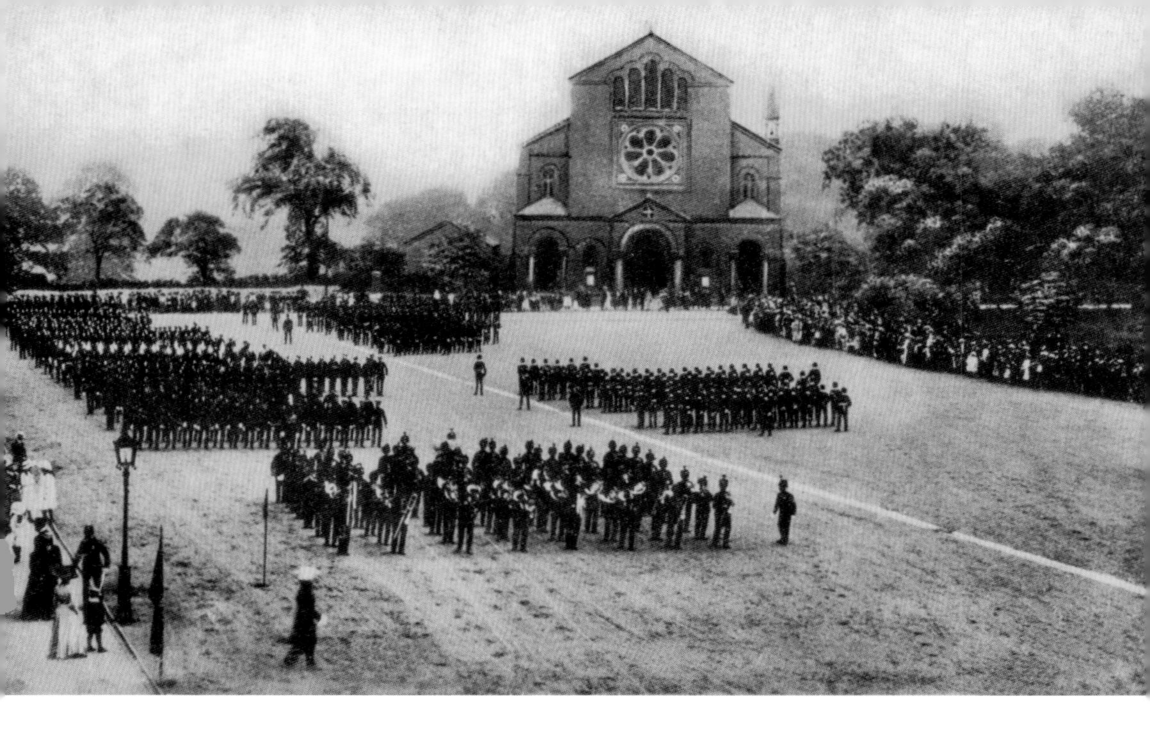

Garrison Church Parade, Woolwich

The Royal Artillery (RA) Parade is the largest in the UK. The central section of its ground, with the Crimean memorial, was extended southward in 2008 to provide a parade ground of the same dimensions as that at Horse Guards, and to accommodate the infantry battalion and companies of guards transferred to Woolwich. Security was also increased: dwarf-walls and iron railings now enclose the parade to the south, the east and the west, while the barracks provide a natural northern boundary. Spaced iron bollards separate the parade from the church approach.

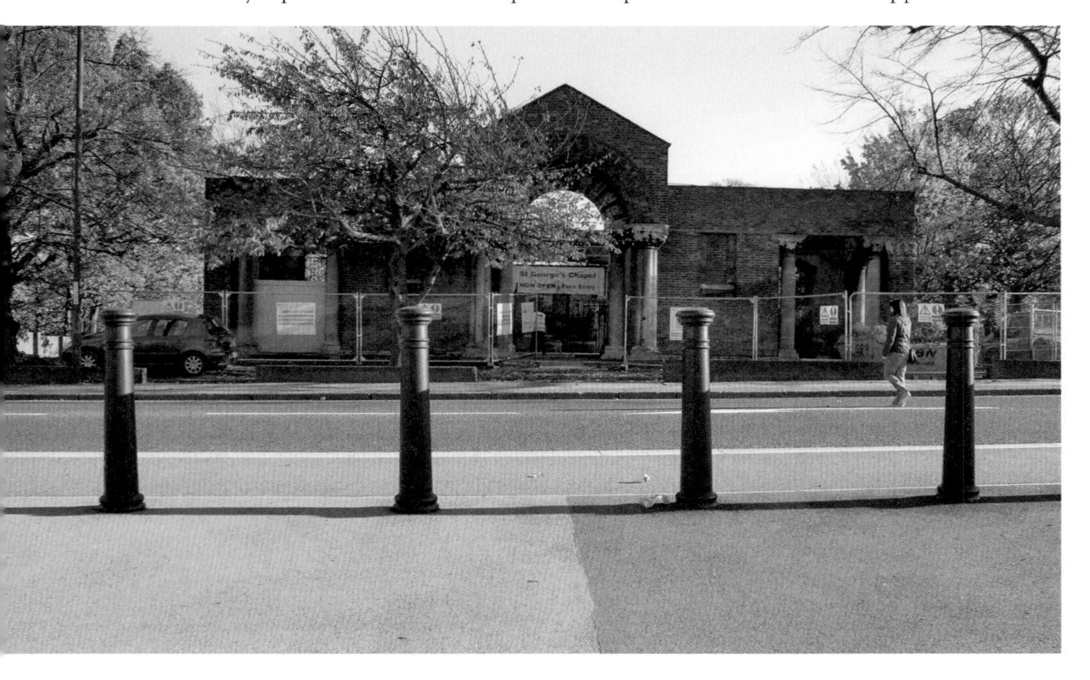

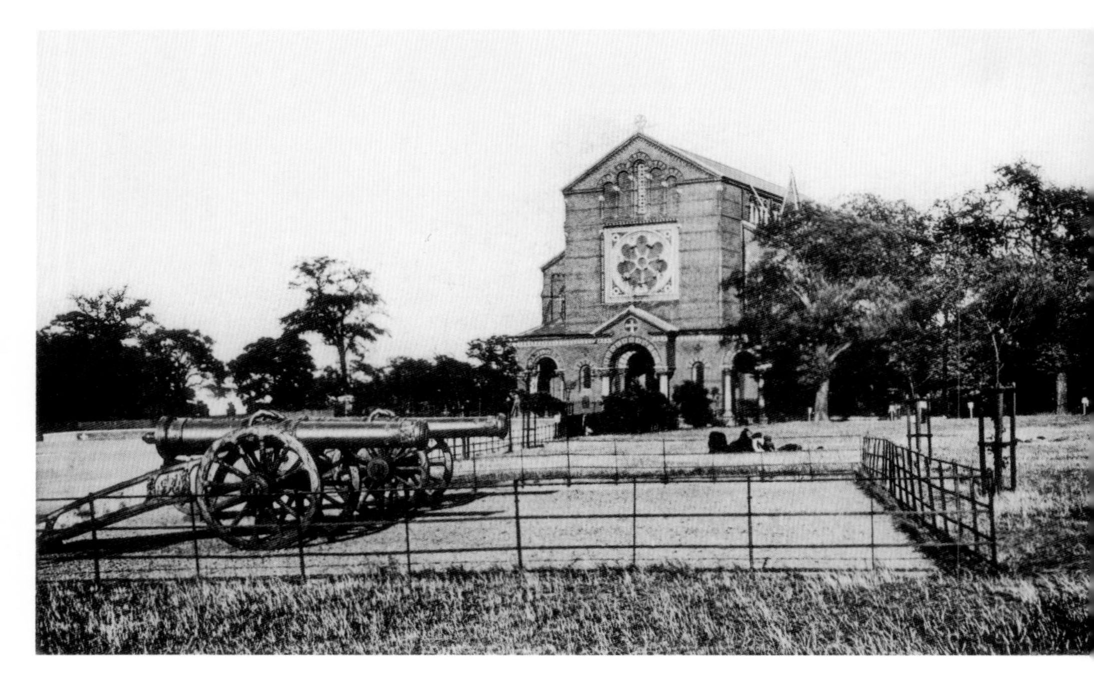

Garrison Church, Woolwich, ***c.*** **1915**

Built in the Lombardi style by Thomas Henry Wyatt between 1863 and 1867 in the Garrison Commandant's garden, St George's became a Royal Garrison church in 1928, following a visit by King George V. Its fabric suffered minor bomb damage during the First World War, only to be reduced to a shell when a flying bomb hit the eastern end of the RA Barracks on 13 July 1944. Its perimeter walls were later demolished to their lower sections, which frame a memorial garden.

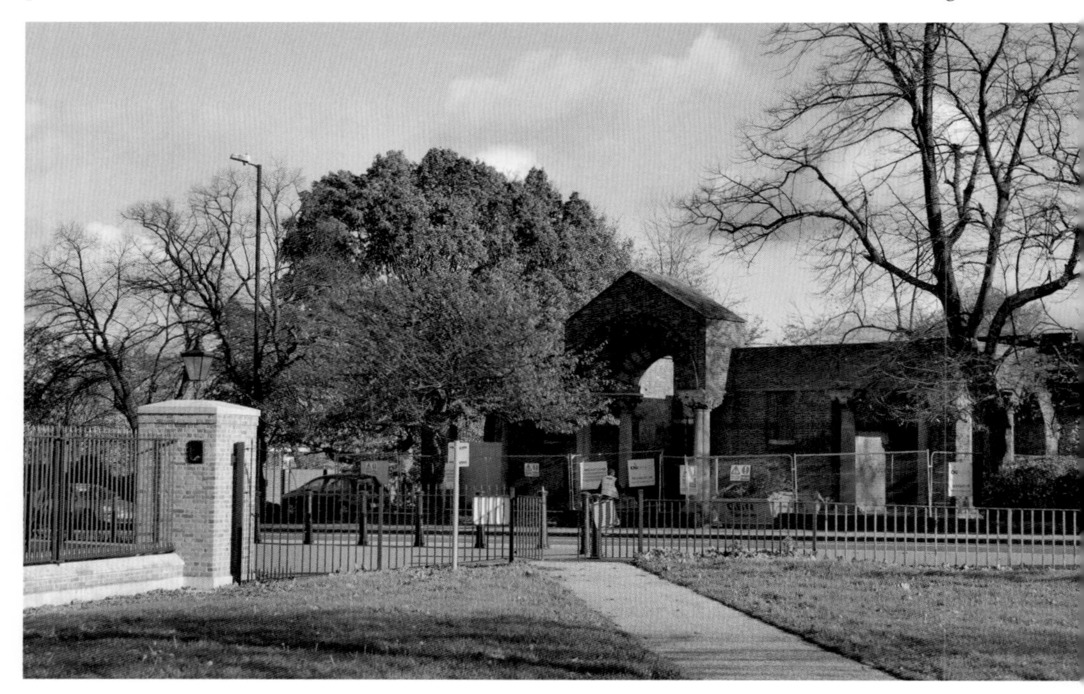

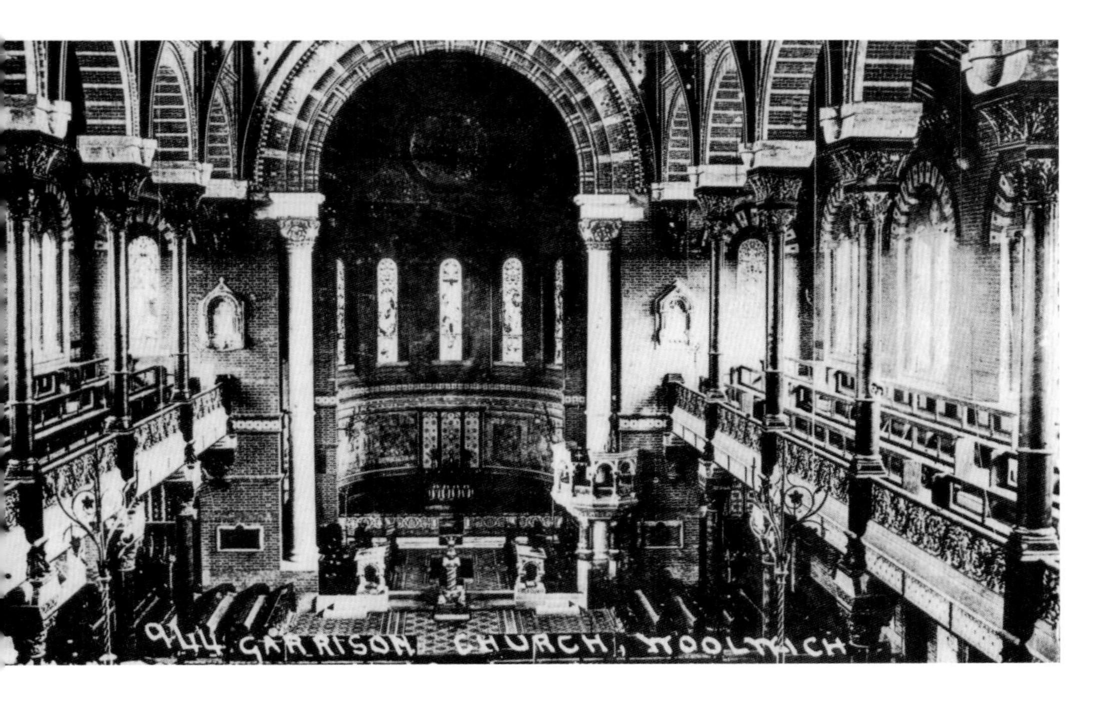

Garrison Church Interior, Woolwich

The church remained consecrated, hosting open-air services for barracks personnel. Surviving features include the altar, Antonio Salviati's mosaic of St George and the Dragon, and the Victoria Cross memorial, flanked by tablets bearing the names of Gunners from the Crimean War to the Second World War. A Grade II-listed building, St George's was on English Heritage's 'At Risk Register' when the Heritage Lottery Fund confirmed its grant of £396,100 towards restoration on 24 October 2011. Works began in 2012 and are still ongoing.

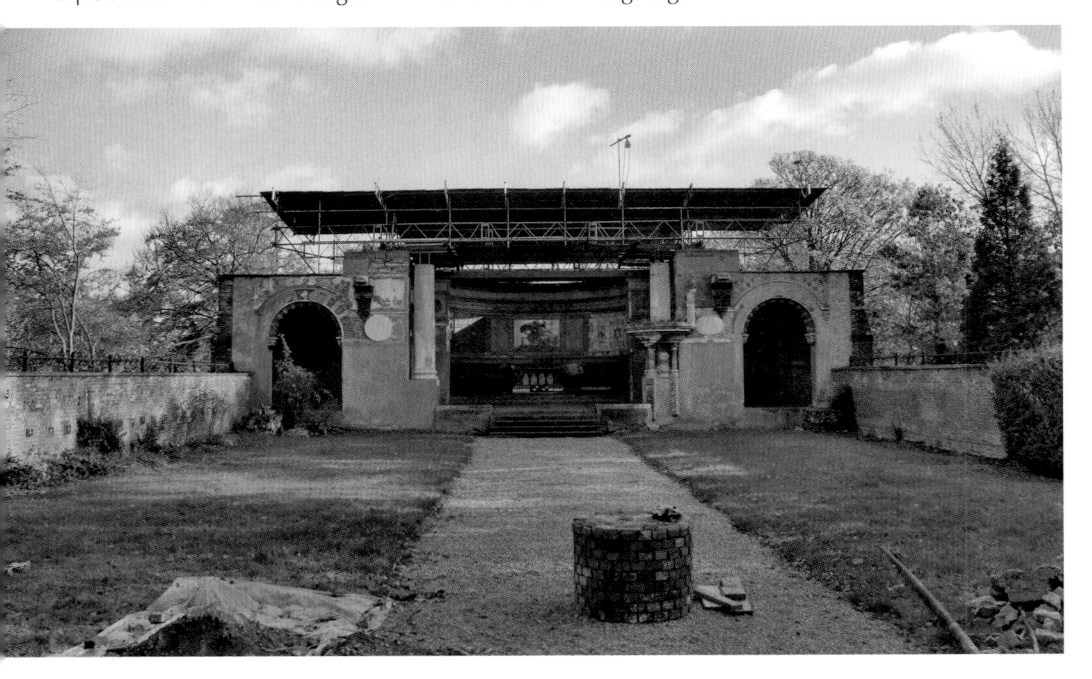

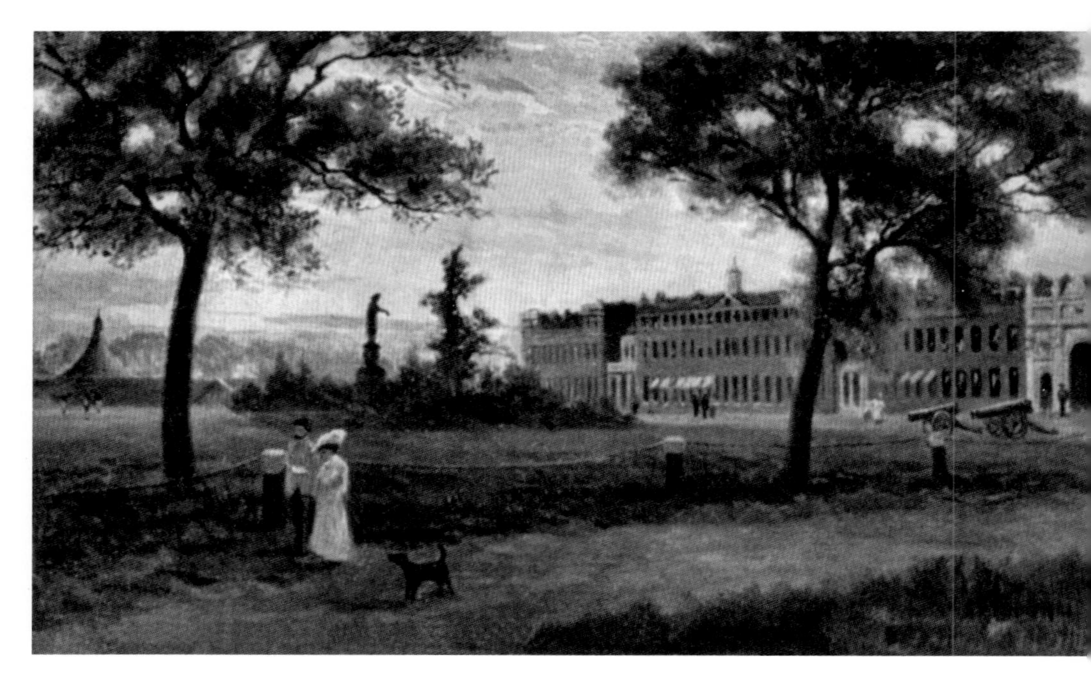

Royal Artillery Barracks, Crimean Memorial, Woolwich, North Kent

The artist who depicted Woolwich Barracks above has allowed himself a substantial degree of license in his painting, including Artillery icons unlikely to have been visible from this vantage point, even allowing for subsequent alterations to the landscape such as Barbara's migration south. The Rotunda dominates centre-left of the tree that the strolling couple and their dog are about to pass, under a romantic, sunset sky – all elements uniting to create an emblem of the grounds at their complete (if semi-fictionalised) best.

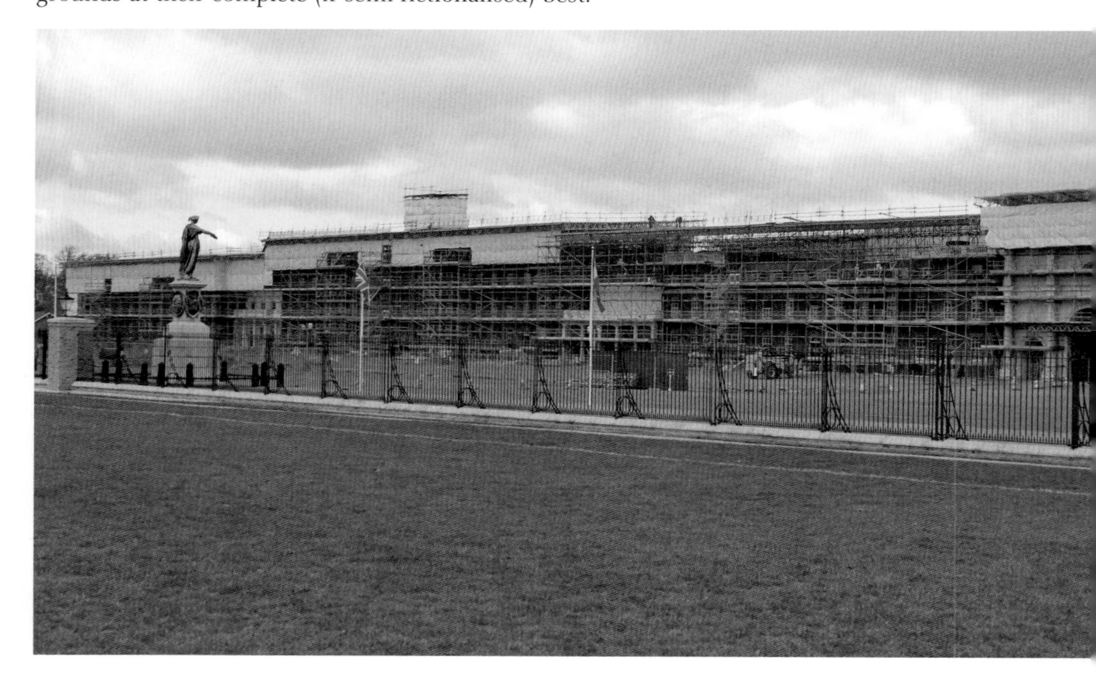

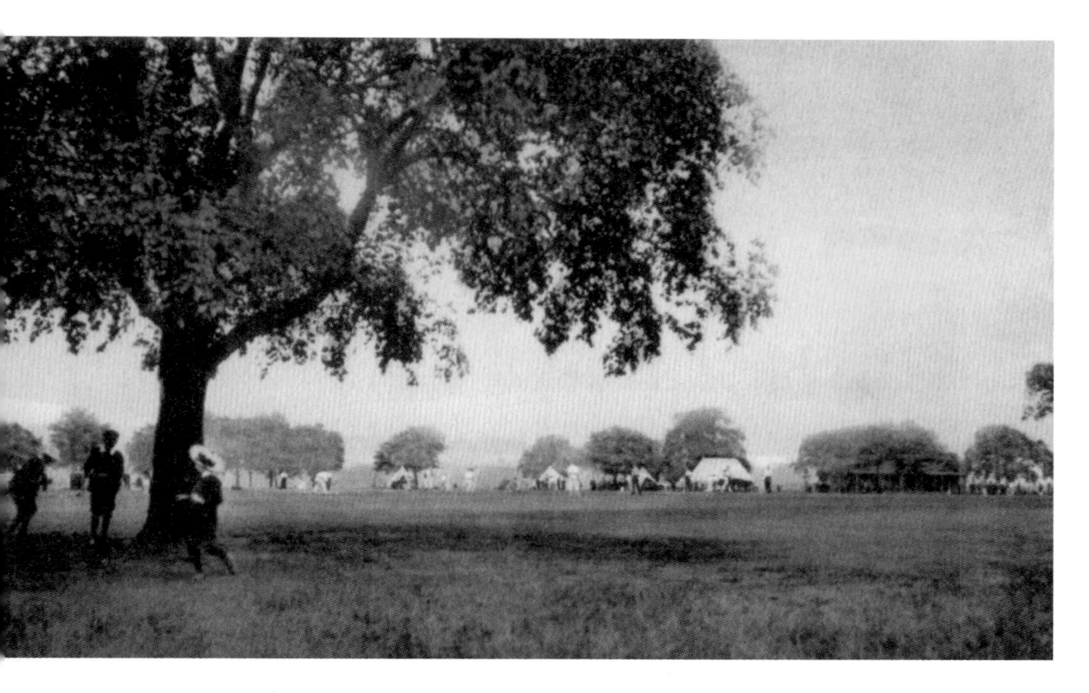

Barrack Field, Woolwich Common

Now separated from the parade ground by a substantial iron fence, Barrack Field was home to Woolwich Cricket Club during the mid-eighteenth century, soon after to Royal Artillery Cricket Club (RACC), whose first recorded match dates to 1765. RACC was constituted as a Regimental Club in 1906, having originally been founded by officers as a private club. Barrack Field is for RA recreational use only, though a public footpath parallel to the railing allows free passage between Repository and Grand Depot Roads.

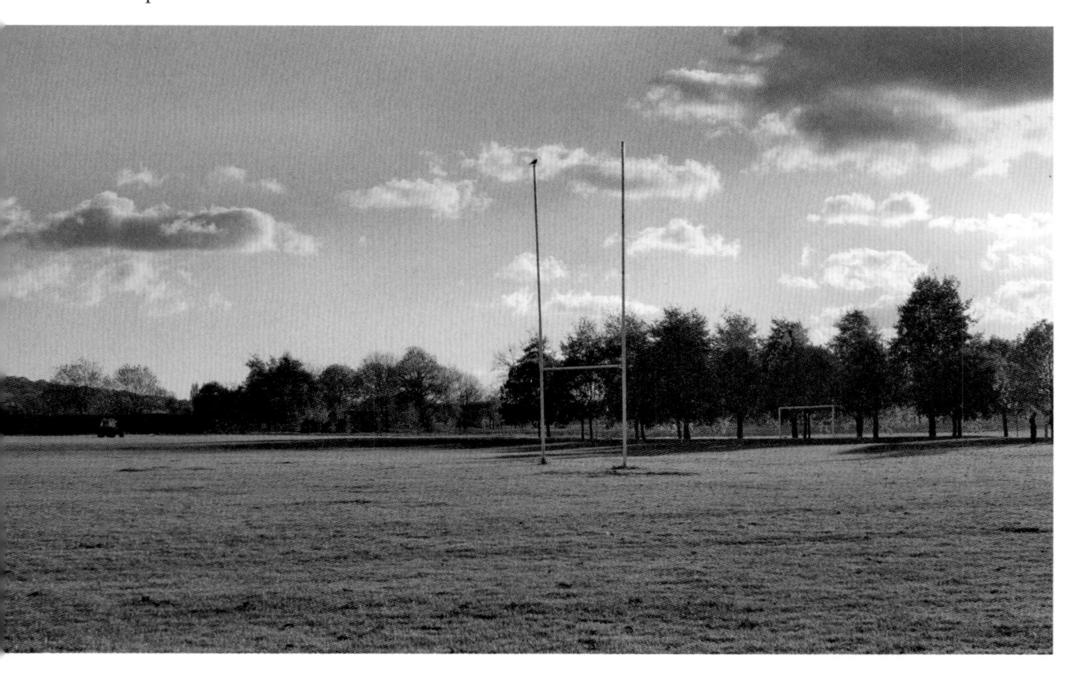

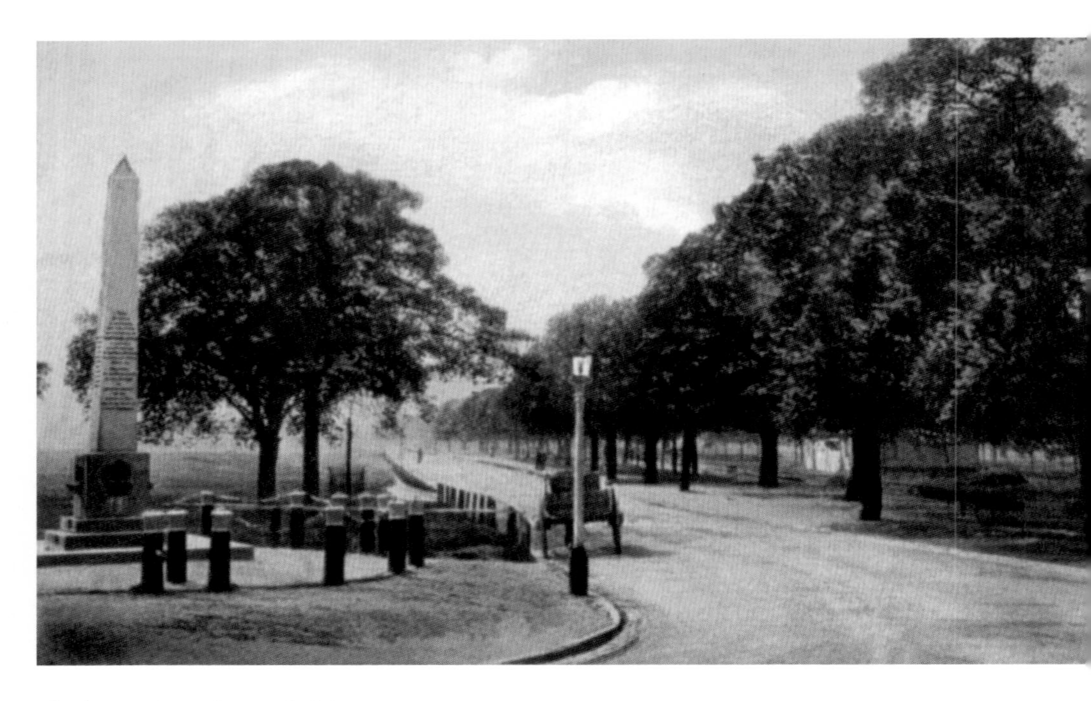

The 'Ha-Ha' Road, Woolwich Common, 1907

Taking its name from the sunken ditch installed in 1774 to separate Barrack Field from Woolwich Common, Ha-Ha Road follows the same path today, providing a transport route rather than protecting the military lands from incursion by wandering cattle, sheep and deer. The original Ha-Ha flanking Barrack Field survives today as a Grade II listed monument, its namesake road running as a continuation of Charlton Park Lane to the west and turning into Plumstead Common Road to the east.

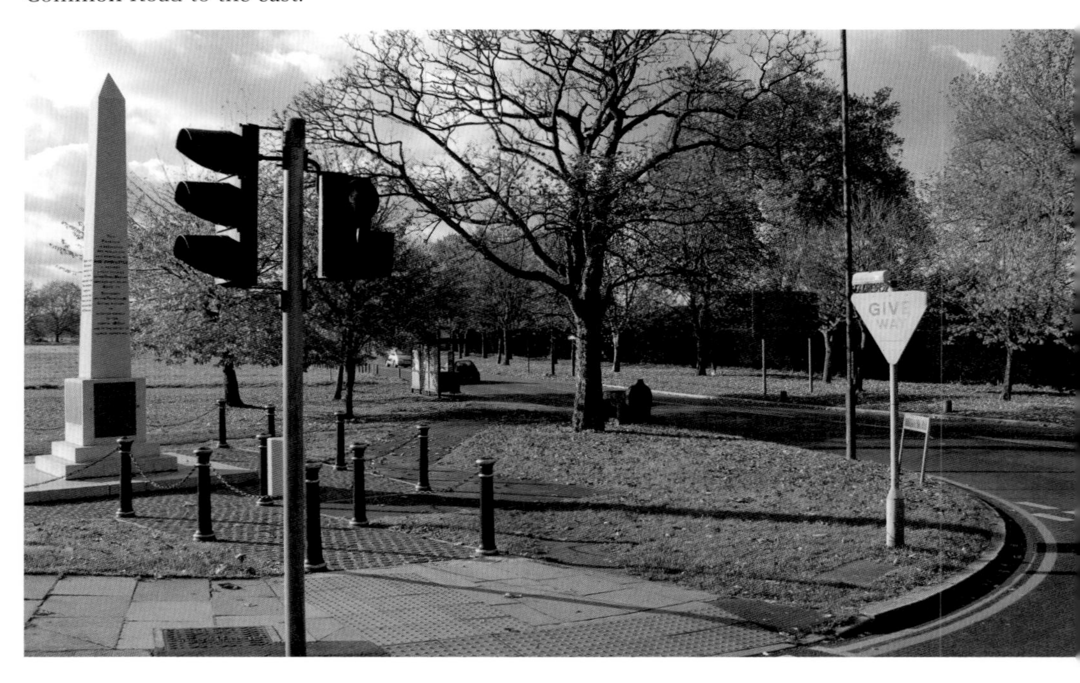

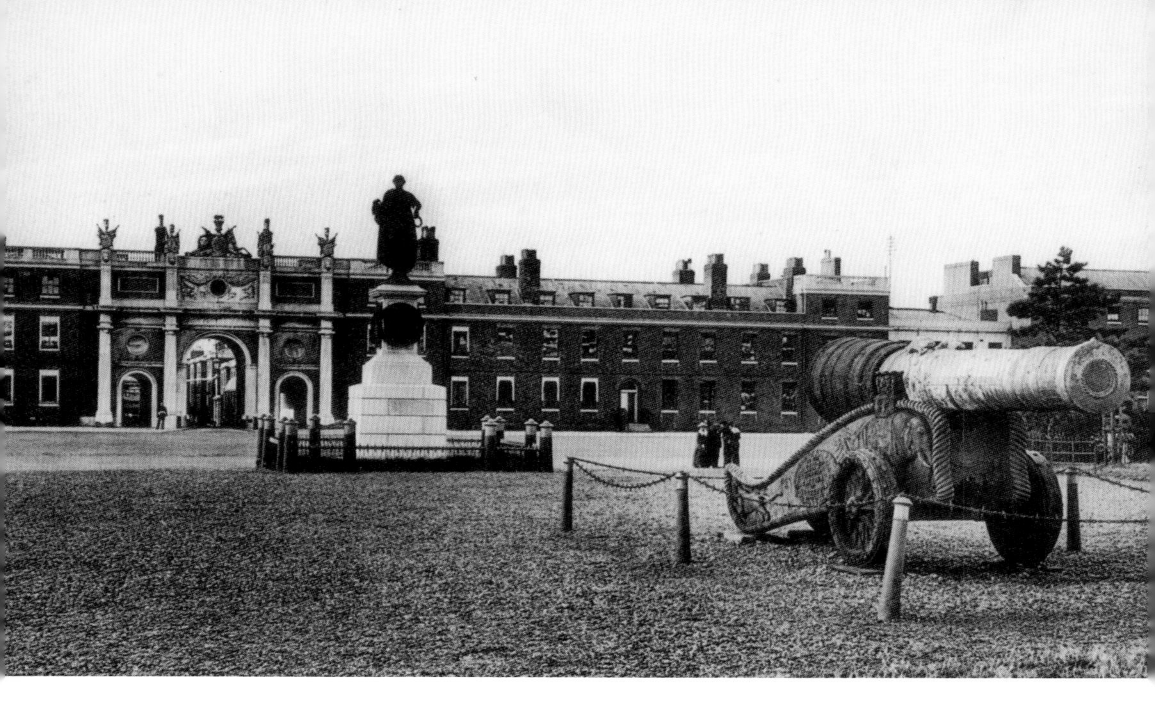

Gun, Monument, and Arch, RA Barracks Woolwich, *c.* 1915

The original displayed cannons, which were a common sight in the district throughout living memory, have been removed from the Royal Artillery grounds since the Gunners' departure in 2007, though a sampling may still be seen outside the Firepower Royal Artillery Museum at the Arsenal, the majority of its historic collection protected from the elements inside. While the parade and field may appear somewhat barren in the short term, redevelopment of the barracks is ongoing, with new sights continuing to appear.

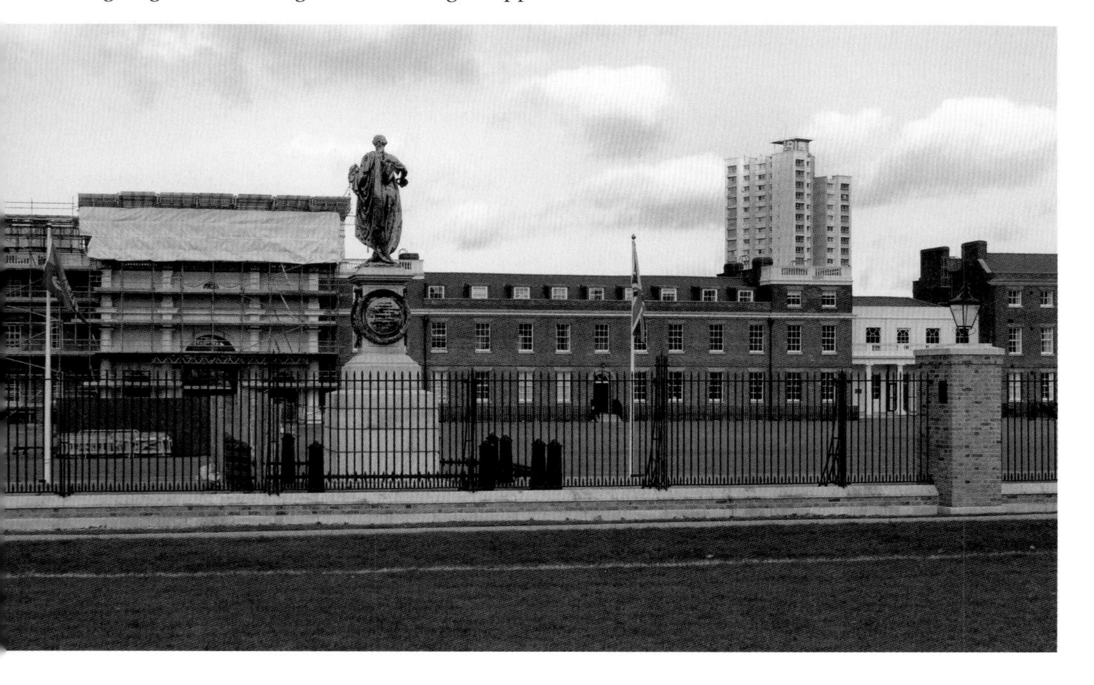

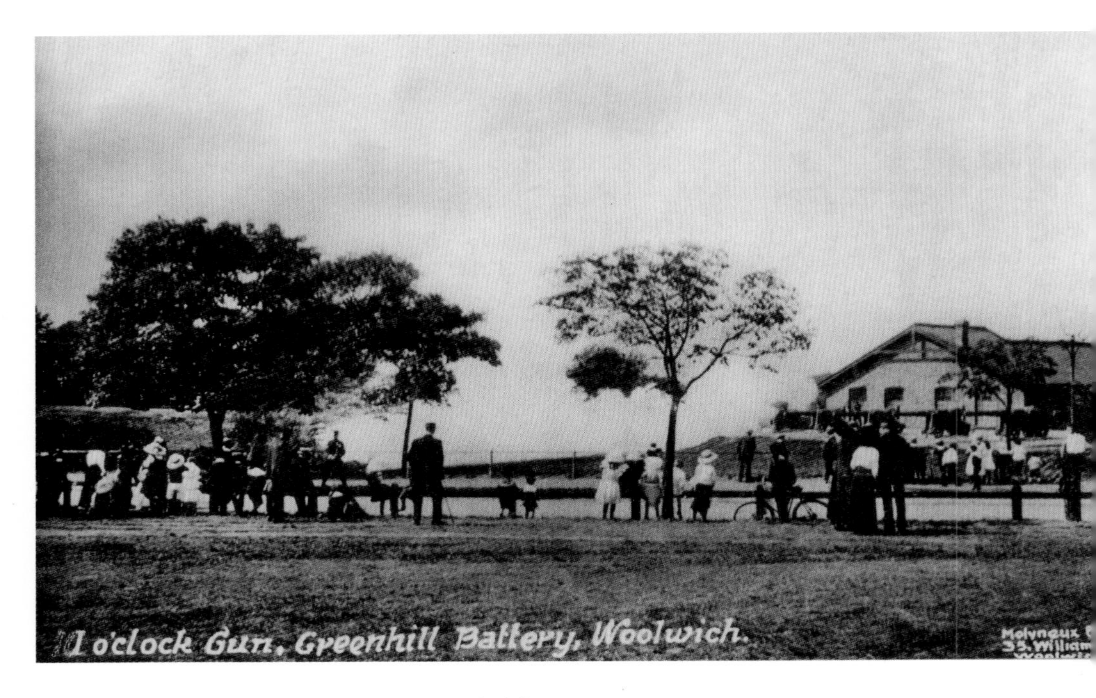

One o'Clock Gun, Greenhill Battery, Woolwich

Time Guns have been cast at the Royal Gun Factory (originally the Royal Brass Foundry) at Woolwich Arsenal for several centuries, exported to cities as far afield as Stanley Park, Vancouver (nine o'clock Gun, 1816) and Edinburgh, at its castle (one o'clock Gun, 1861). Today, the gun on display at Greenhill Court is a 42-ton 36-inch mortar, the largest built in England, as designed by Robert Mallet in 1854. It has fired nineteen shells in total, 'but never in war'.

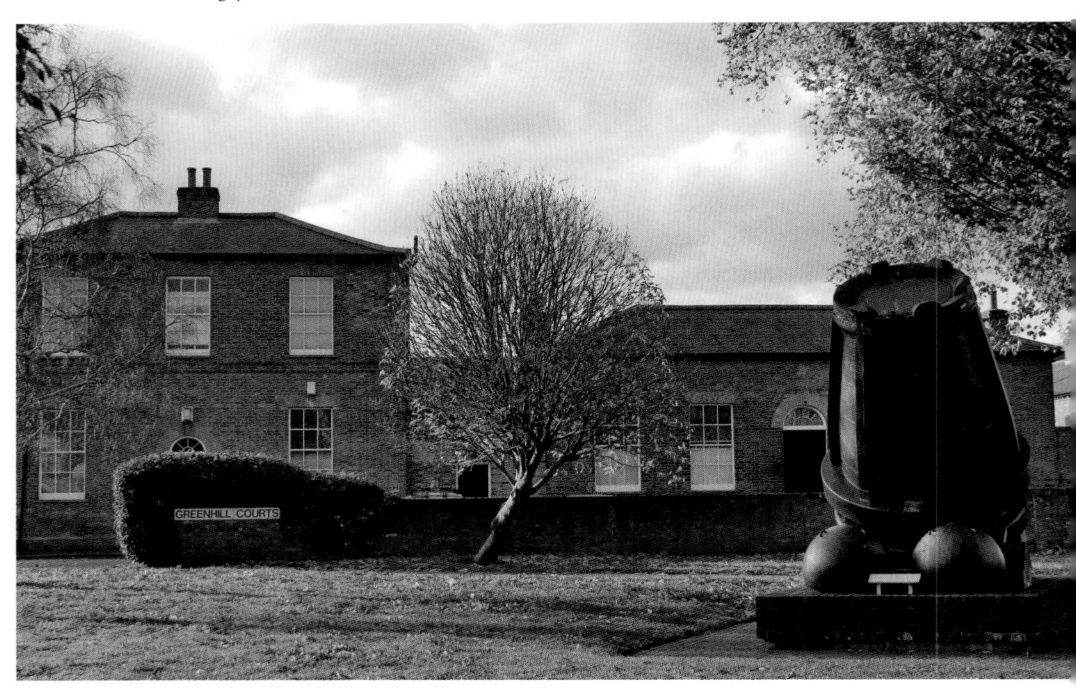

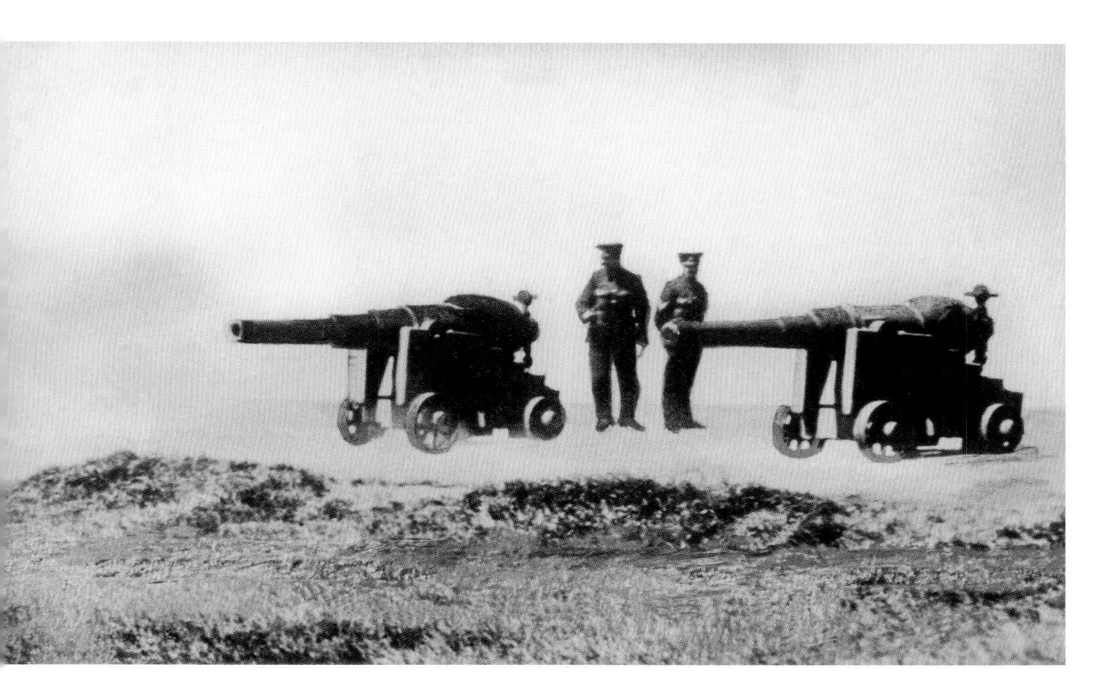

One o'Clock Gun, Woolwich, 1918, and Early Eighteenth-Century Iron Gun Discovered in 2011
According to the plaque at its foot, the iron cannon discovered during development at Napier Lines in 2011 'is an example of the first type of gun to be cast at Woolwich ... made under the direction of Colonel Albert Borgard (1659–1751) First Colonel of the Royal Regiment of Artillery and Firemaster of the Royal Arsenal.' Napier Lines has been home to The King's Troop, Royal Horse Artillery, since 2012. The iron gun is on display south-east of the Rotunda.

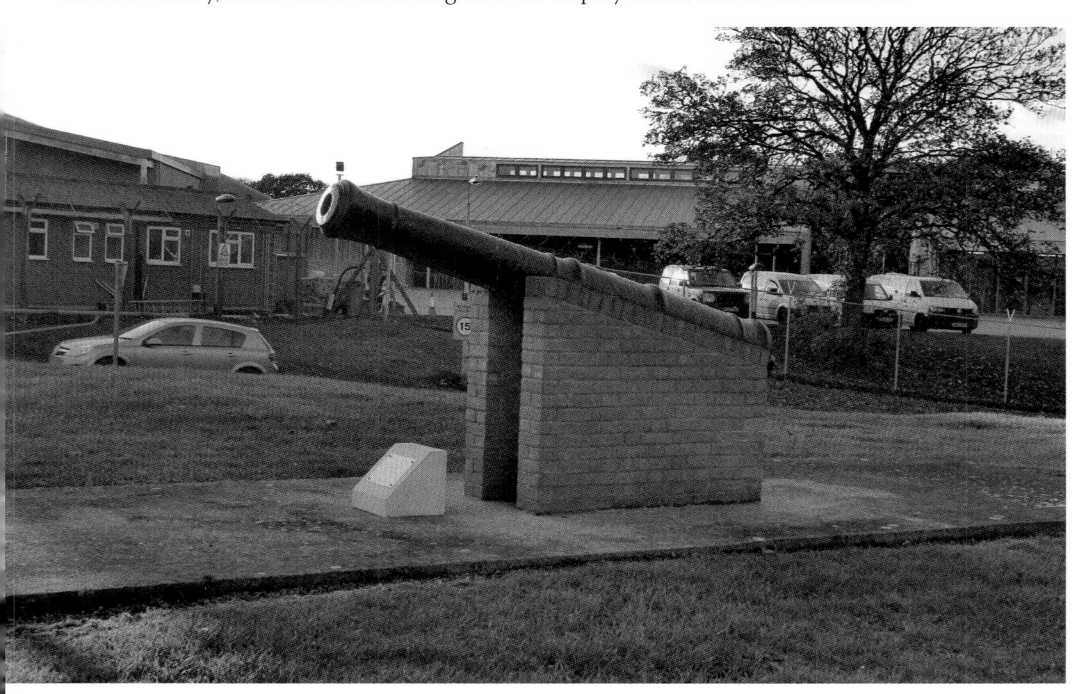

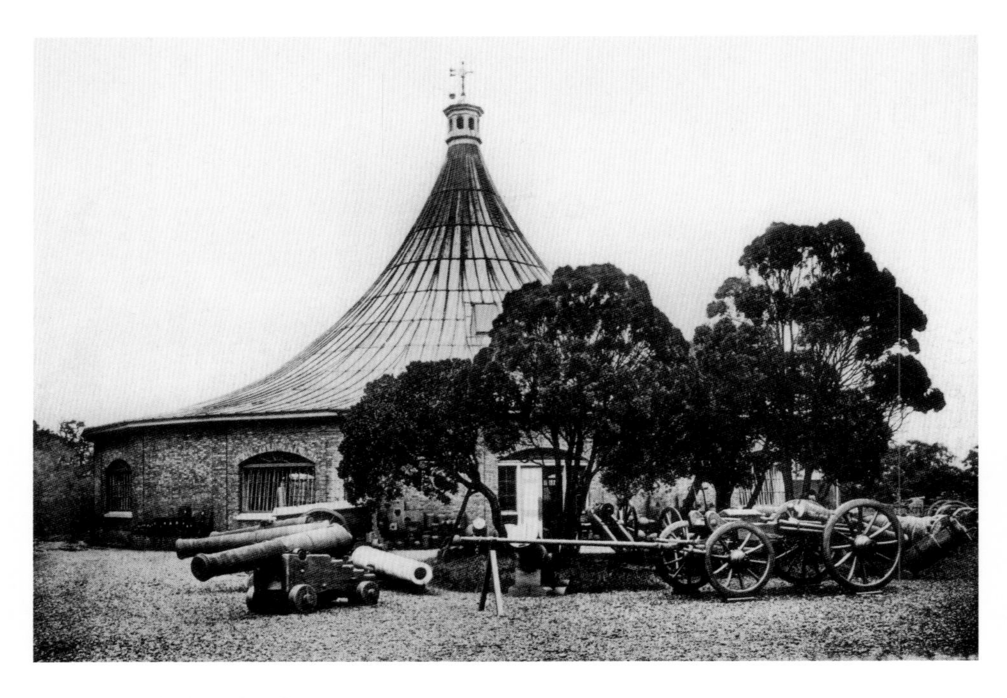

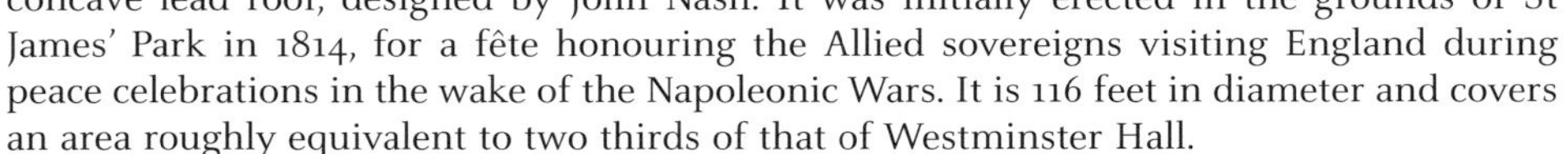

The Rotunda, Woolwich, *c.* 1915
Standing at the eastern boundary of Repository Woods, but approached through a separate entrance, the Rotunda is a twenty-four-sided, single-storey building, with a pagoda-style concave lead roof, designed by John Nash. It was initially erected in the grounds of St James' Park in 1814, for a fête honouring the Allied sovereigns visiting England during peace celebrations in the wake of the Napoleonic Wars. It is 116 feet in diameter and covers an area roughly equivalent to two thirds of that of Westminster Hall.

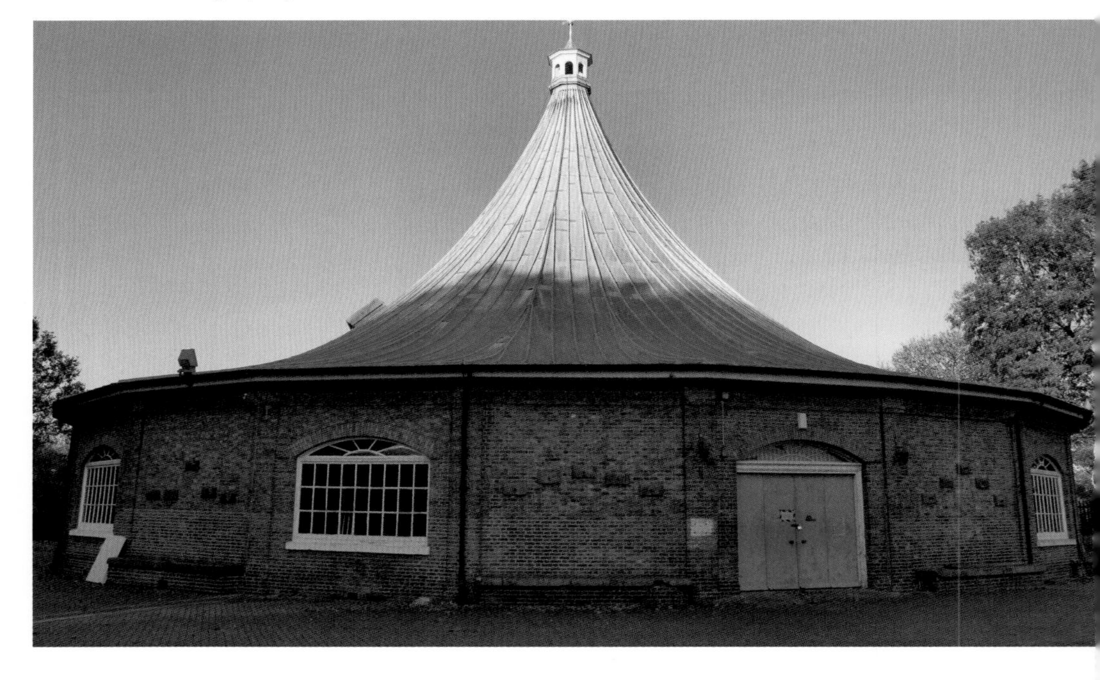

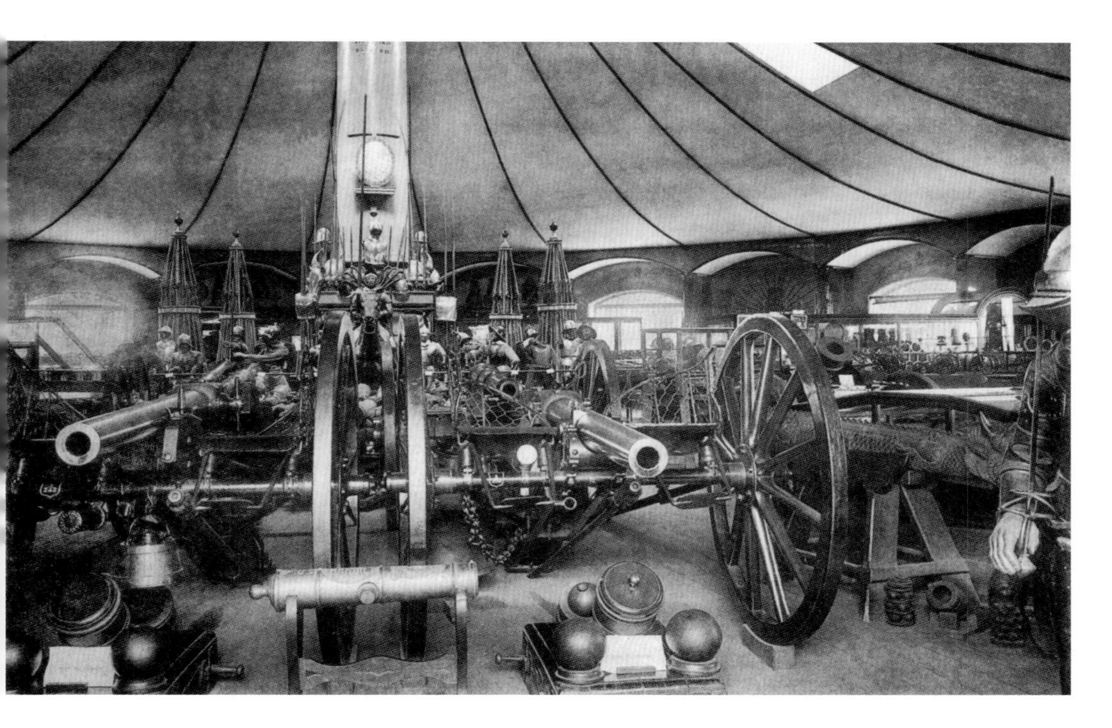

Interior of the Rotunda, Woolwich, *c.* 1915, and Firepower, 2013
The Rotunda was moved to Woolwich from Carlton House in 1819, 'given by his Royal Highness to the Royal Military Repository, for the reception of ... Arms and other Trophies taken by the British Army in Paris, on the triumphant entry of Field Marshal the Duke of Wellington into that city in 1815.' It grew into the Royal Artillery Museum, but closed to public access when its collection was transferred to the Firepower Museum at the Royal Arsenal in 2011.

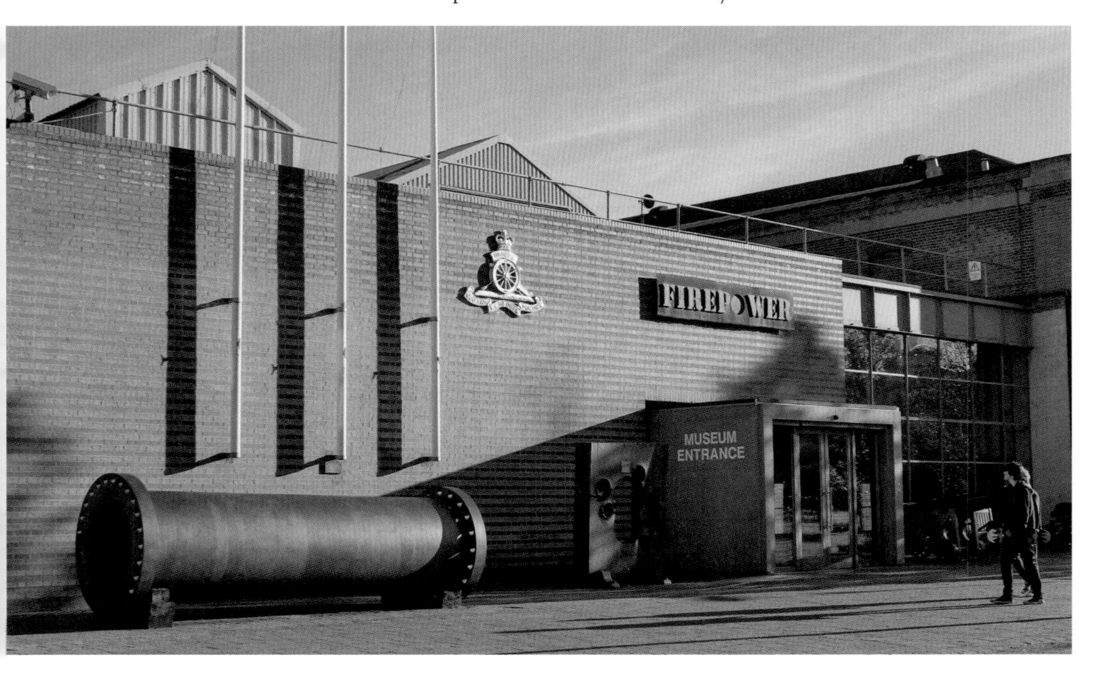

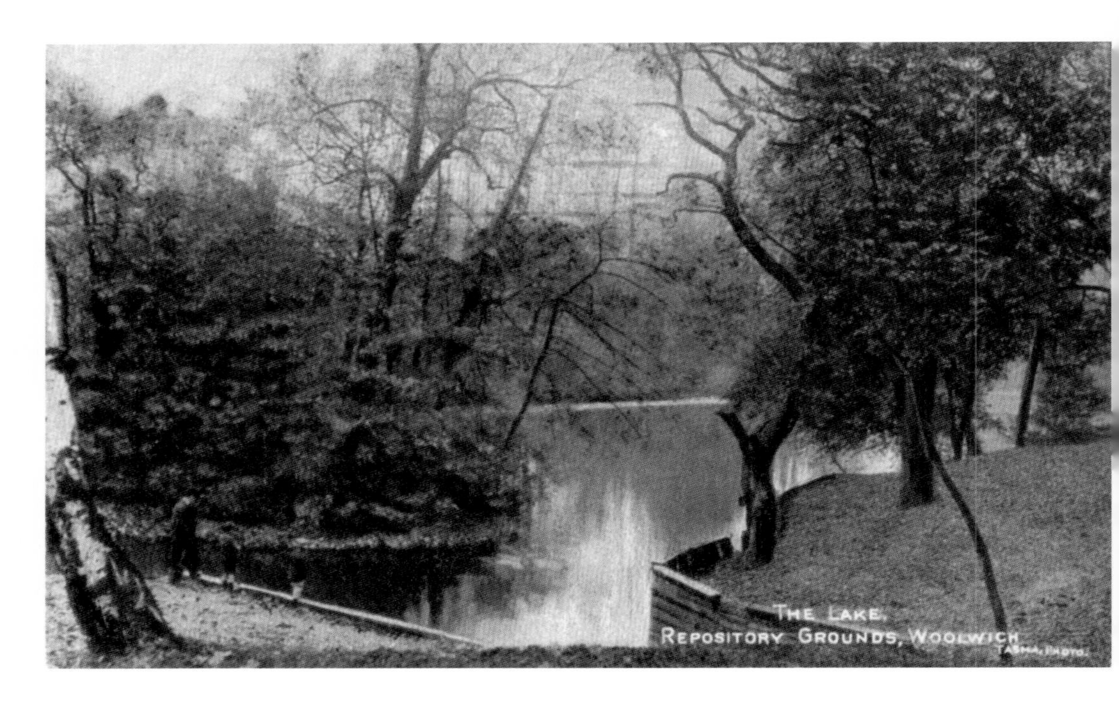

The Lake, Repository Grounds, Woolwich

English Heritage made a detailed archaeological survey of Repository Woods in 2008. Its findings uncovered the Royal Military Repository's unique role in training soldiers to mount and move heavy artillery at the beginning of the nineteenth century, revealing that the surviving landscape of tracks and ponds, which were to provide an attractive backdrop for the nearby Rotunda, was a military construction, combining practical and recreational uses. Repository Woods is owned by the Ministry of Defence, with no public access allowed.

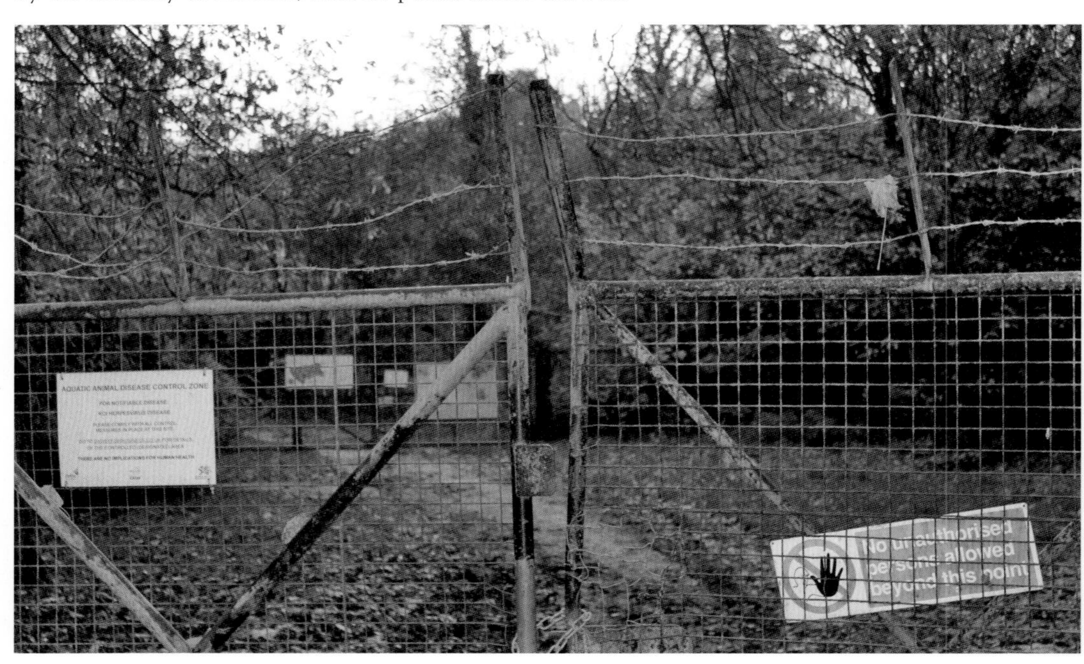

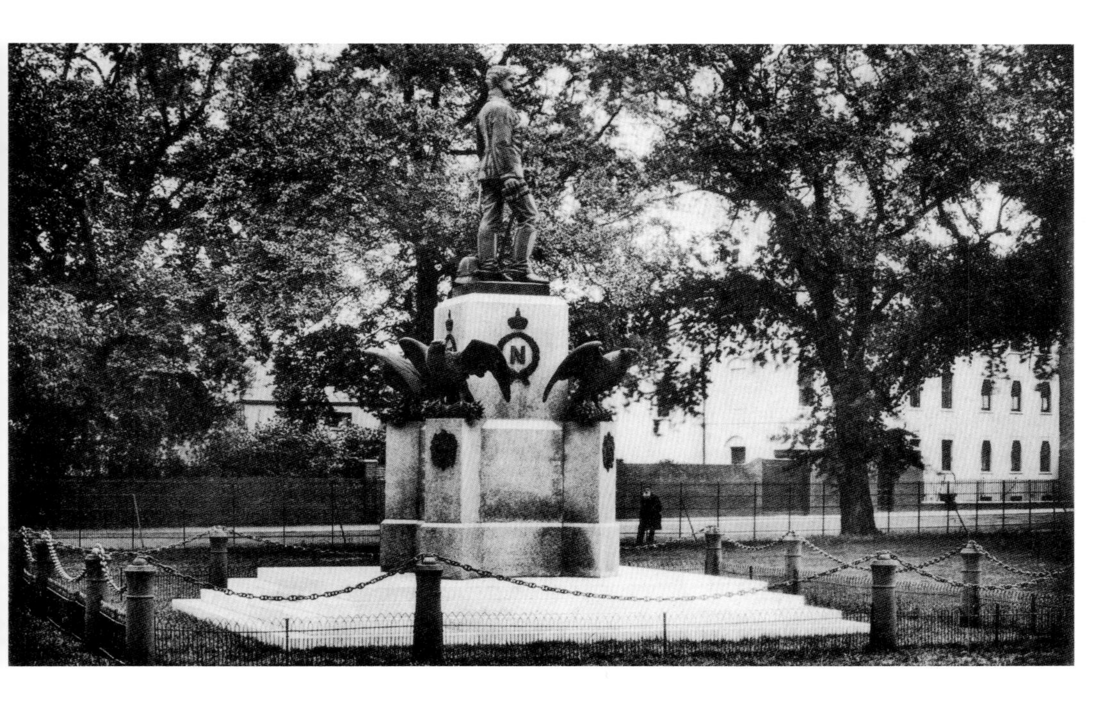

Prince Imperial Monument, Woolwich, *c.* 1915, and Lee Rigby Memorial, 2013

Commemorating the namesake son of Napoleon III, a Woolwich cadet killed with spears during the Zulu War on 1 June 1879, the Prince Imperial Monument was erected at the Royal Military Academy in 1883, moving to Sandhurst in 1955. Drummer Lee Rigby was ambushed by two British Islamic converts of Nigerian descent at Artillery Place, Woolwich, on 22 May 2013, and was hacked to death with knives and a cleaver. His memorial is maintained outside the RA Barracks Headquarters on Repository Road.

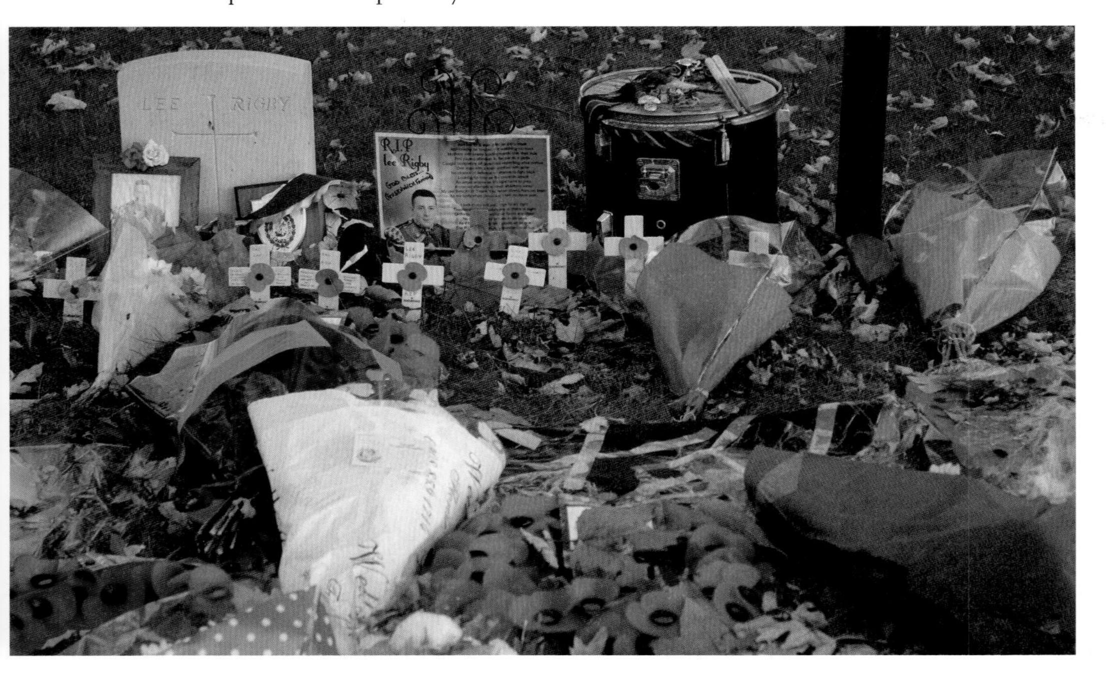

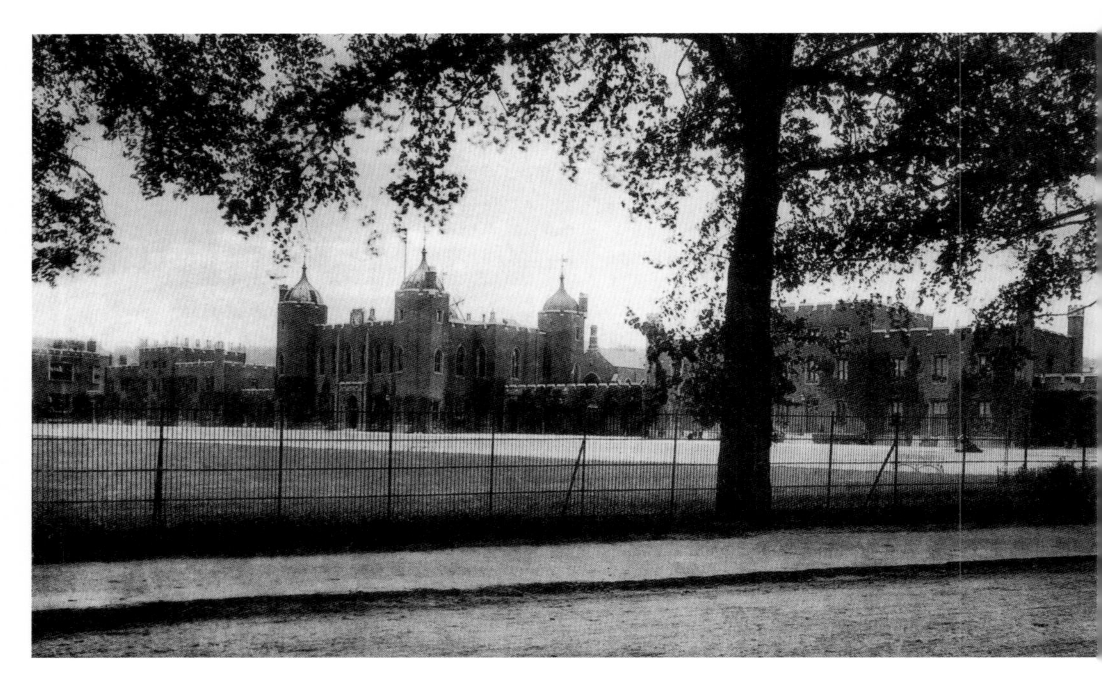

Royal Military Academy, Woolwich, *c.* 1915

Founded in 1741, the first Royal Military Academy was a converted workshop in Woolwich Warren. Designs for a larger building were underway from 1796, the common's south-west field selected as its site in 1803. When the parish refused to sell its ancient rights to herbage and turbary, these were circumvented by Act of Parliament, likewise Charlton Common. Although the parish was awarded £3,000 compensation, with Charlton Common's former freeholders Lady Jane Wilson and Sir Thomas Maryon Wilson granted £8,770, acrimony lingered.

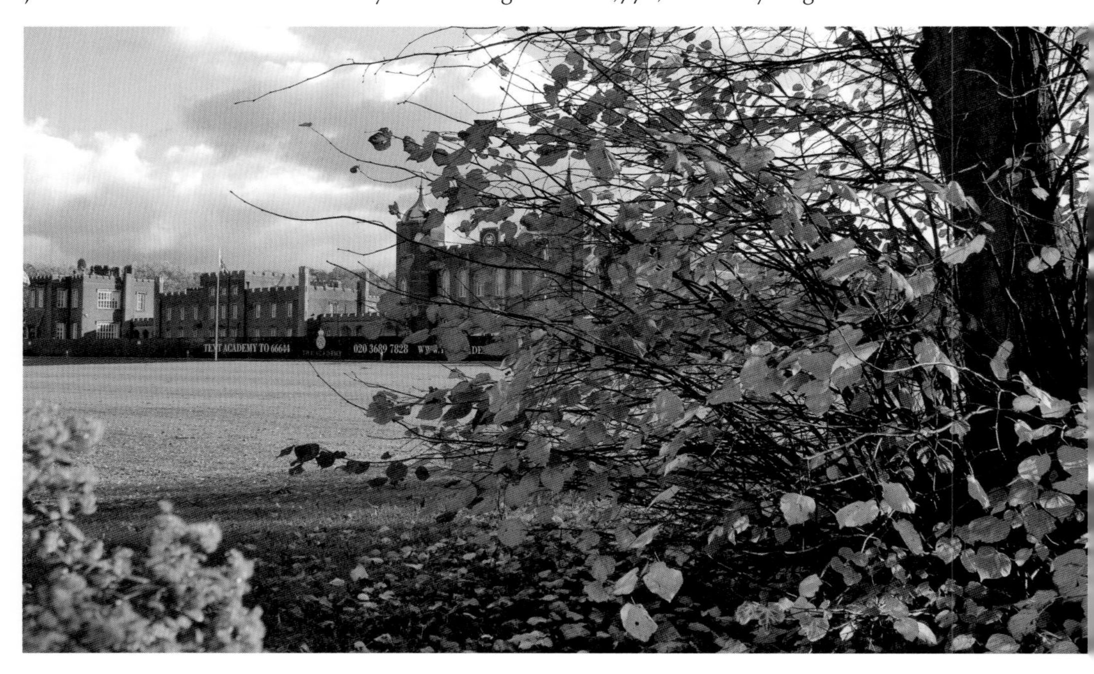

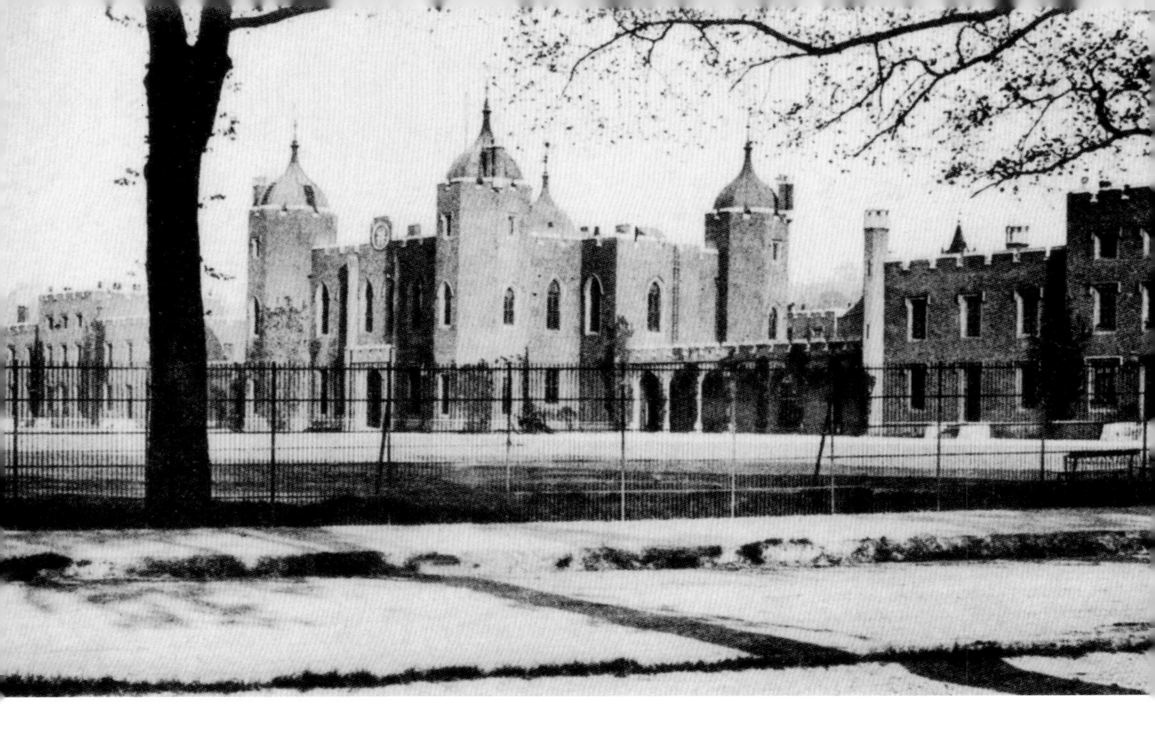

Royal Military Academy, Woolwich, *c.* 1905

Construction of the Royal Military Academy began in the summer of 1803. James Wyatt's design is notable for its Tudor-Gothic style, exemplified by the central octagonal ogee-topped corner towers, echoing the Tower of London's White Tower and contrasting with the barracks' classical frontage. The four eldest classes and resident officers moved into their new quarters in August 1806. The academy closed in 1939, its cadets transferred to Sandhurst. Durkan Estates purchased the site in 2006 for conversion into residential flats.

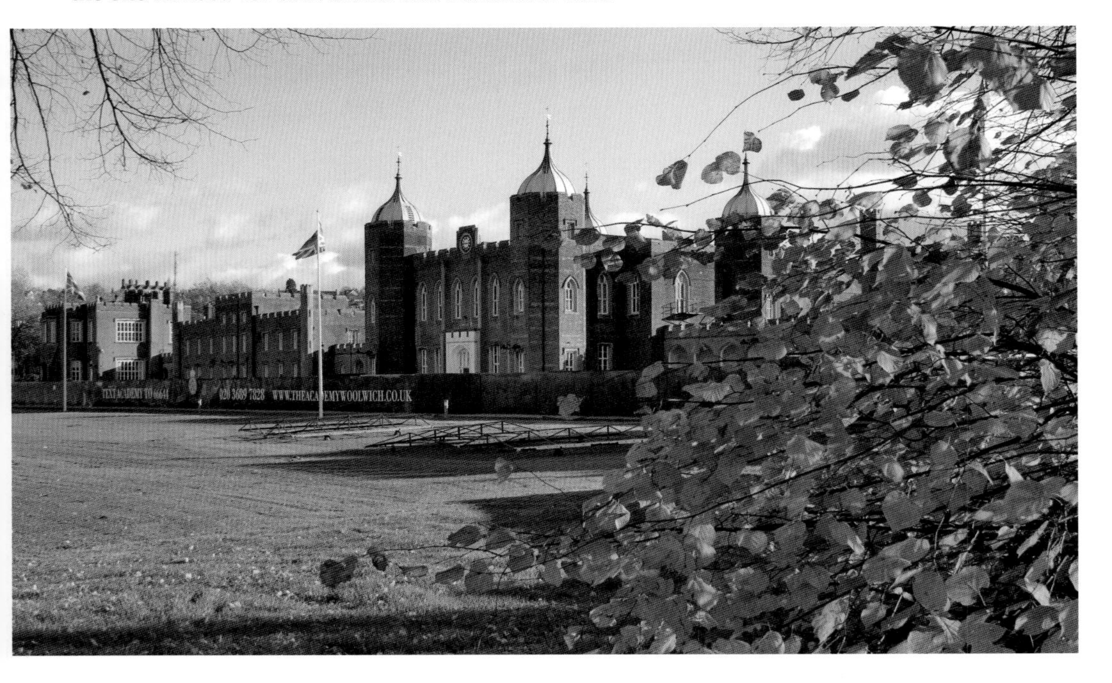

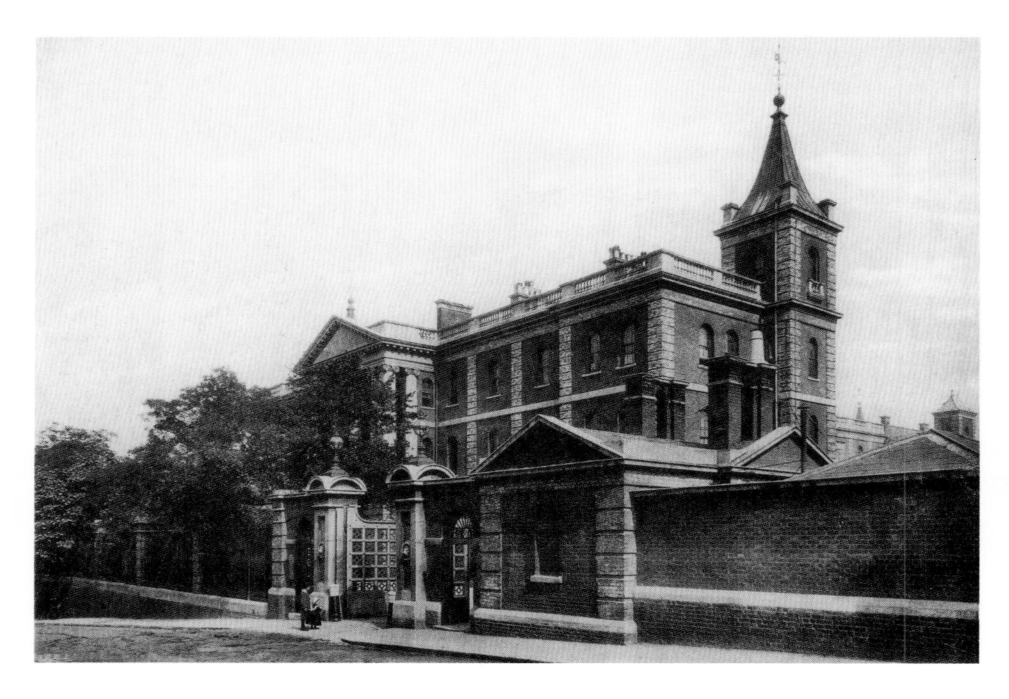

Red Barracks, Woolwich, *c.* 1915
The red-brick Royal Marine Infirmary on Frances Street was built between 1858 and 1860, one of the first two pavilion-plan hospitals erected in England after the Crimean War. Following closure of the Woolwich Dockyard and opening of Royal Herbert Hospital, it passed to the Army in 1869. It was rechristened as Red Barracks, and later housed the Artillery College from 1888, and the Military College of Science between 1927 and 1939. Demolished in 1975, despite its 1972 listing, it was redeveloped as residential housing. Only the perimeter wall survives.

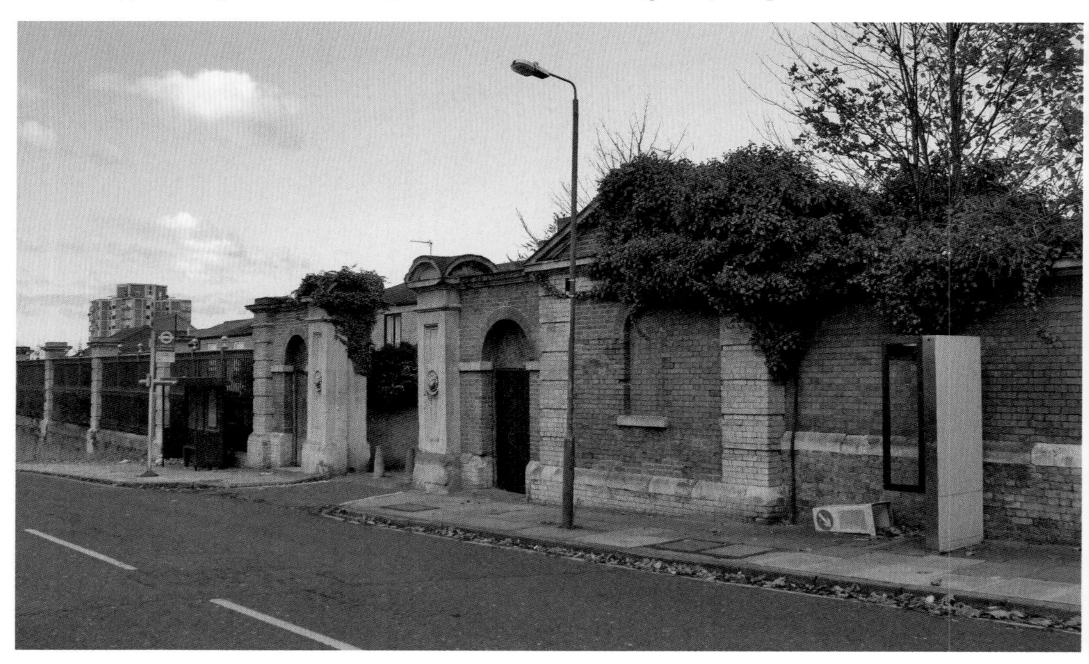

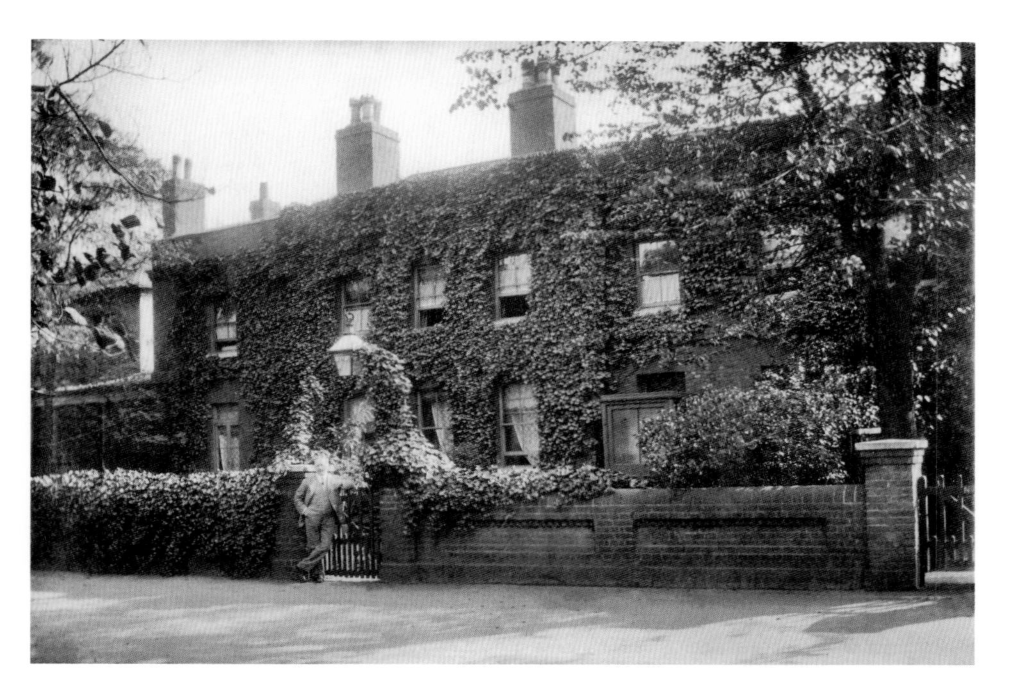

No. 12 Quarters, Woolwich Arsenal, and Cambridge Barracks Gate
It has not been possible to identify which barracks No. 12 Quarters would have belonged to, but it was probably among those deemed surplus to requirements and demolished, like Red Barracks, or neighbouring Royal Marine Barracks, which originally housed the personnel who provided a military presence in the Dockyard. Rechristened Cambridge Barracks after Woolwich Dockyard's closure, it provided additional accommodation for Army troops until its demolition in 1972. The surviving gatehouse today functions as a police office and community centre.

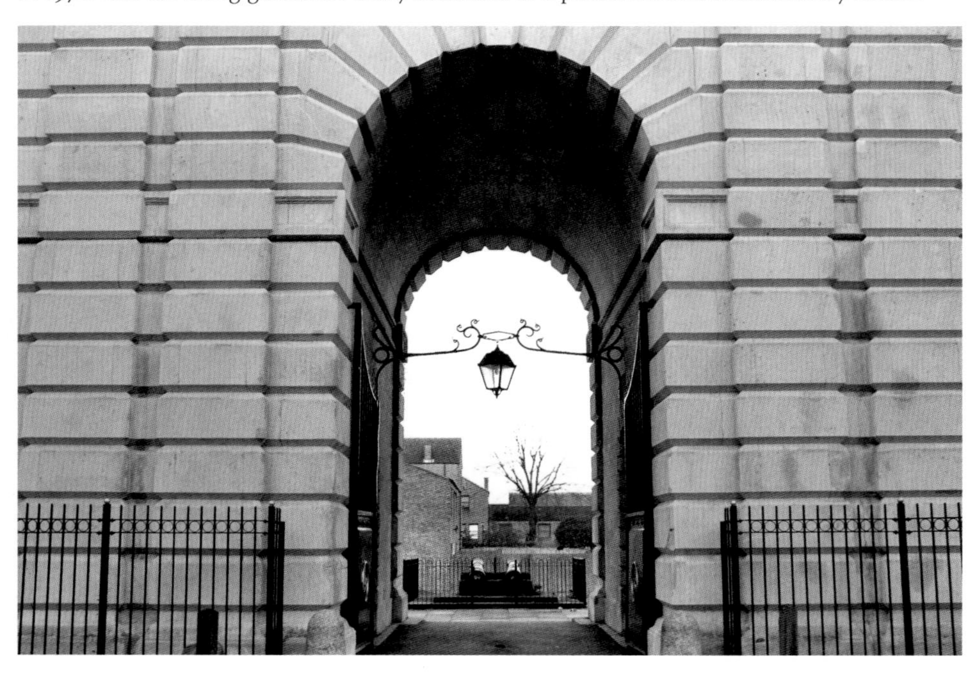

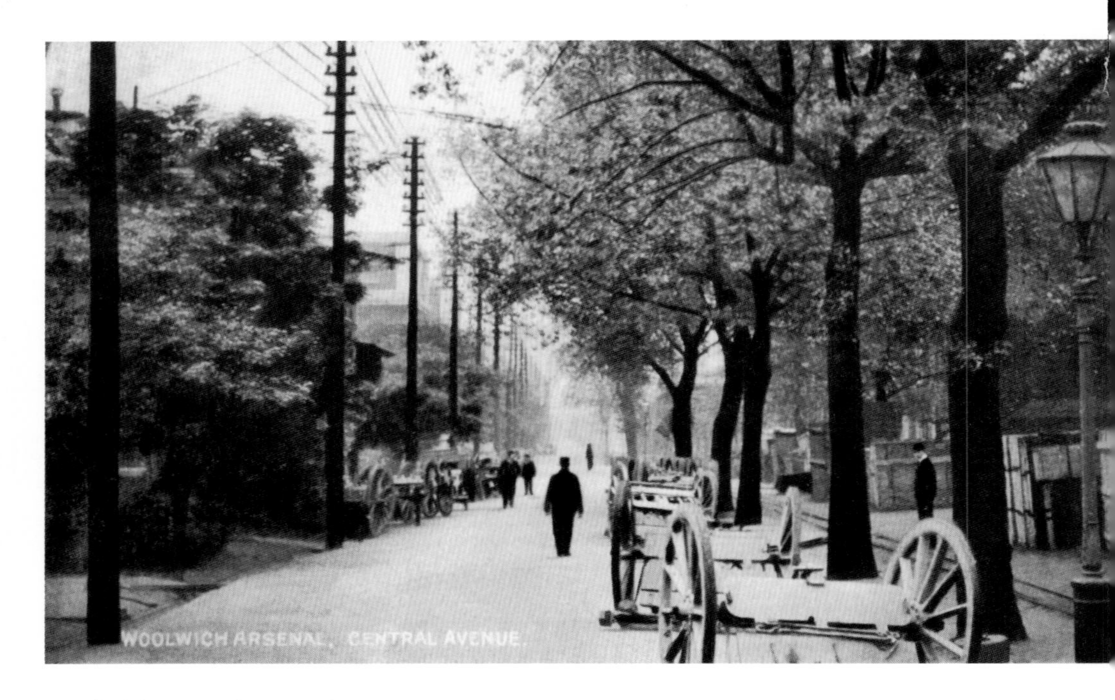

Woolwich Arsenal, Central Avenue

While no reference to Central Avenue has been discovered outside the title of this postcard, the vista bears a striking resemblance to today's No. 1 Street, which runs down Woolwich Arsenal from Dial Arch Square to the riverfront. New housing complexes have been springing up in this area as part of Woolwich's regeneration; here, Stephen Marshall Architects' designs for Berkeley Homes sympathetically blend in with the historic buildings, while adding vibrant colour suggested by the detailing on field Navy weapons.

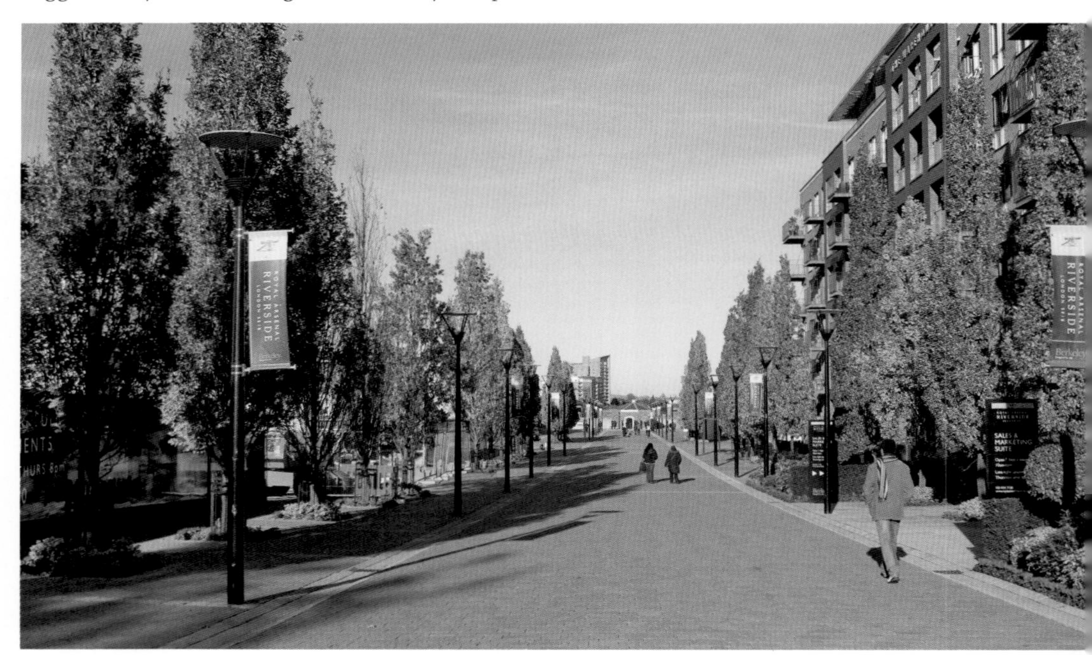

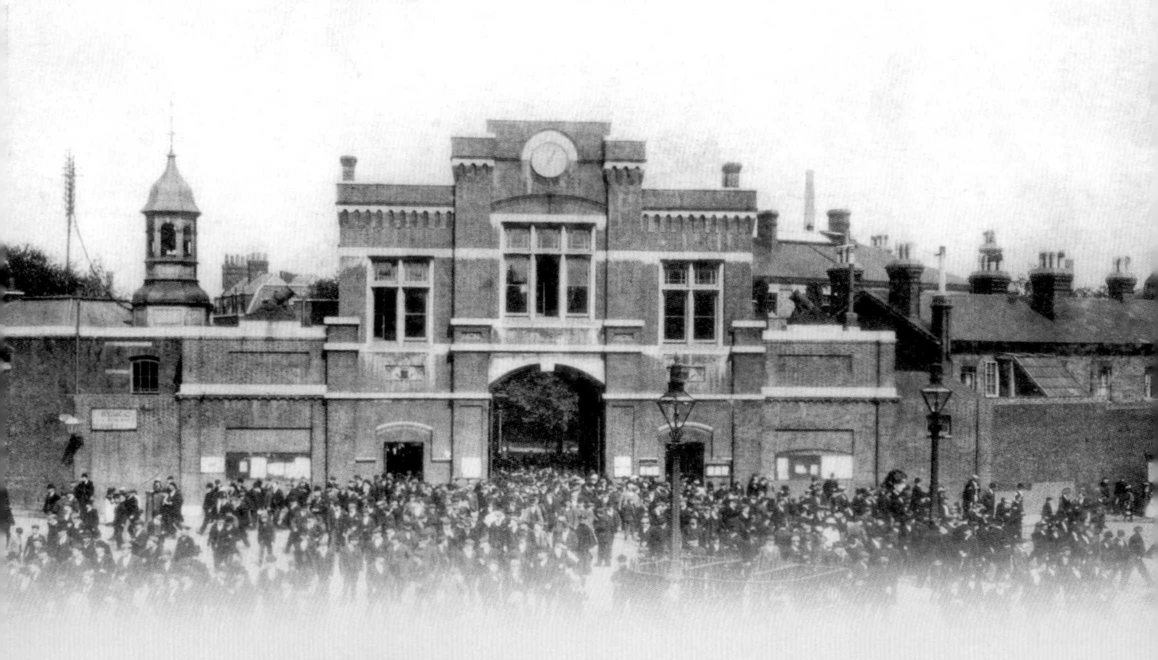

CHAPTER 2

Woolwich Village

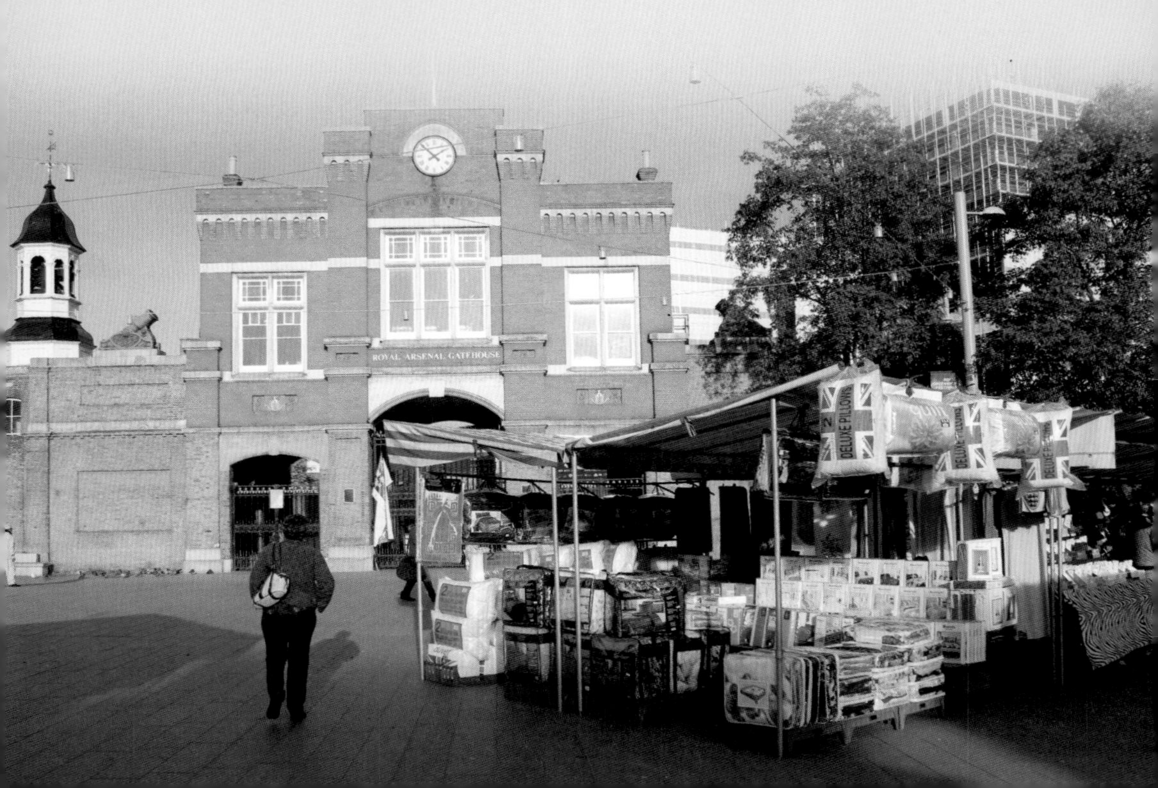

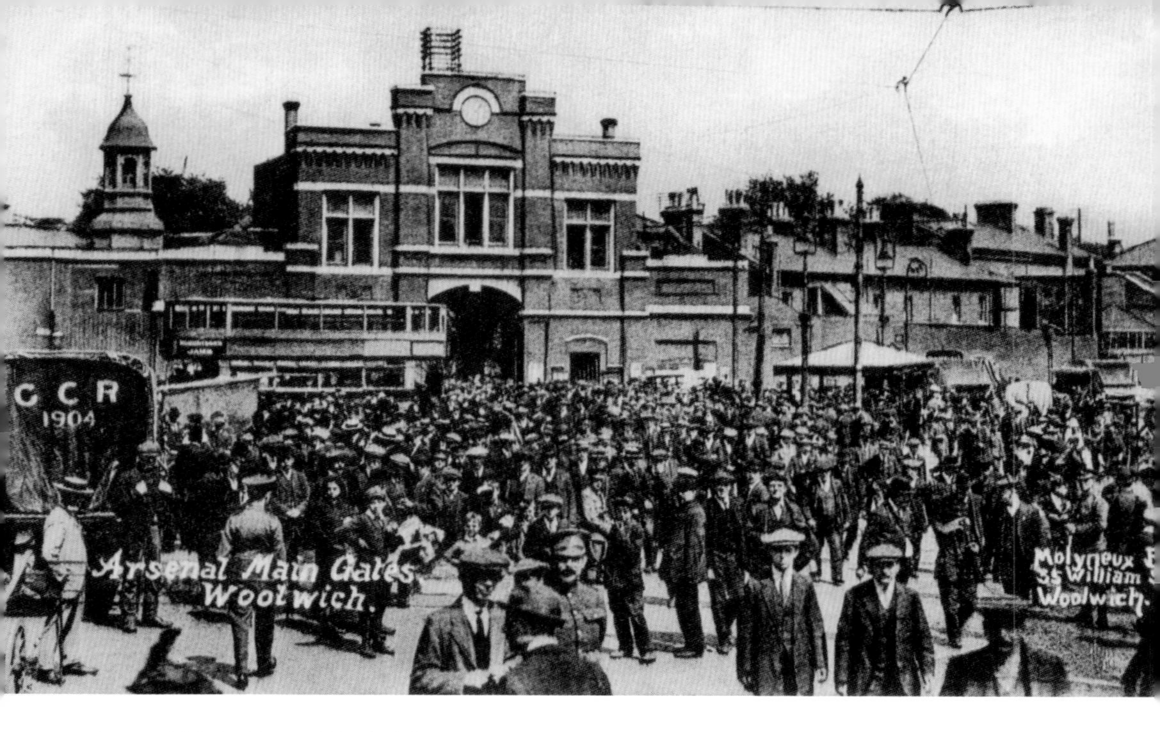

Arsenal Main Gates, Woolwich, 1915

Although Royal Arsenal is famous as a munitions factory, it began life as Woolwich Warren – originally a rabbit warren in the eastern grounds of a Tudor house named Tower Place – and was used for the proving of guns. The Board of Ordnance purchased the lands in 1671 to house a large storage depot. From 1691, when the Laboratory was relocated from Greenwich, ammunition was made there. Above, workers stream from the main gates onto Beresford Square, a quieter prospect since the factory was demolished.

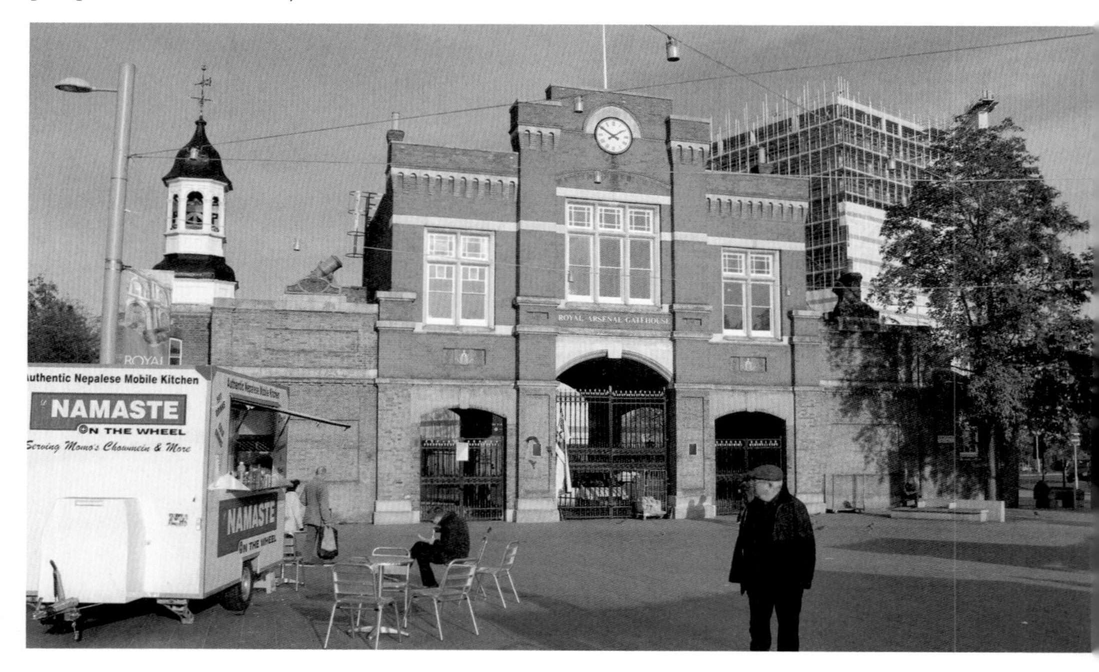

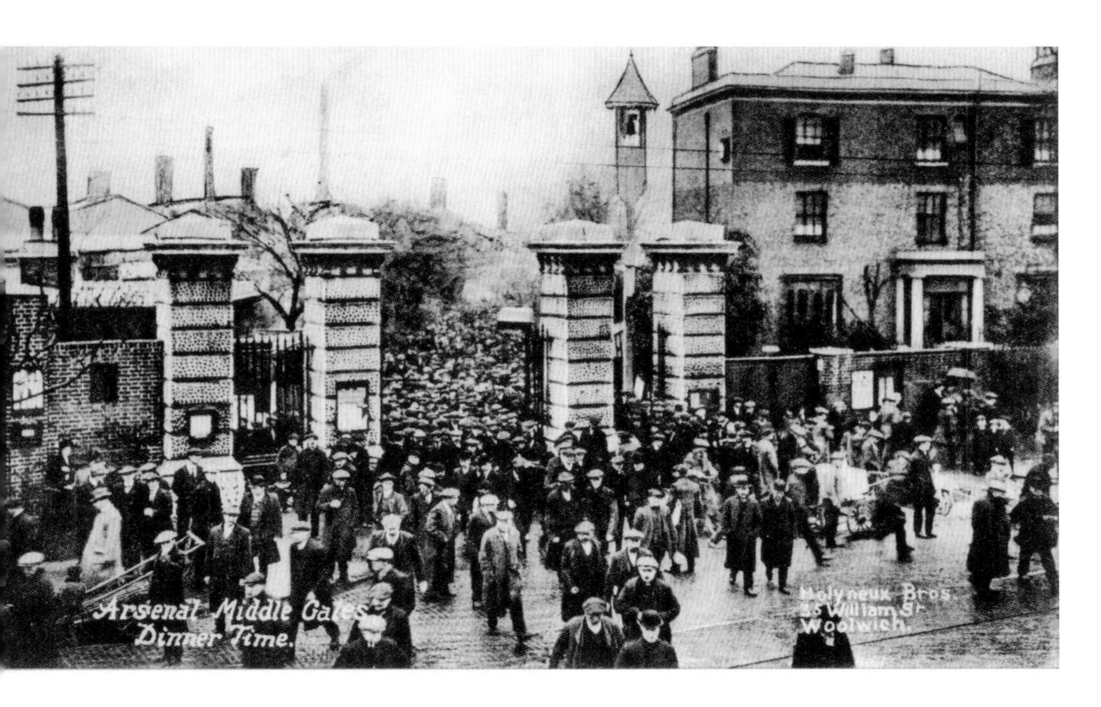

Arsenal Middle Gates, Dinner Time, 1915

Its design alternatively attributed to Sir John Vanbrugh and Nicholas Hawksmoor, the Royal Brass Foundry (later Royal Gun Factory) was constructed in 1717, bringing large-scale gun-making to Woolwich. Further works led to the development of dedicated departments, including the Royal Carriage Department and Storekeeper's Department. The Arsenal eventually covered a vast terrain, with its middle gates located on Plumstead Road, today at a distance of several bus-stops from the main gates, obscured from the street by a thick pyracantha hedge.

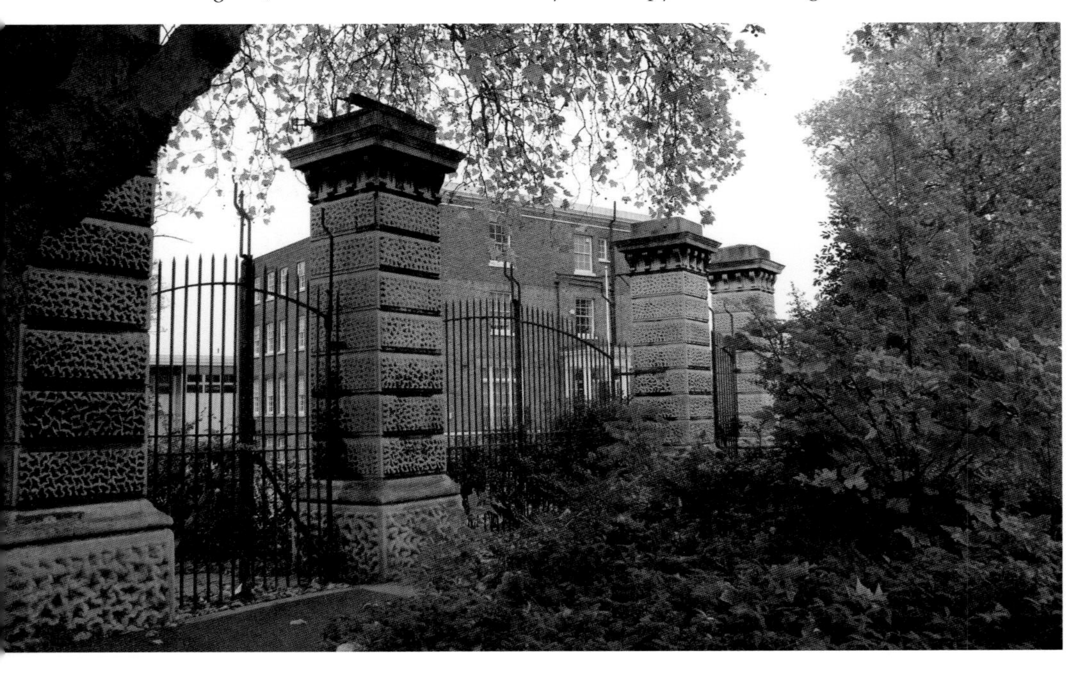

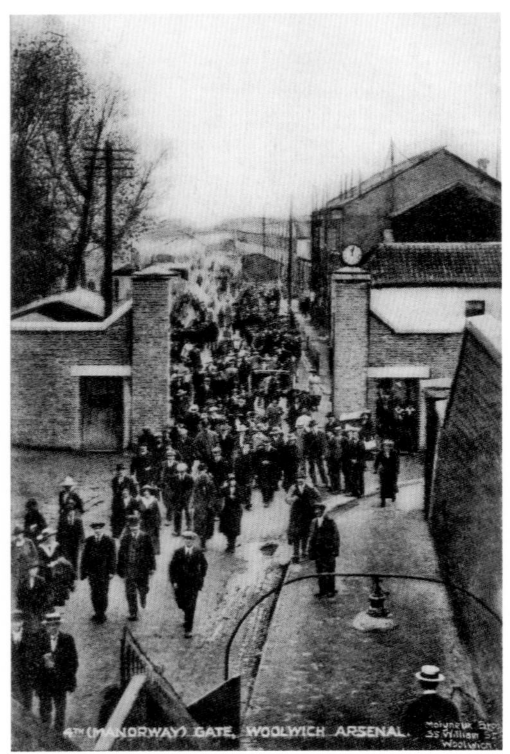

4th (Manorway) Gate, Woolwich Arsenal, 1915

With lands on Plumstead marshes annexed to the rapidly growing complex, it was designated Royal Arsenal in 1805. The 1850s saw another intensive spurt of construction following the Crimean War, extending ever further eastwards. Royal Arsenal reached its peak of production and employment during the First World War, then covering 1,285 acres. The demolished Manorway Gate stood on Griffin Manor Way, nearer the river than can be photographically conveyed, the path today only existing as a stub of its former self after the area's redevelopment.

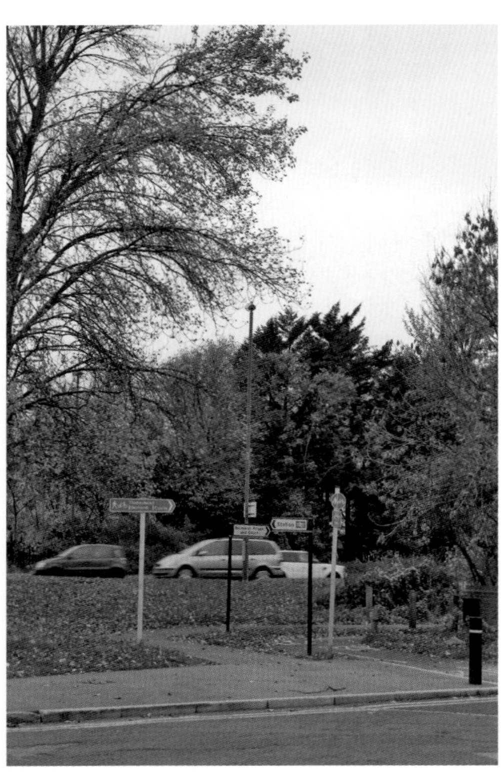

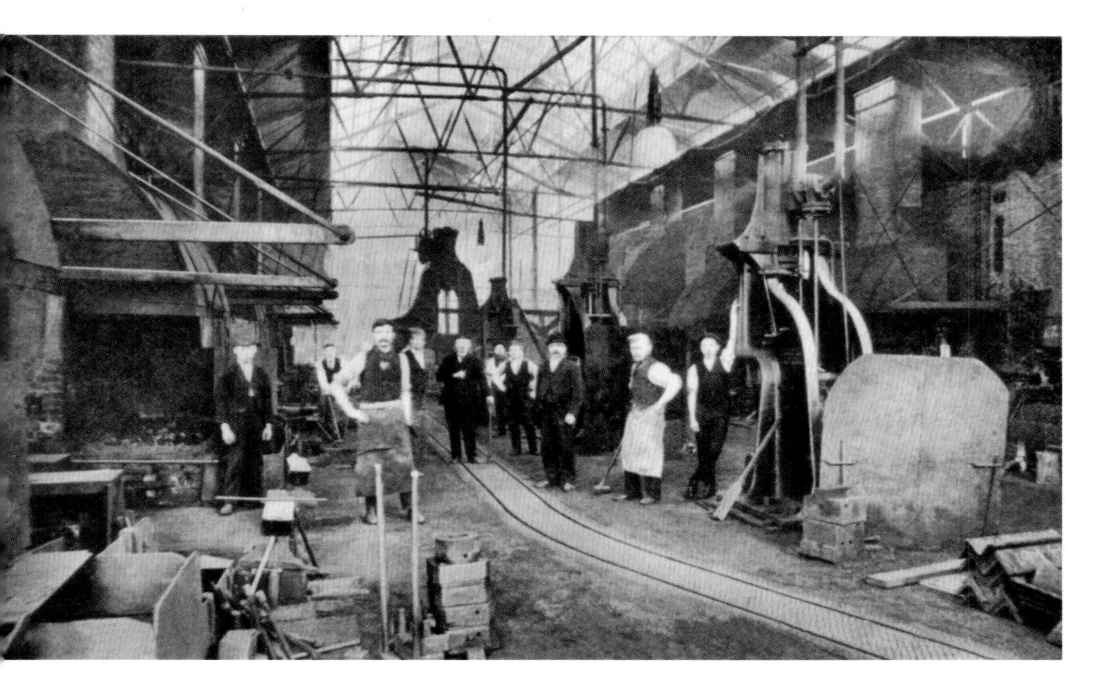

Woolwich Arsenal, Blacksmiths' Shop and *Assembly*
The Second World War brought a further boost to the Arsenal, though less dramatic than that of the First World War, with a steady decline setting in afterward. The Royal Ordnance Factory closed in 1967, the majority of its eastern lands ceded to the Greater London Council, providing the site for the town of Thamesmead. A scaled-back Ministry of Defence presence remained on its western grounds until 1994. Peter Burke's 2001 cast-iron sculpture *Assembly* now stands at the riverside once occupied by factory workers, including blacksmiths.

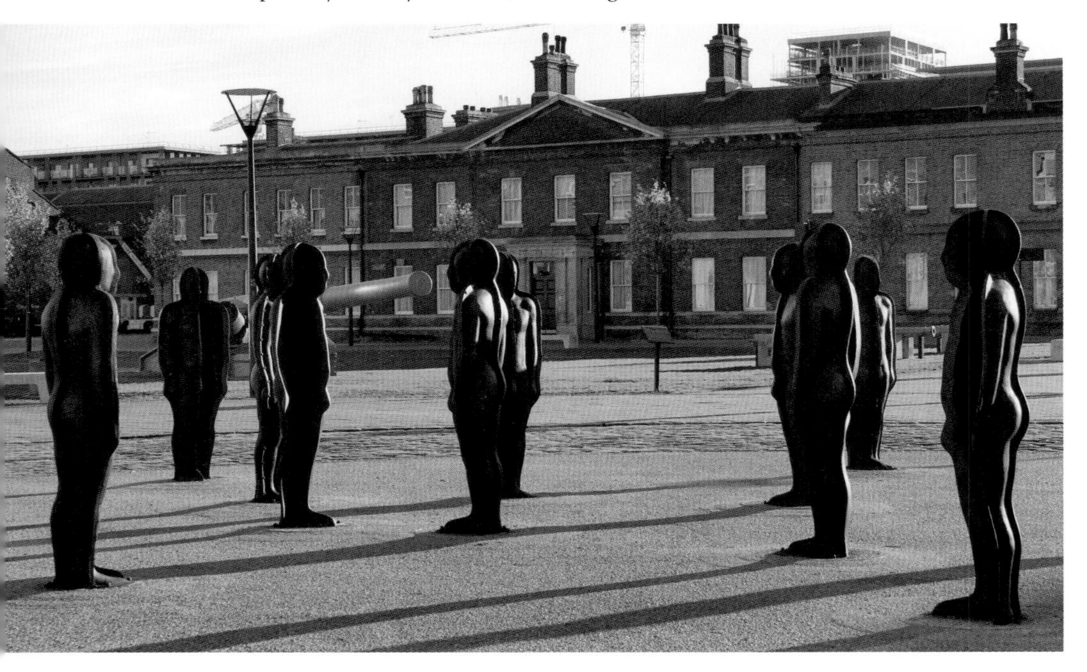

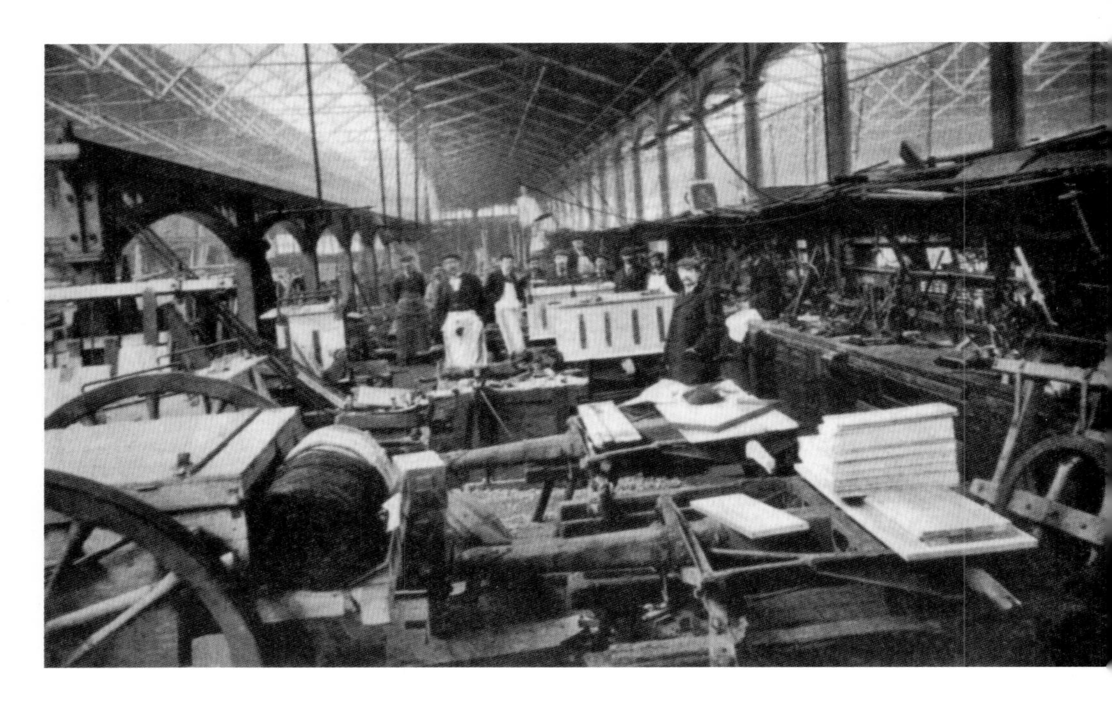

Woolwich Arsenal, Wheelers' Shop and Artillery Square Displays

The former Arsenal site in Woolwich was first passed to a state development agency in 1997 and then on to the private sector in 2011. The economic downturn of 2008 delayed regeneration plans. However, a new high-rise project was initiated in 2011 on the southern side of the Arsenal Main Gate, interrupted by the riots that erupted throughout London, including in Woolwich. Royal Arsenal grounds in Artillery Square are now shared by Firepower and the Greenwich Heritage Centre (see page 33).

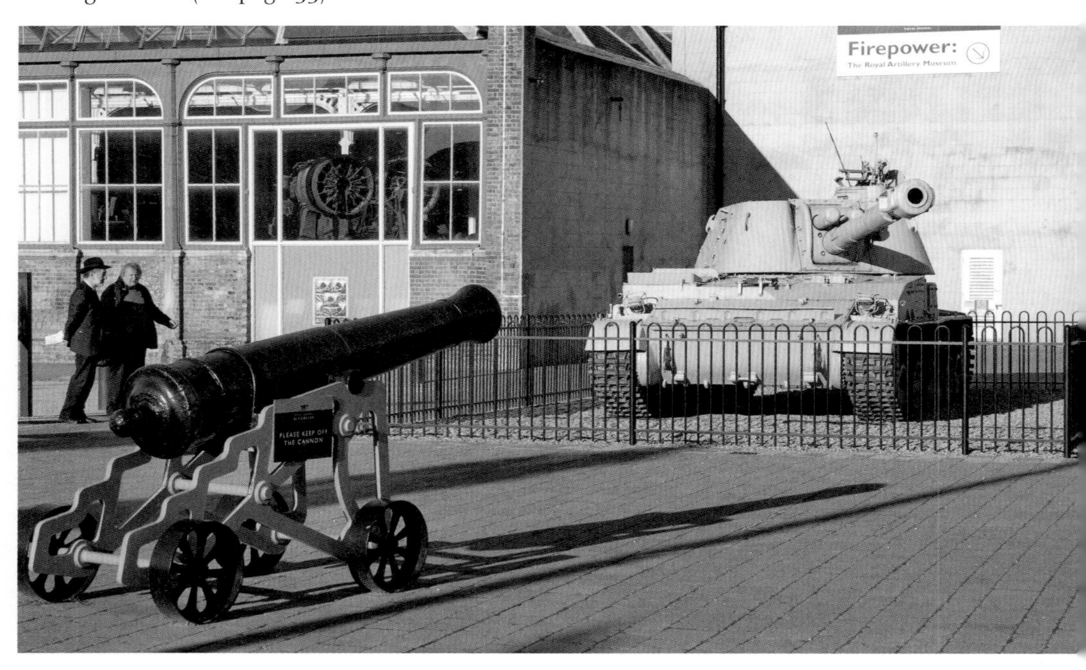

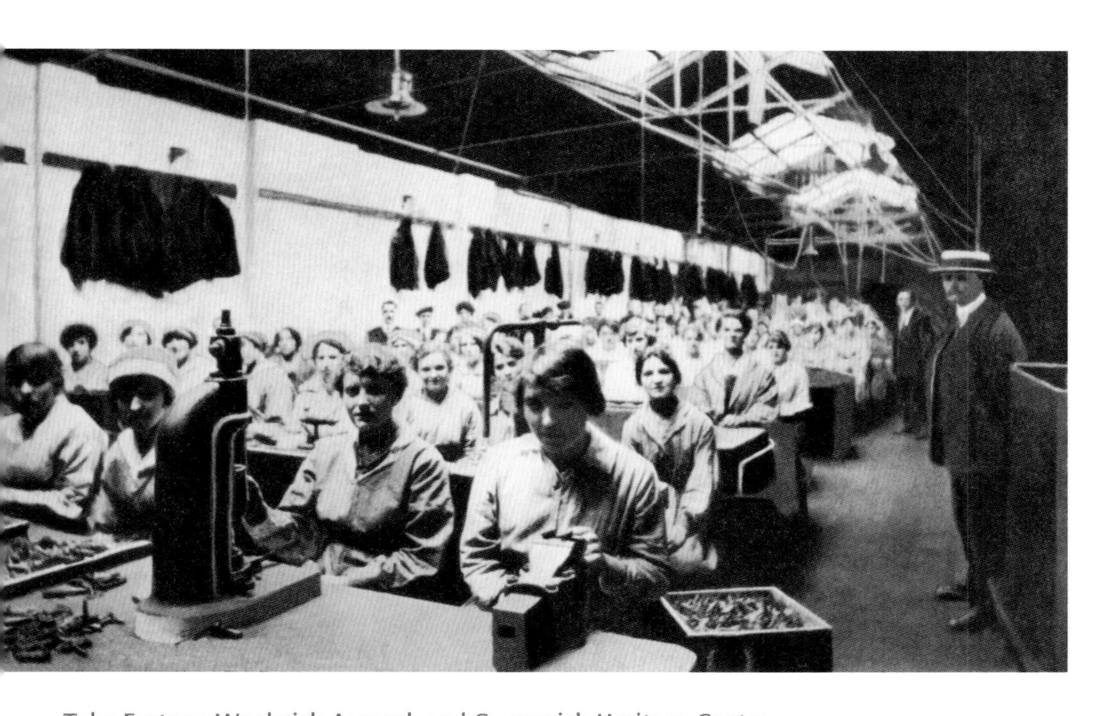

Tube Factory, Woolwich Arsenal, and Greenwich Heritage Centre
Women and children worked in the Arsenal, in addition to large numbers of unskilled labouring men and skilled artisans. Earlier cutbacks at the Arsenal following the Crimean War fuelled trade unionist Will Crooks' by-election victory in March 1903, when he became the country's fourth Labour MP. Woolwich went on to become the first borough in England to be represented by Labour at all levels of government, when its two Labour representatives were elected to the London County Council in March 1904.

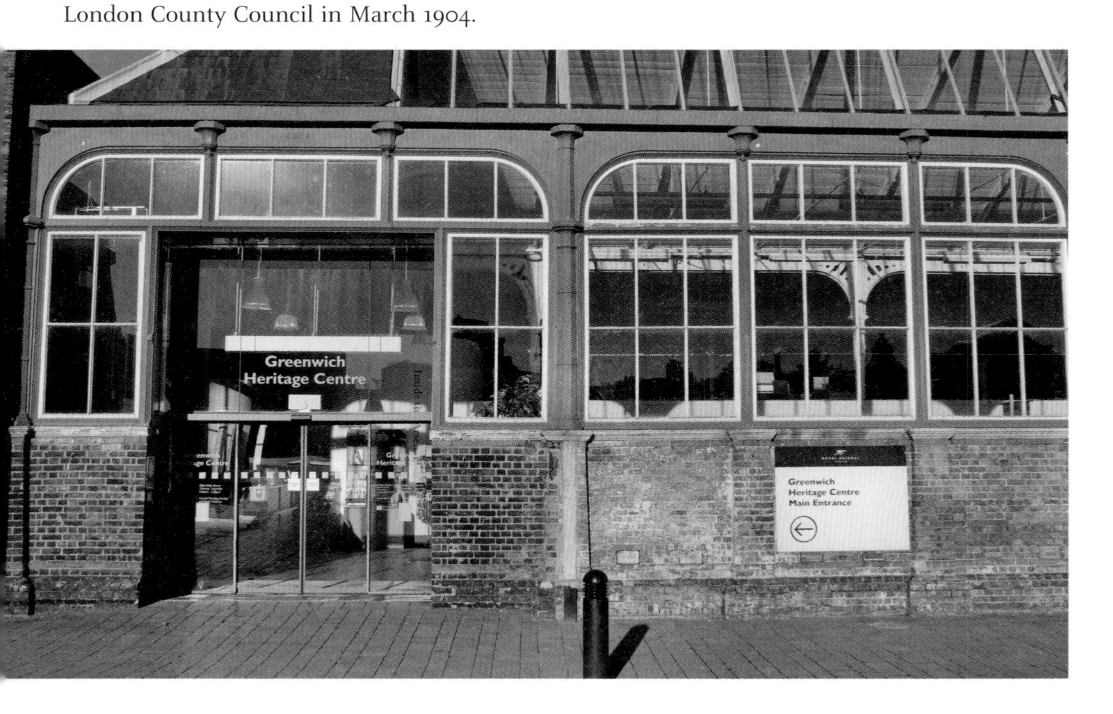

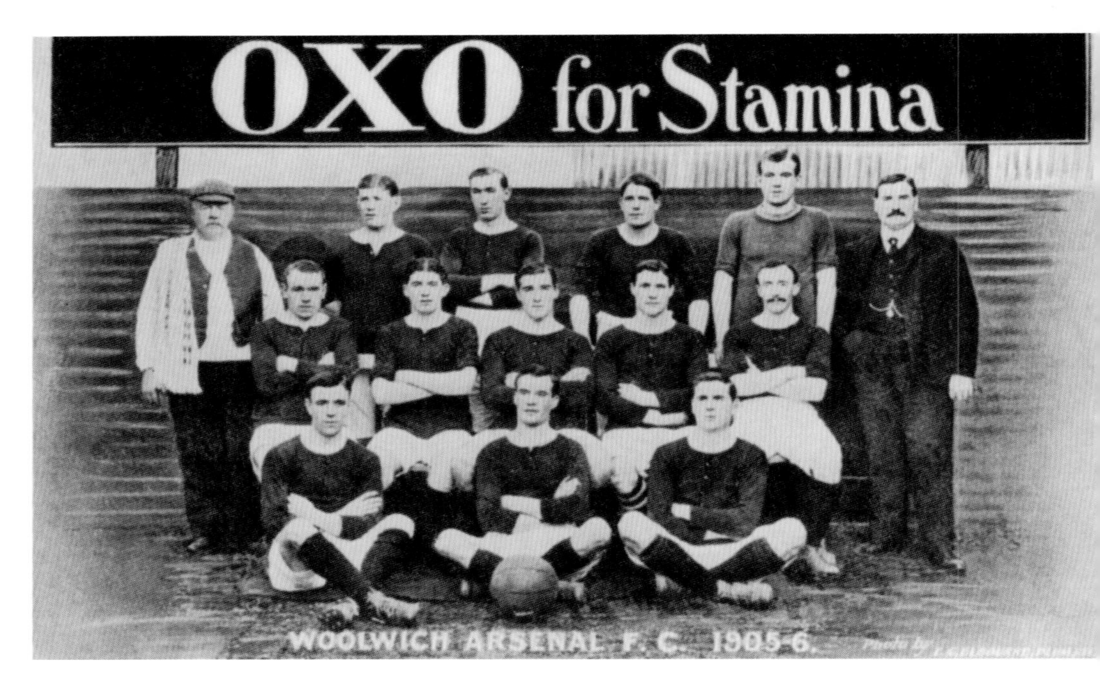

Woolwich Arsenal FC, 1905/06, and the Manor Ground Site, 2013
Formed as Dial Square FC in 1886 by munitions factory workers, the club changed its name to Royal Arsenal later that year, and was subsequently rechristened Woolwich Arsenal prior to joining the Football League in 1893. At that time, they purchased the Manor Ground, which was their home until they moved to North London in 1913. The stadium soon fell derelict and was demolished; its site (off the present Griffin Manor Way) became an industrial estate, itself now semi-derelict and scheduled for redevelopment.

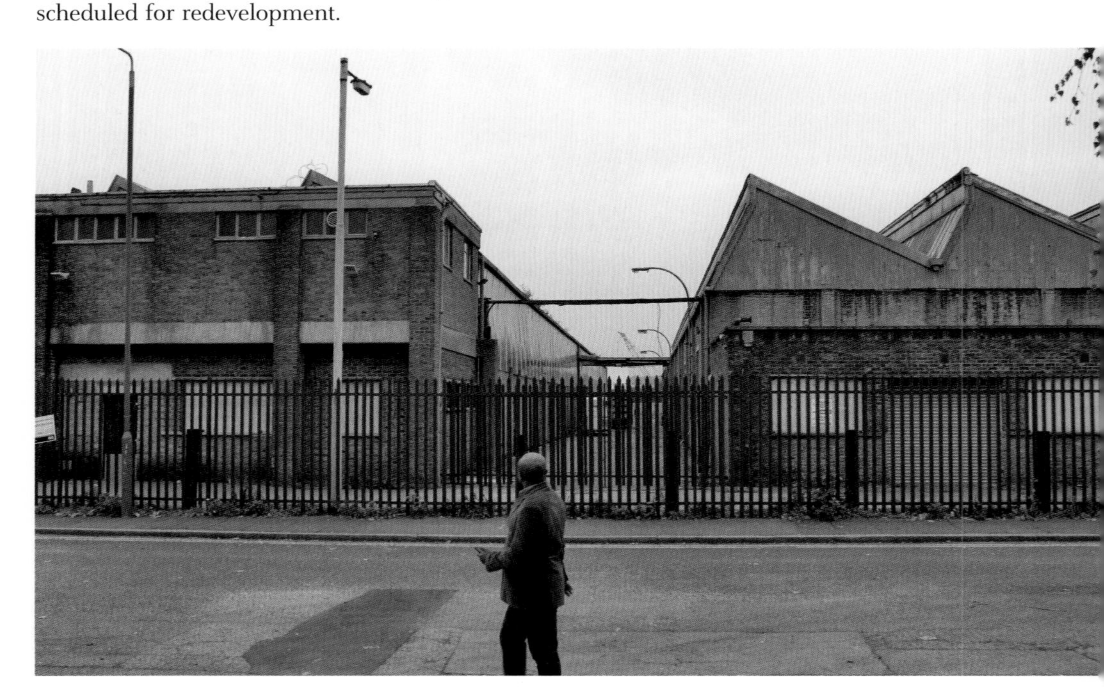

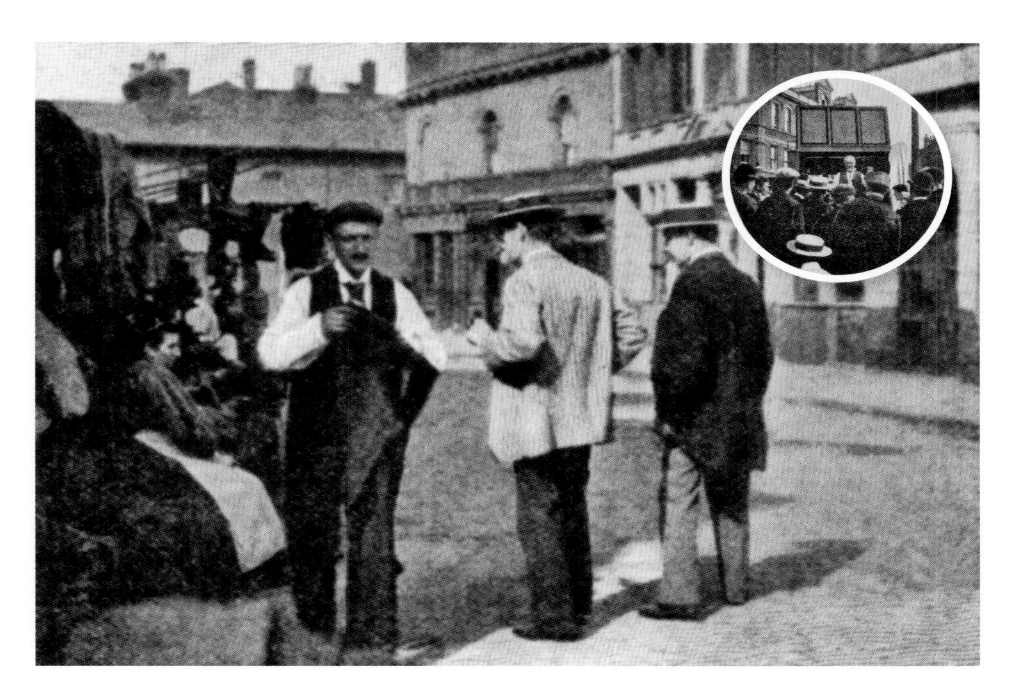

Street Auctions of Military Woolwich, 1900
Although a weekly market was held on Fridays, Woolwich had no annual fair, as neighbouring villages did. Incorporated by Royal Charter of King James I & VI in 1618, the market at Woolwich had no doubt already existed unofficially for some considerable time. A seventeenth-century market house stood near the north-east corner of the ropeyard, south of the high street (later identifiable as the corner of Warren Lane and Ropeyard Rails) – a prime location, as it was on the only route through Woolwich.

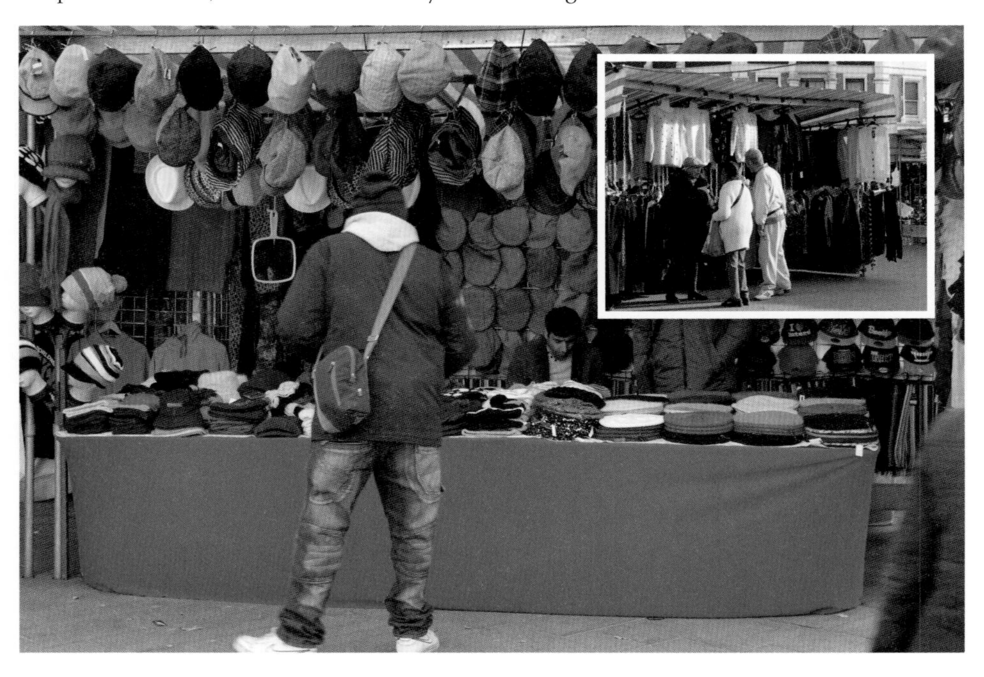

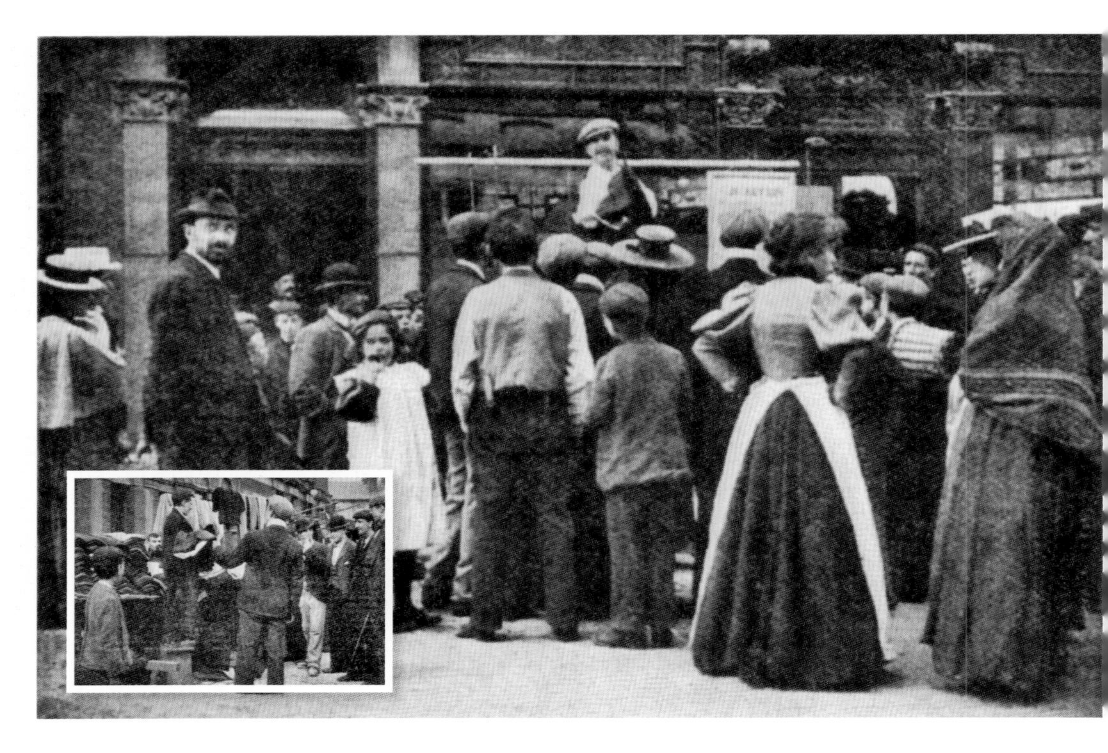

Woolwich Market Street Auction, 1900

Sir William Pritchard gifted the market house to the parish of Woolwich in 1679 for the benefit of the poor. The market may have already migrated to waste ground where the high street widened south of Bell Water Gate by the 1670s, spilling onto the southern end of the old gun yard. Sir William Langhorne acquired Pritchard's property in 1707, including right to the market tolls, and the site of Market Hill, built up between 1723 and 1726 as part of the Manor of Charlton.

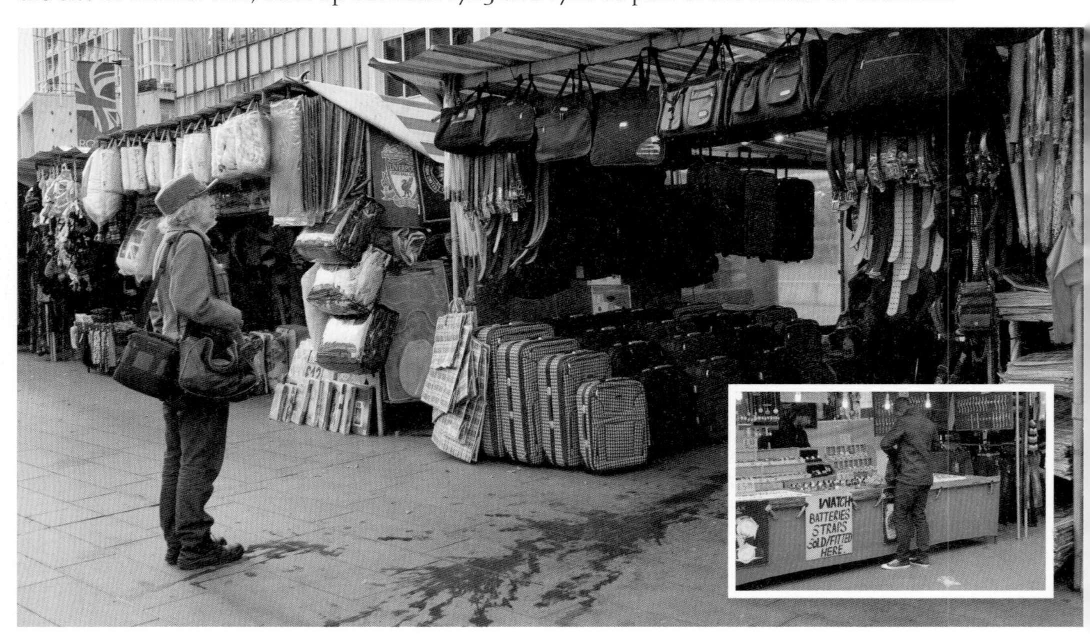

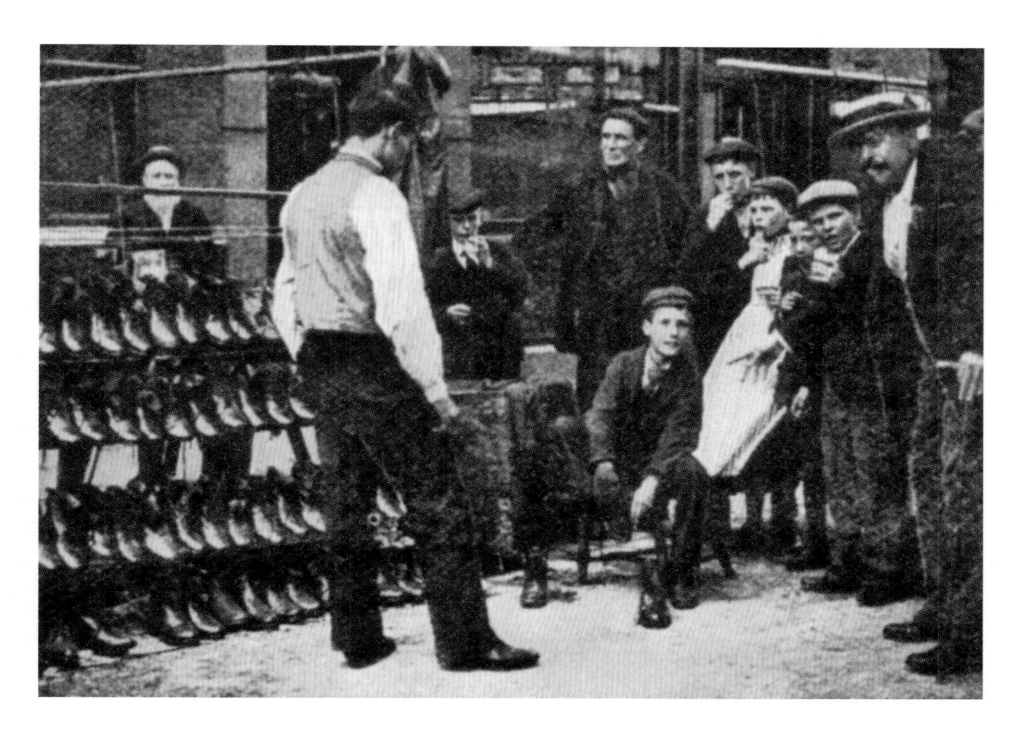

Woolwich Market Shoe Stall, 1900

A new marketplace was laid out during the 1720s, designed as an open square with a central office and shops in perimeter sheds. Lined with new houses on three sides, it adjoined the wharf to the north. As the town was redeveloped, its market expanded into the high street. Legislation was established in 1807/08 authorising Woolwich Town Commissioners to reform the market on a new site, claiming the old one was disused as dilapidated (perhaps more worrying to authorities, it was unregulated).

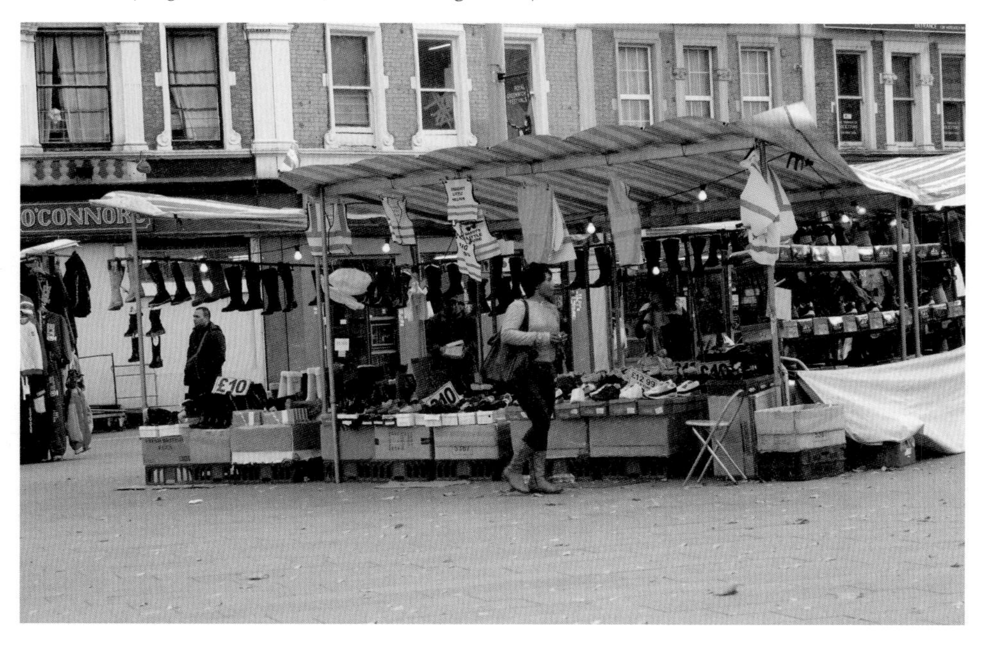

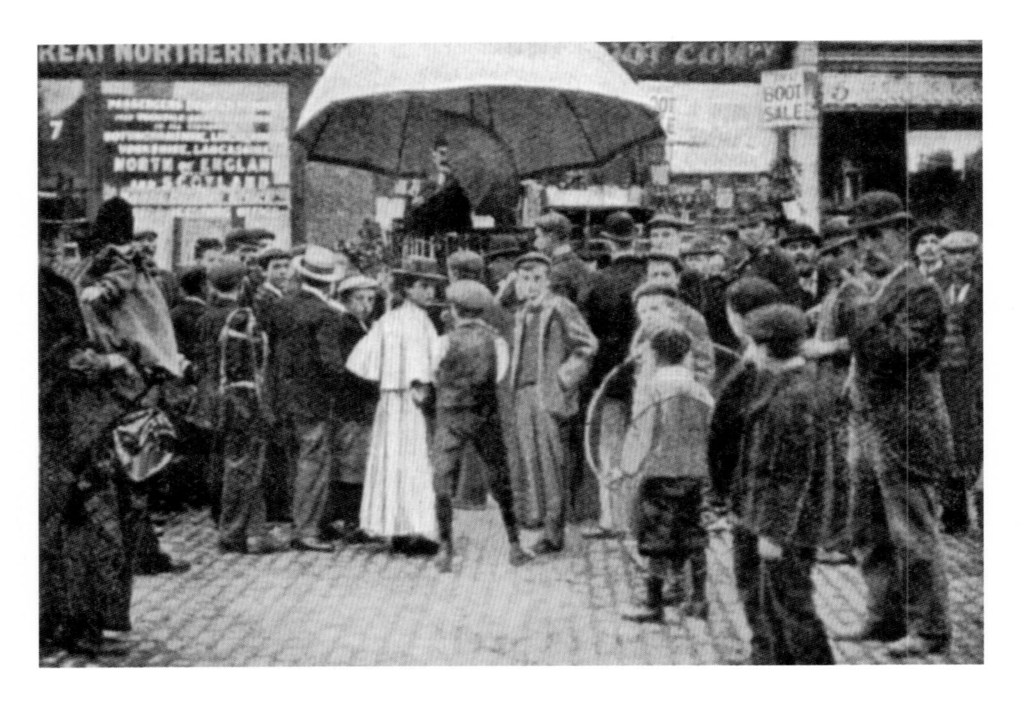

Woolwich Market Stalls, 1900

An attempt was made to establish a new market on William Street, parallel to today's Wellington Street, toward the north. This area is now at the heart of civic Woolwich, but was then too far out on the town's periphery to make for a commercially viable location. The experiment failed, with the name of Market Street (running off Wellington), then called Brewer Street, its sole survivor. Meanwhile, the unregulated market had continued trading at Market Hill and at the old market house.

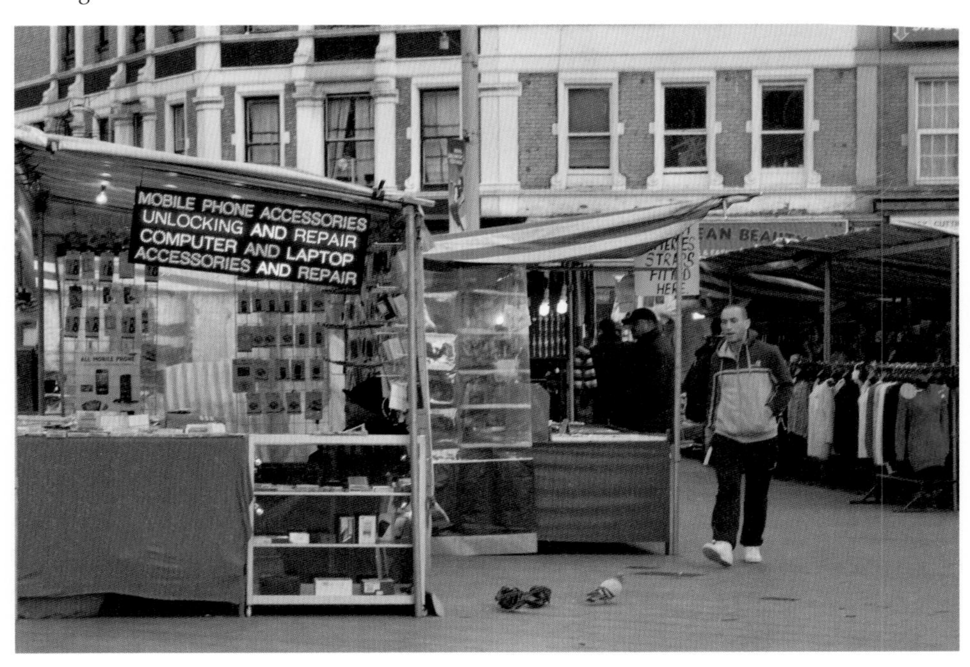

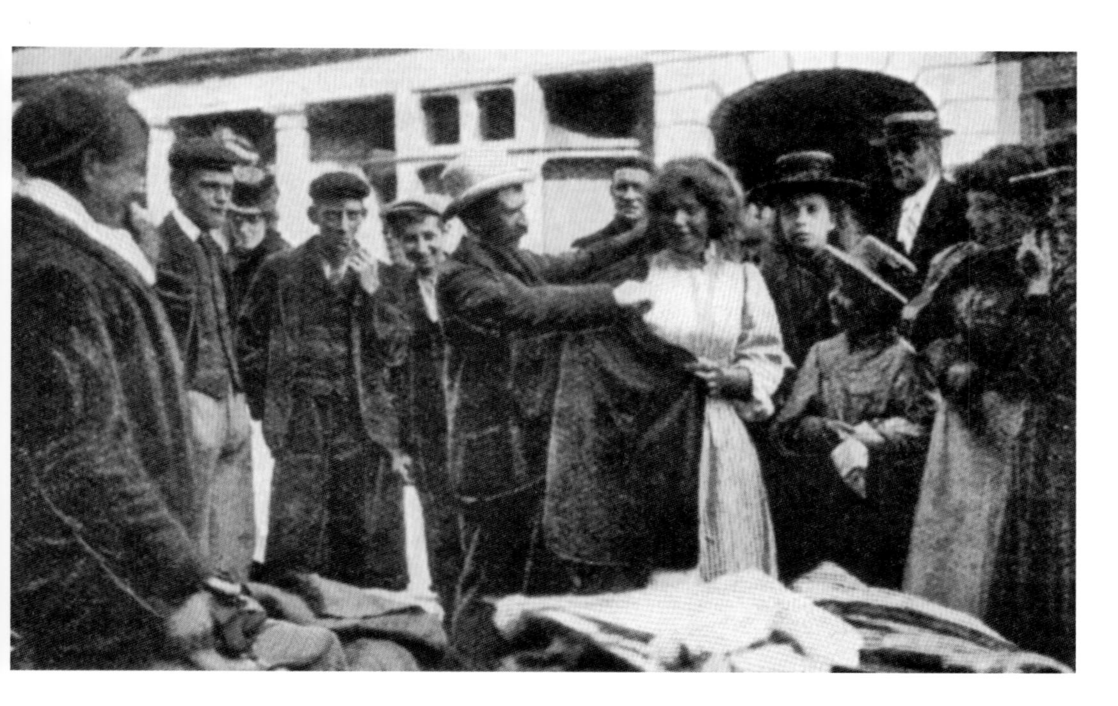

Woolwich Market Clothing Stall, 1900, and Woolwich Market Food Stall, 2013
The Pritchard lands developed under Sir William Langhorne during the 1720s were cleared in around 1830 by Sir Thomas Maryon Wilson, who had inherited the Manor of Charlton. Although this provided a large open space, there was another comparable area towards which the market now began to migrate: Beresford Square (see page 43). Despite concerted efforts made in 1868 to entice traders back to Market Hill, Beresford Square remained the market's home. Market Hill's grounds were consequently later reduced in size.

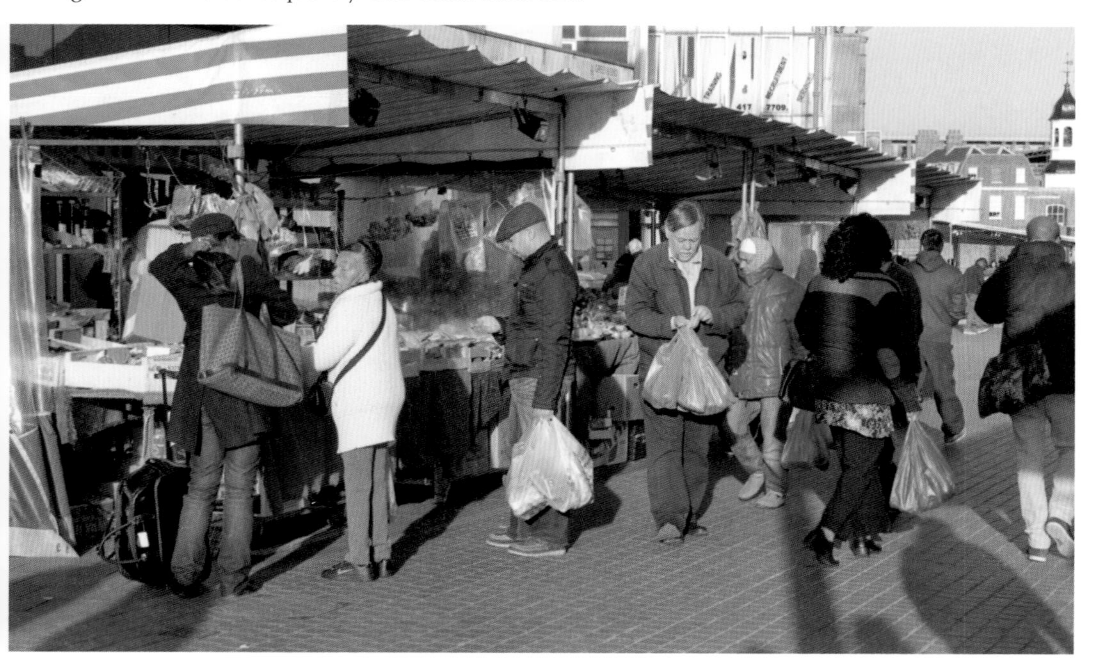

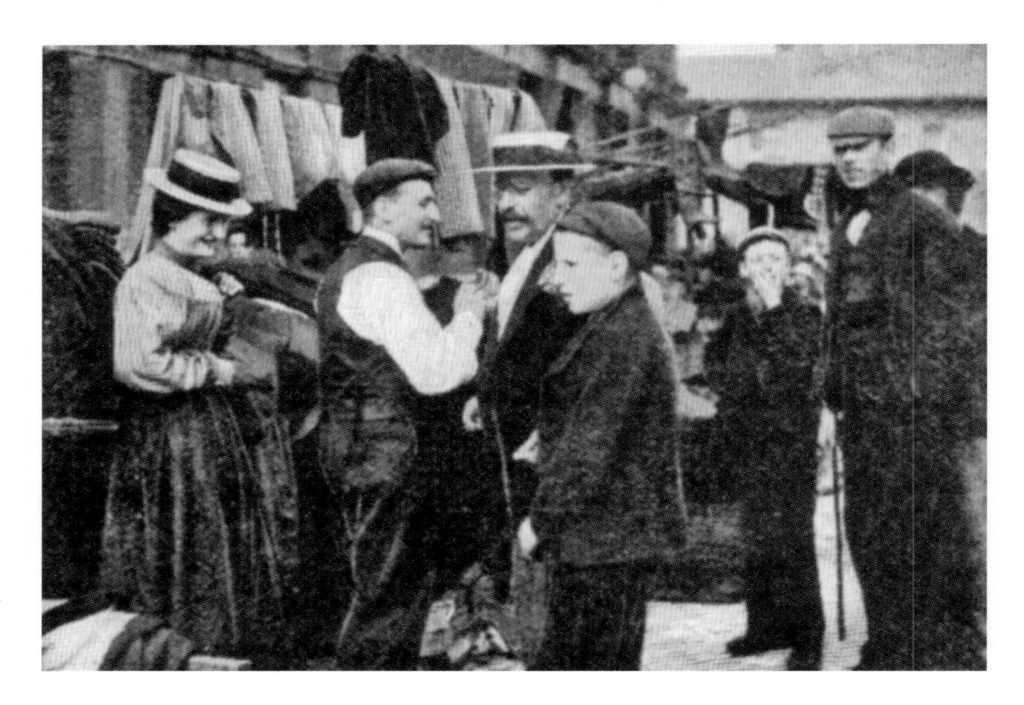

Woolwich Market Clothing Stall, 1900, and Woolwich Market Food Stall, 2013
By 1900, Woolwich Market had an international reputation, with a seven-page heavily illustrated article titled 'The Street Auctions of Military Woolwich', published in *The Royal Magazine* in the USA. Arthur Goodrich recounts with outrage how local authorities, who had purchased right to the market tolls from the Lord of the Manor, determined to levy tolls on all the stands in Beresford Square. Today, stalls are greatly depleted in number, many unfit for purpose, with traders fearing their market is under threat.

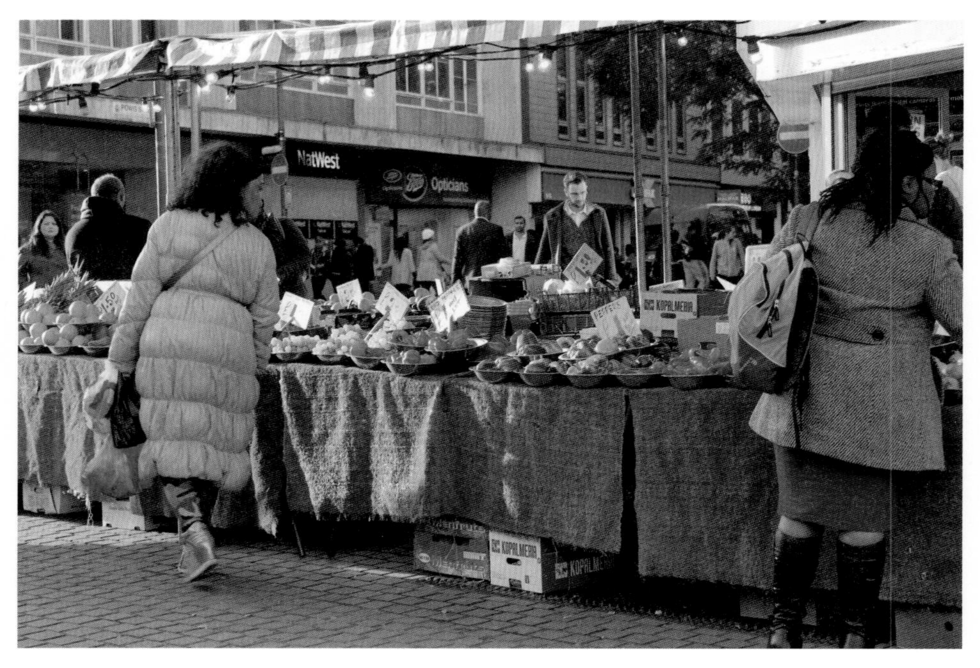

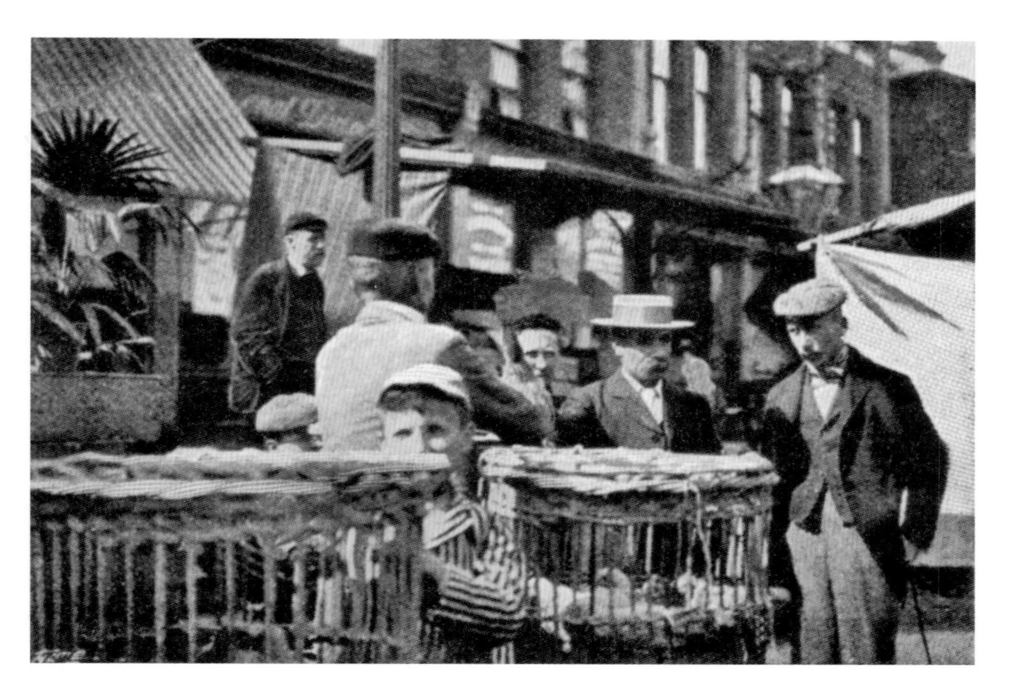

Woolwich Market Bird Stall, 1900, and Woolwich Market Fruit and Veg Stall, 2013
With a complex system of letting and subletting in place by 1888, producing hierarchical feudal relationships similar to landlord, tenant and subtenant, disgruntled market traders paid the tolls to avoid eviction. Their investment paid dividends: the market flourished, with customers able to stock up on anything from crockery to clothing and bric-a-brac to foodstuffs – everything except bar furniture (considered unsuitable for outdoor display) and poultry (for reasons unknown). In today's market there is noticeably less activity around the textile stalls, but digital items attract.

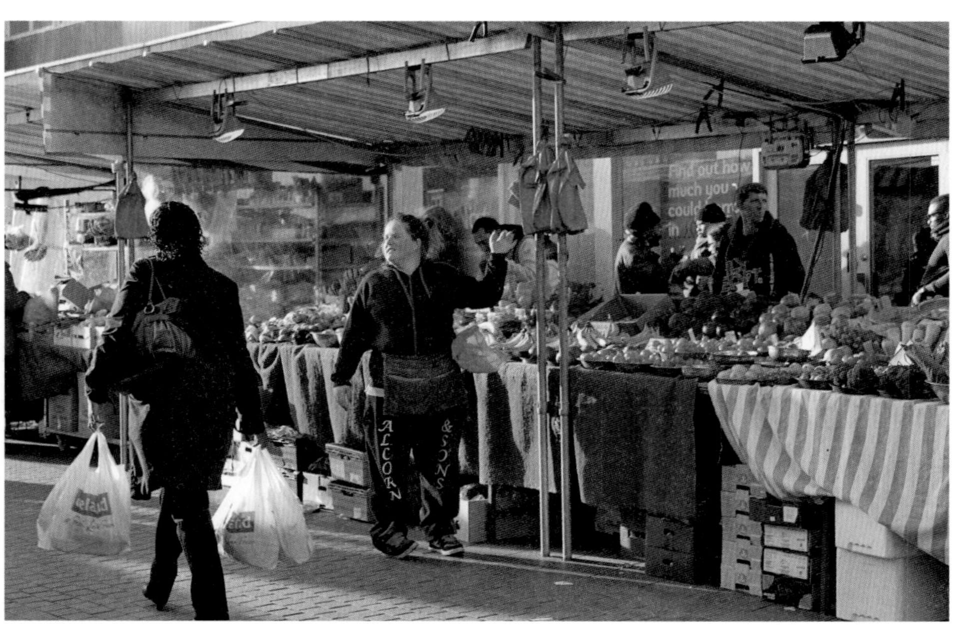

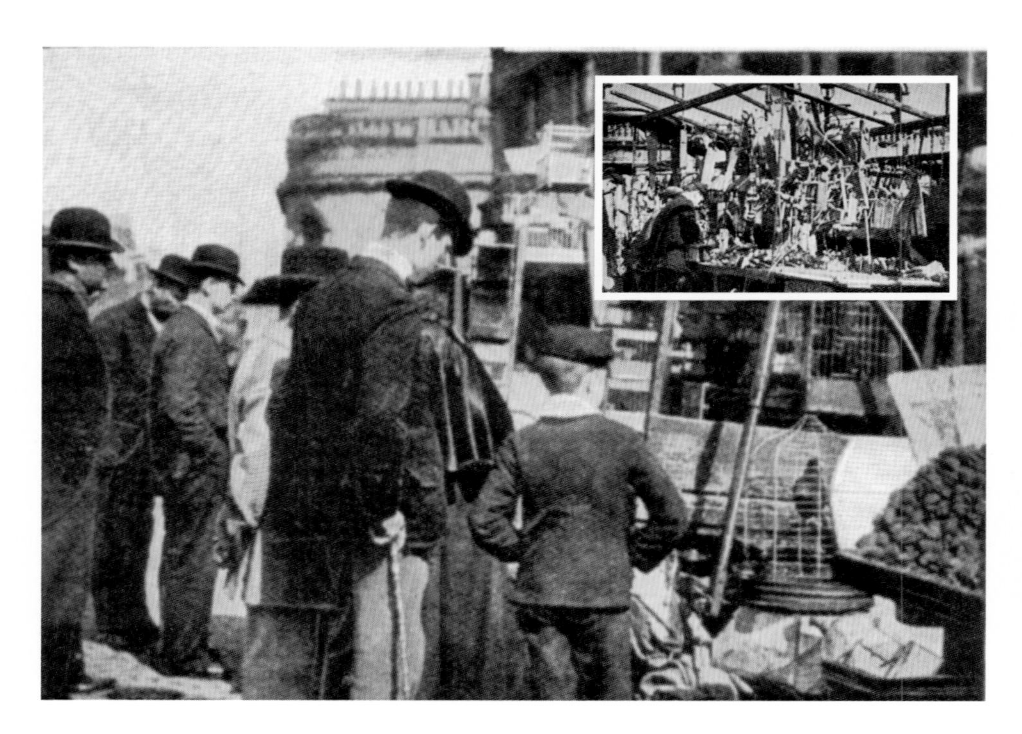

Woolwich Market Bric-a-Brac, 1900, and Woolwich Market Food Arcade, 2013
Today's Woolwich Market is a scaled-down version of its former self. Shops still line the perimeter, the square's centre housing twenty-eight (of a possible seventy) stalls. Auctioneering is a thing of the past and bartering is an illusion, but the banter and witty calling by traders manning the vibrantly colourful fruit and veg stalls add a rhythmic energy to the liveliest part of the market, whose operation is currently under review. It is to be hoped 'regeneration' will reinvigorate, rather than dismantle, the market.

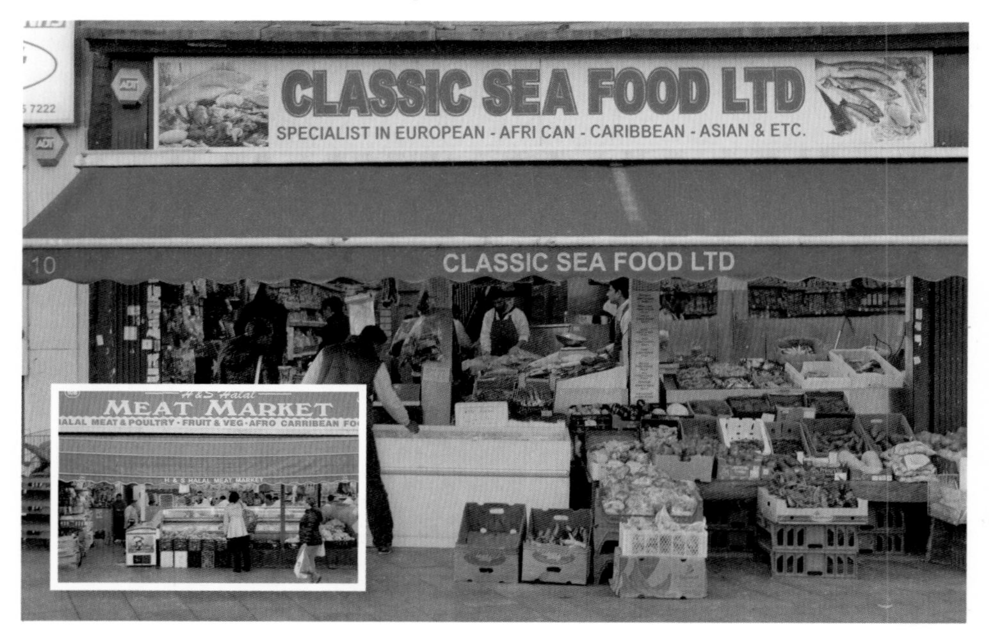

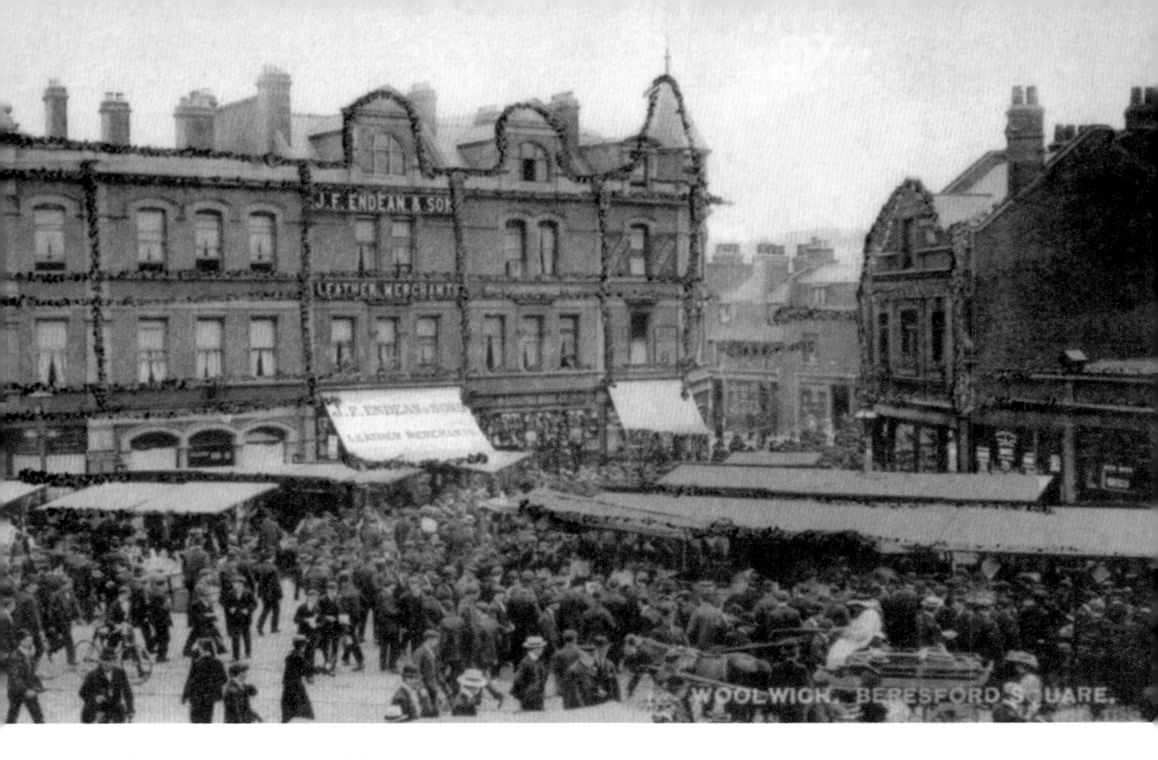

Beresford Square, Woolwich
Site of today's Woolwich Market, Beresford Square has functioned as a commercial centre for two centuries, since the foot of Green's End was cleared in 1812/13, creating the large open space named in 1837 for Army officer 1st Viscount William Carr Beresford (1768–1854), Master General of the Arsenal between 1828 and 1830, when its new entrance was built. Woolwich Market was legally established here in 1888, although its unofficial presence dates substantially earlier. Permanent shops soon sprang up to line the streets.

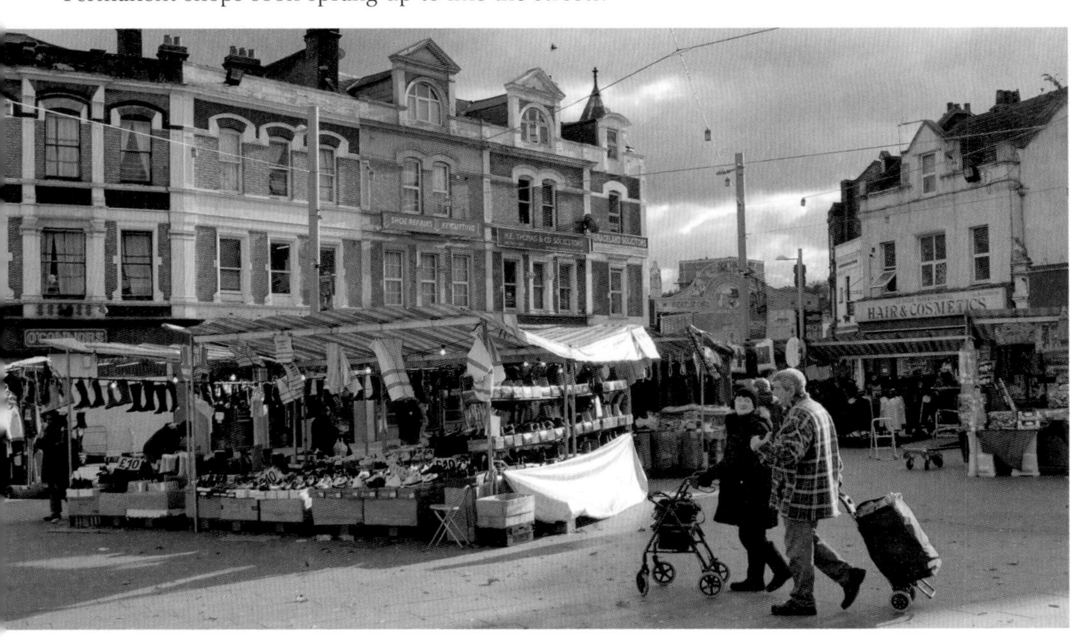

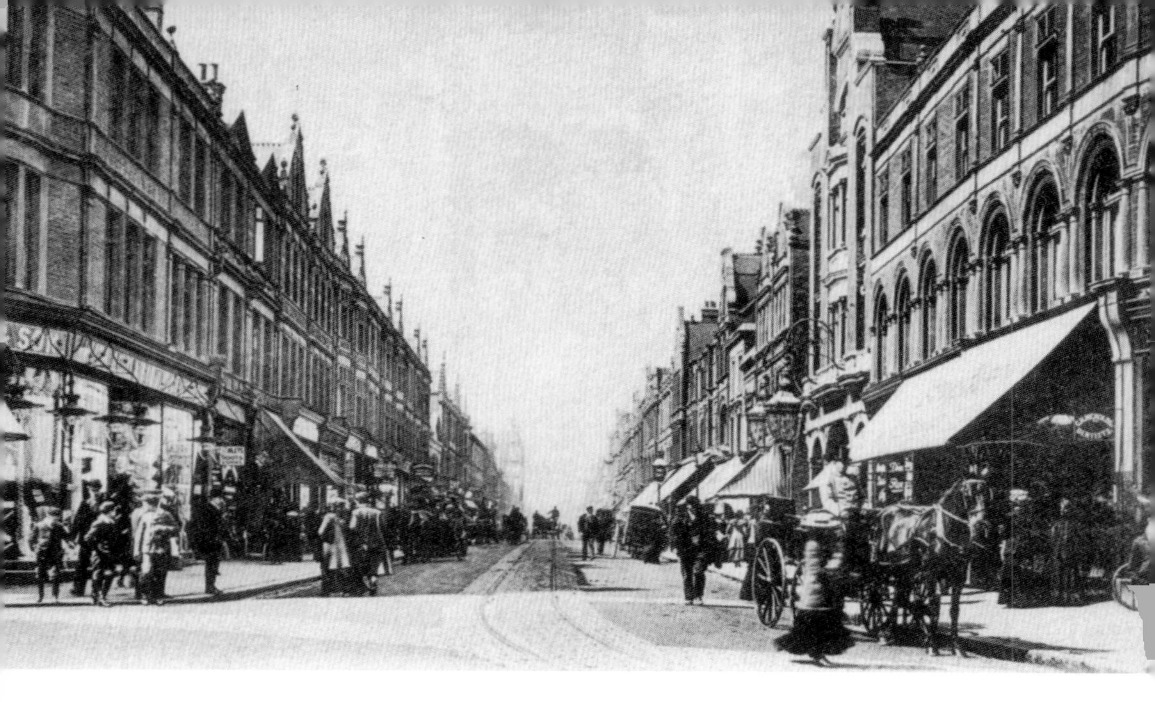

Powis Street, Woolwich, 1907

As the Arsenal expanded during the mid-nineteenth century, and its housing pushed further into Plumstead, Powis Street – between Beresford Square and the high street (today's A205) – became a magnet for consumers. Five shopfronts were approved between 1848 and 1852, four in 1858, and between 1861 and 1866, more than twenty shops were erected, mostly to the south. Now, only Nos 51–53 and 79–81 survive. Powis Street was named for the family of Greenwich brewers who purchased Bowater Estate, providing the sites for commercial and municipal Woolwich.

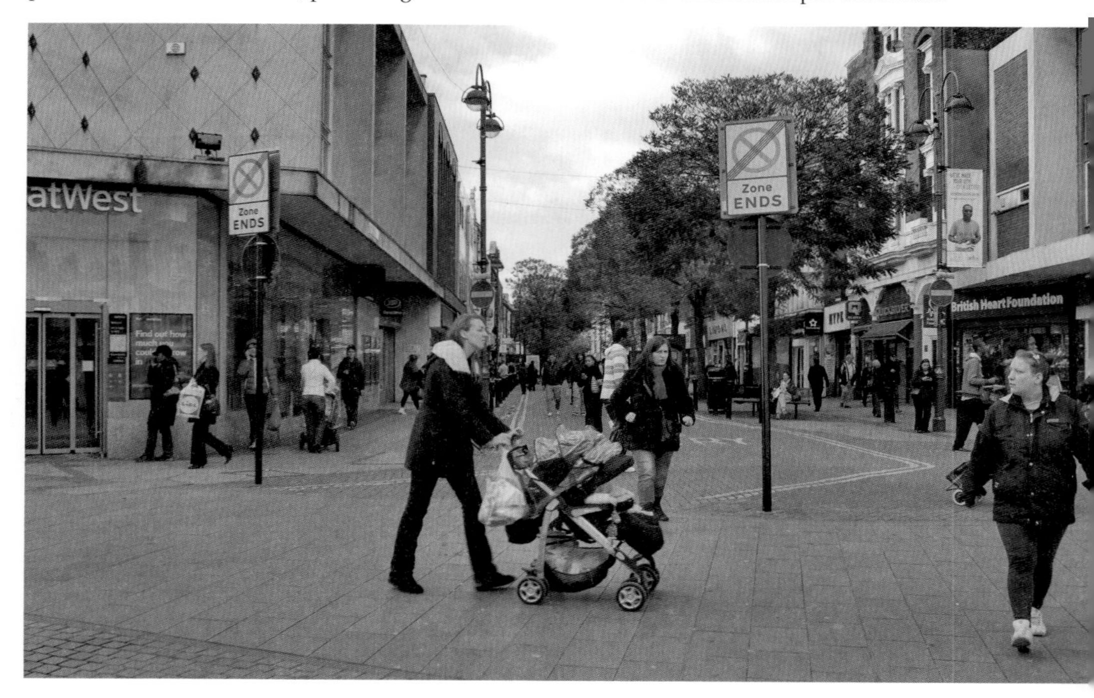

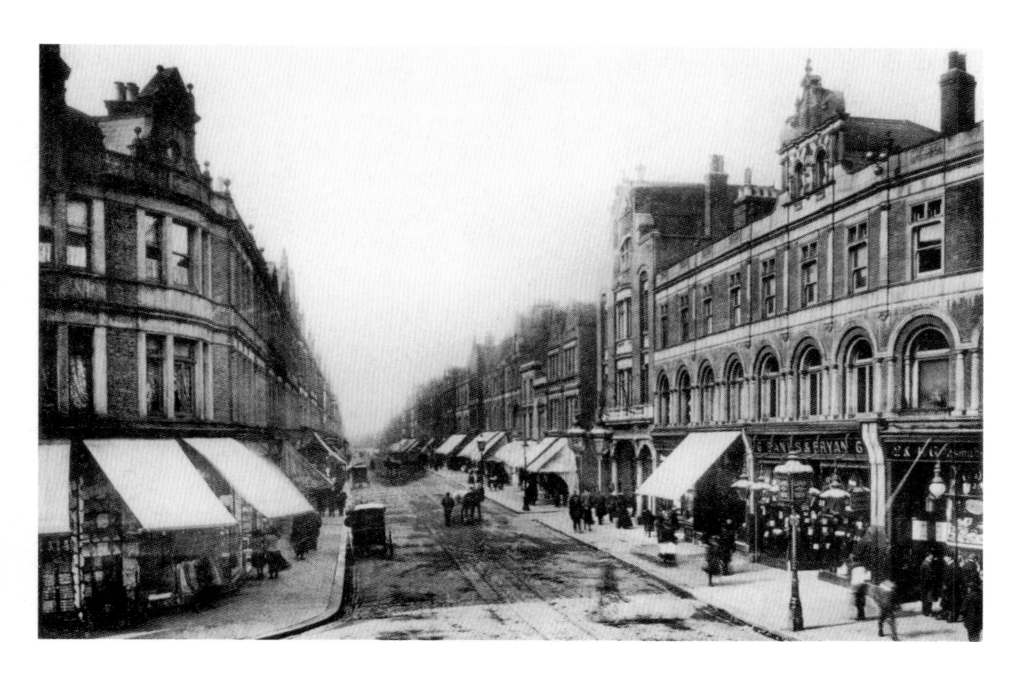

Powis Street, Woolwich, *c.* 1915

One surviving frontage on Powis Street is the former William Shakespeare pub. Built in 1853 and rebuilt in 1900, its façade dates to around 1894. The building is identifiable in the modern photograph as the three-storey, red-brick edifice topped by the figure of a monkey perched on the white triangle framed by urn finials. A bust of Shakespeare is carved within the triangle but is obscured from view by the camera angle. Fellow poet Richard Lovelace was born to a high-status family 'of Woolwich' in 1617.

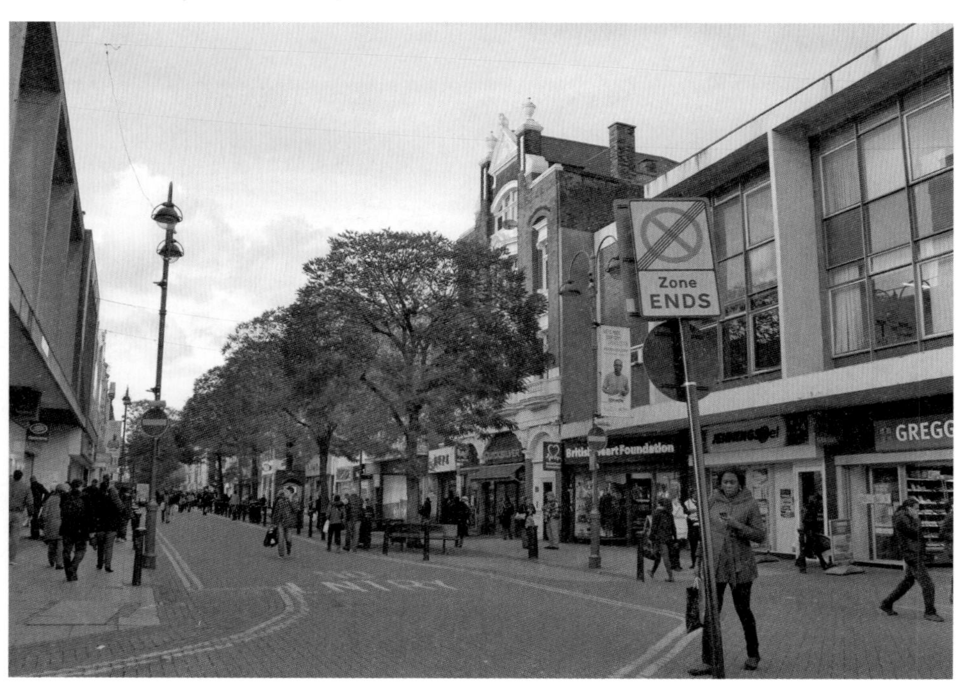

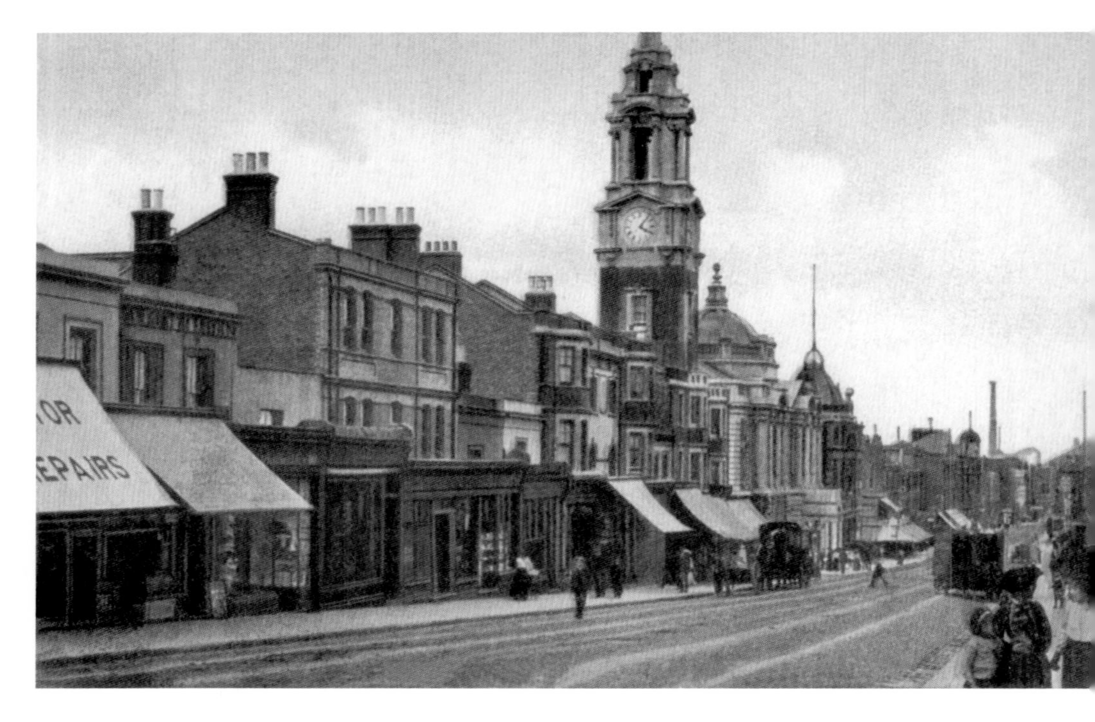

Wellington Street & Town Hall, Woolwich, 1905

As the nineteenth century progressed, Wellington Street developed into the heart of Woolwich's Municipal District, its first town hall having been erected in nearby William Street during the 1840s. The new town hall was built in Wellington Street between 1903 and 1906 in grand Baroque style – a much larger edifice to suit the requirements of a rapidly expanding borough. Its eastern neighbour was the Grand Theatre and Opera House; to the west stood a line of Victorian shops, since replaced by Job Centre Plus.

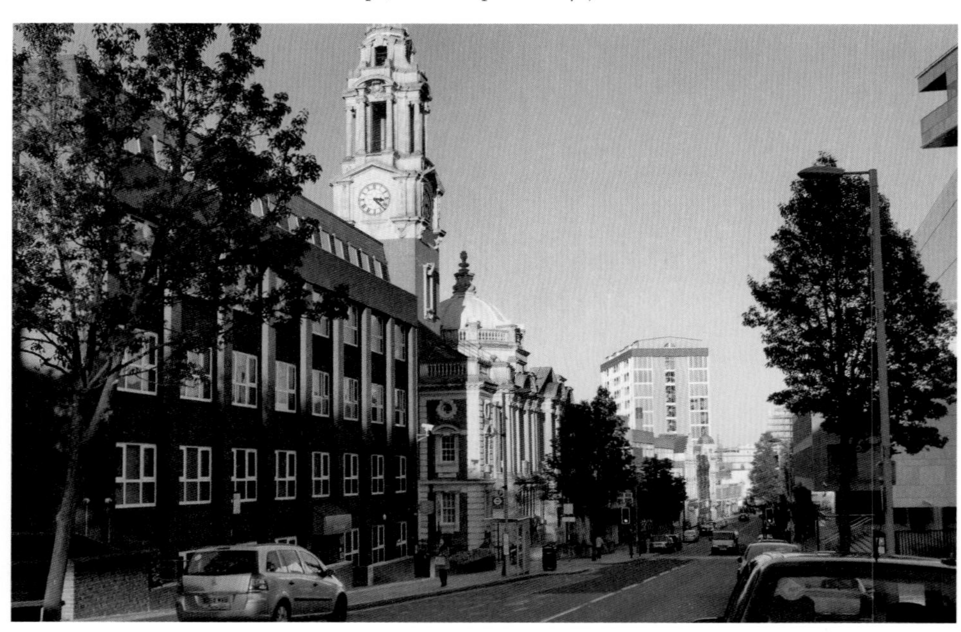

New Town Hall, Woolwich, 1905
Built by J. E. Johnson & Sons to Alfred Brumwell Thomas' design (believed to be based on his earlier plan for Plumstead Town Hall, which remained unbuilt), Woolwich Town Hall taps into classical tradition, rather than the Gothic revival still favoured outside London. It projects a confident Edwardian energy, following on from the Industrial Revolution and consequent urban expansion. The site cost £15,000 and construction cost £80,000. Thompson was later knighted for his work on Belfast City Hall and he also designed Deptford Library.

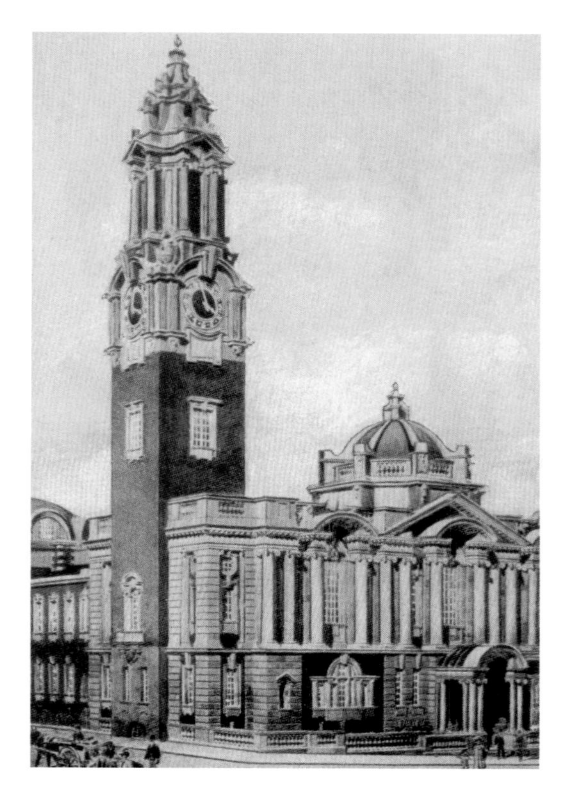

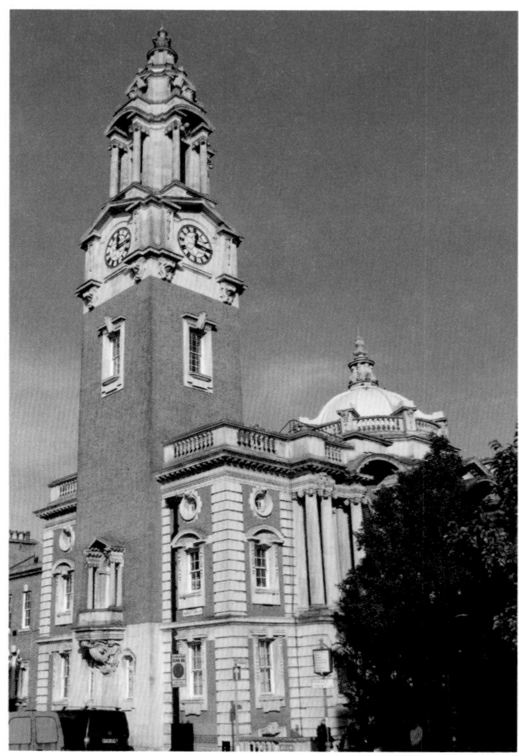

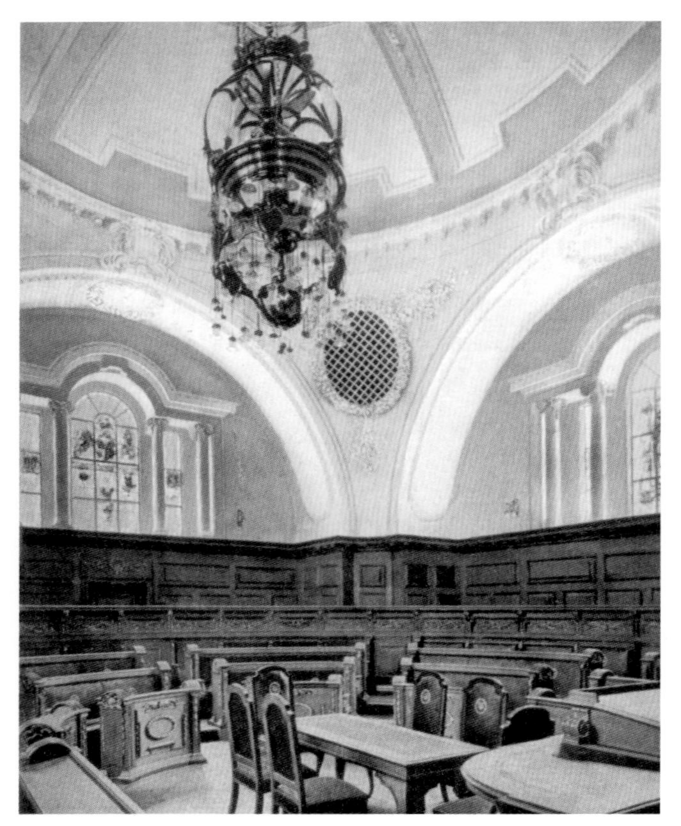

Interior of Council Chamber, Woolwich Town Hall, 1910
The town hall's council chamber boasts a domed ceiling, oak wall-panelling, and matching seats semi-encircling a dais, opposite to which is a central stained-glass window bearing the arms of the previous Boroughs of Woolwich and Greenwich, the more recent Borough of Greenwich (prior to its Royal status) and the monarch under whom Woolwich gained stature as 'the Mother Dock of England'. Windows left and right depict King Henry VIII and Queen Elizabeth I, with medallions of their namesake Tudor ships.

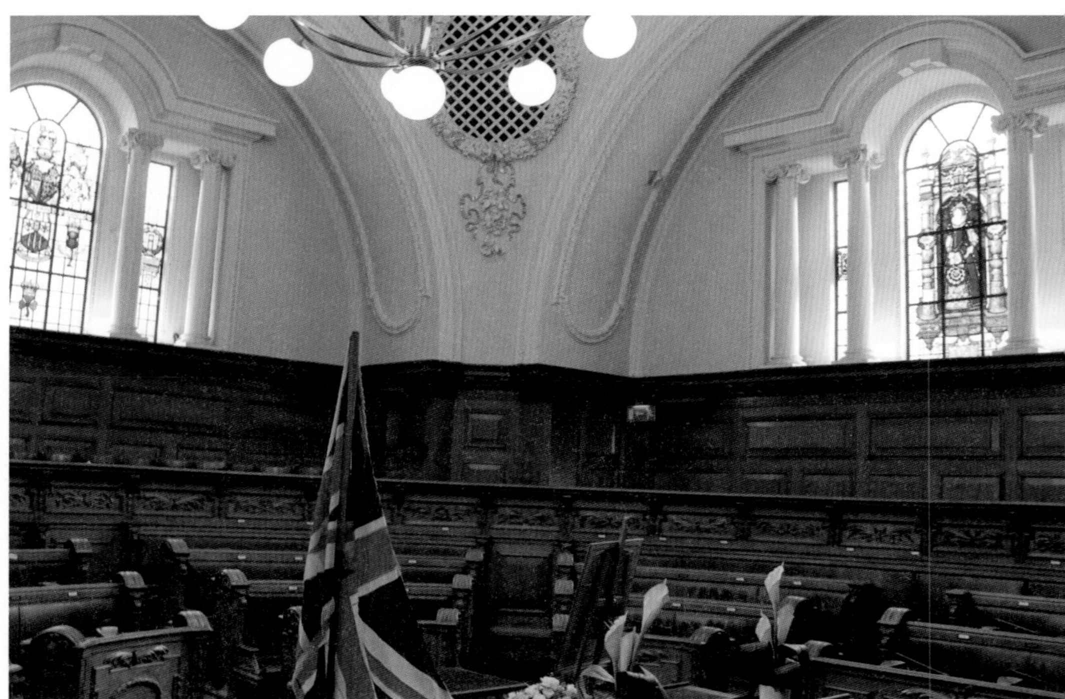

Will Crooks & Nick Raynsford, MPs for Woolwich, 1906 and 2013
In 2006, the centenary year of the Parliamentary Labour Party, MPs representing the twenty-nine seats held by the founding Labour MPs elected in 1906 were invited to contribute an extended obituary for *Men Who Made Labour*, with Nick Raynsford celebrating the achievements of Will Crooks (1852 Poplar – 1921 Whitechapel). Crooks harnessed his gift for the witty retort to champion improved conditions, pay and healthcare for workers at Woolwich – key issues again faced by Mr Raynsford since the global recession of 2009.

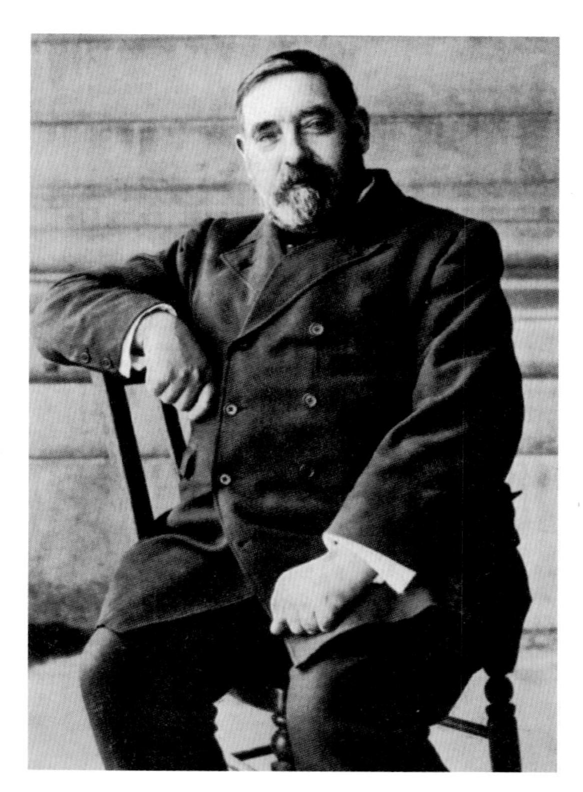

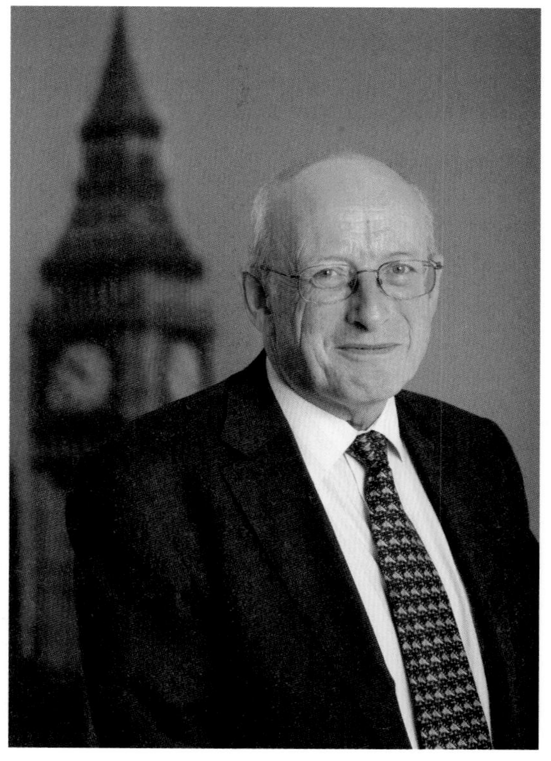

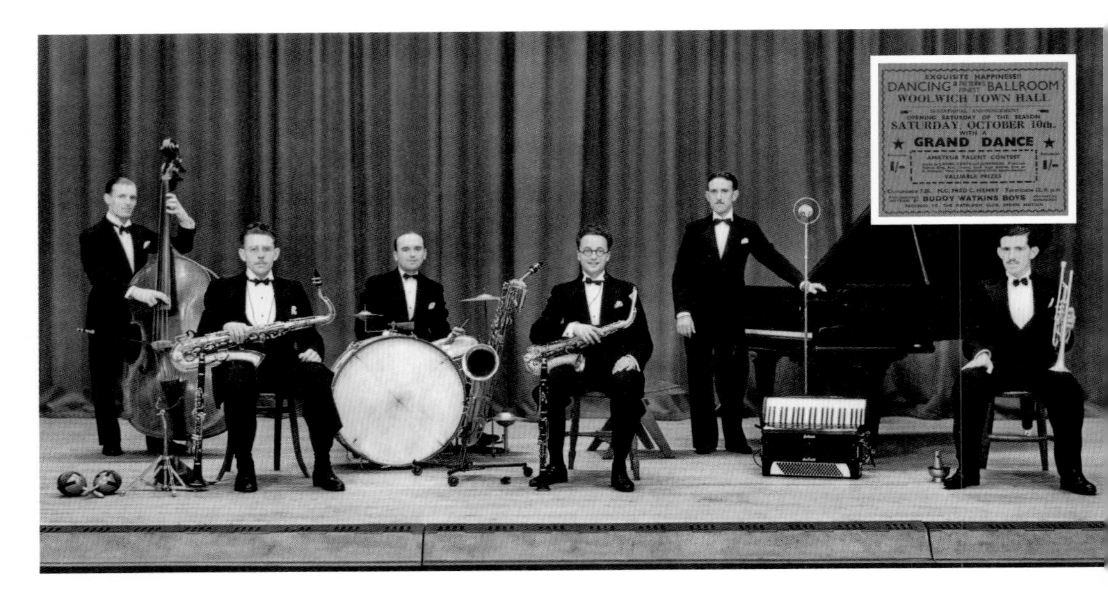

Buddy Watkins Boys Play Woolwich Town Hall and Flamenco Dancers at The Grand

A local musician, whose business card records him as 'Buddy Watkins, Rhythm Pianist 10 Earlswood Street, E. Greenwich, S.E.10', Buddy led a band that performed at dance competitions as well as concerts. Woolwich Town Hall has continued to host themed dances to the present day, the most recent being a Jingle Bell Rock Disco on 4 December 2013. The neighbouring Grand Theatre has likewise broadened its repertoire to include entertainments in all genres from Flamenco dancing to stand-up and film screenings to seasonal pantomime.

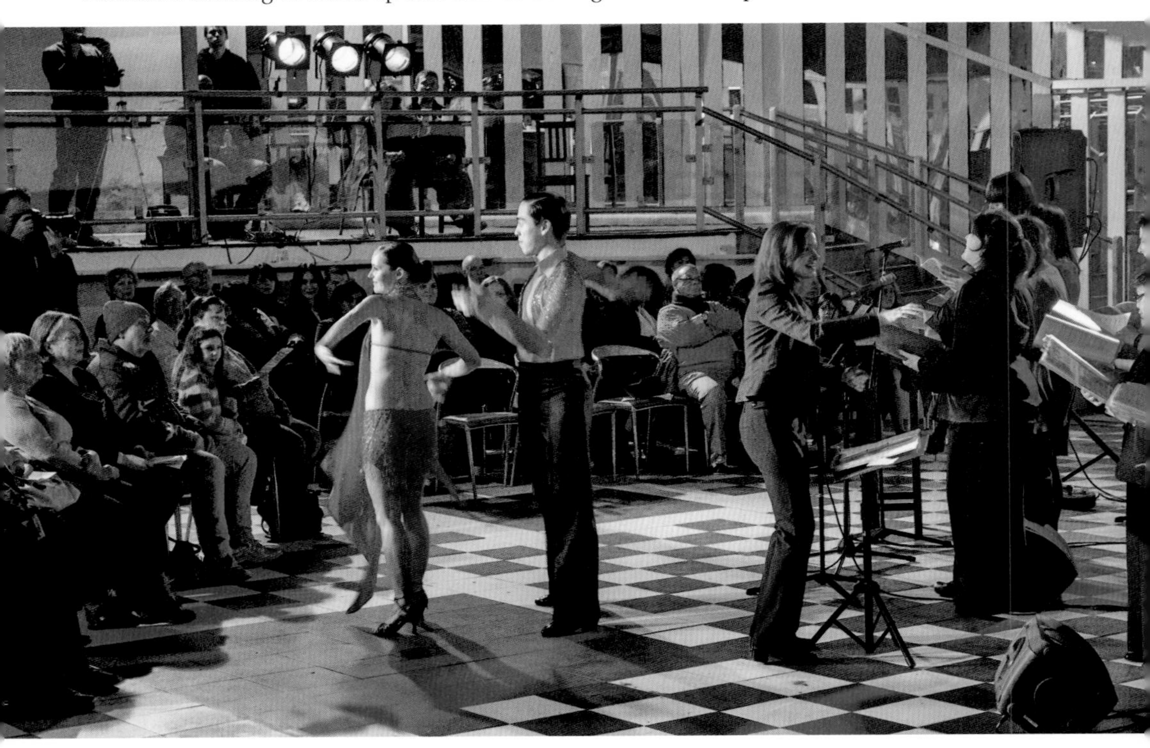

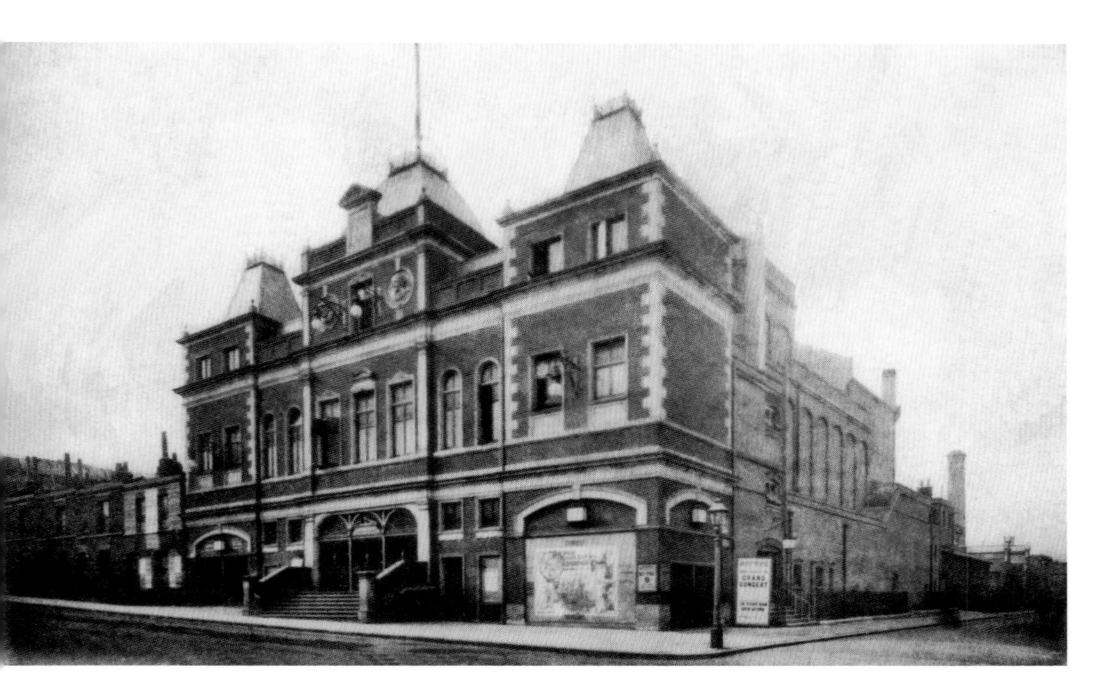

The Grand Theatre, Woolwich, *c.* 1915
The original Grand Theatre and Opera House was opened by Sir Henry Irving in 1900, producing dramatic and musical performances, later adding 'variety'. It was transformed into a cinema by 1925, before closing for demolition in 1939 to make way for a new cinema. This was finally completed in 1955 but closed in 1982. It reopened as a nightclub in 1985, lost its license, and was again sold for reopening as an arts venue in 2011, although it is sadly once more at risk of being demolished.

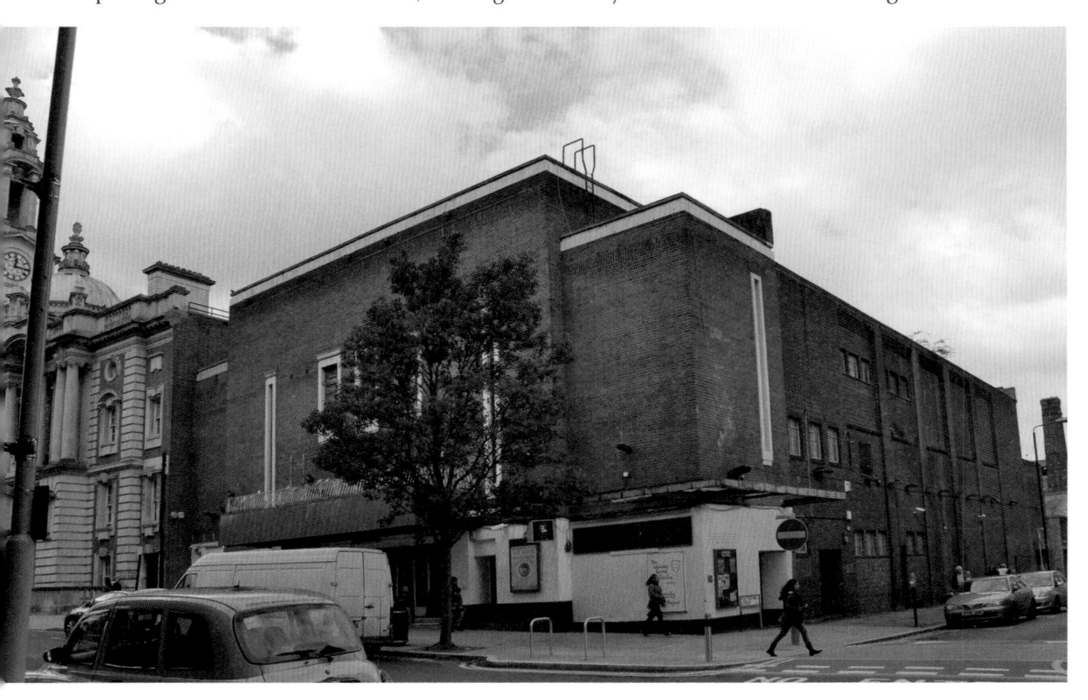

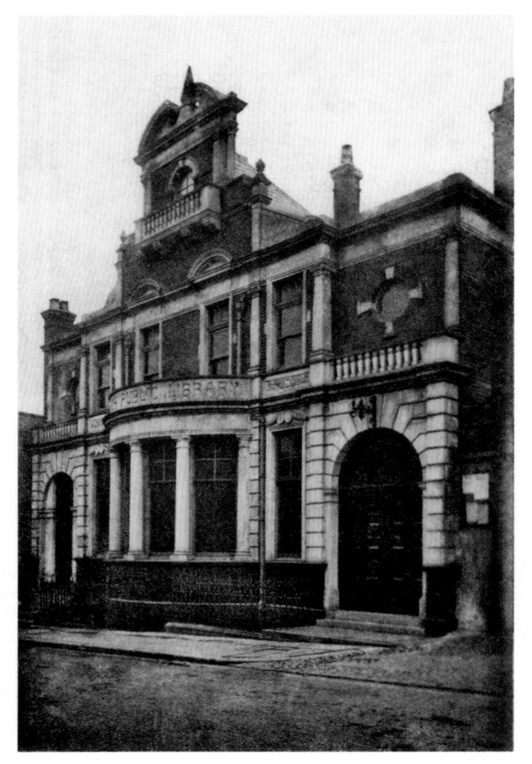

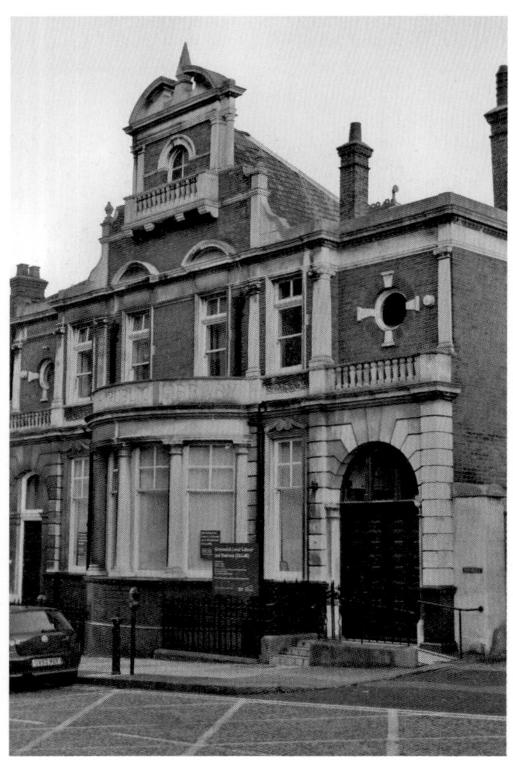

Public Library, Woolwich, *c.* 1915
A municipal works yard next to the police station on William Street, now Calderwood Street, was mooted as the site for a new town hall, but was in fact used for the public library, which was opened by Lord Avebury on 8 November 1901. It has been accorded a Grade II listing by English Heritage. The building survives intact, but has been superseded by a new public library, four times its size, which opened in the Woolwich Centre complex at No. 35 Wellington Street in 2011.

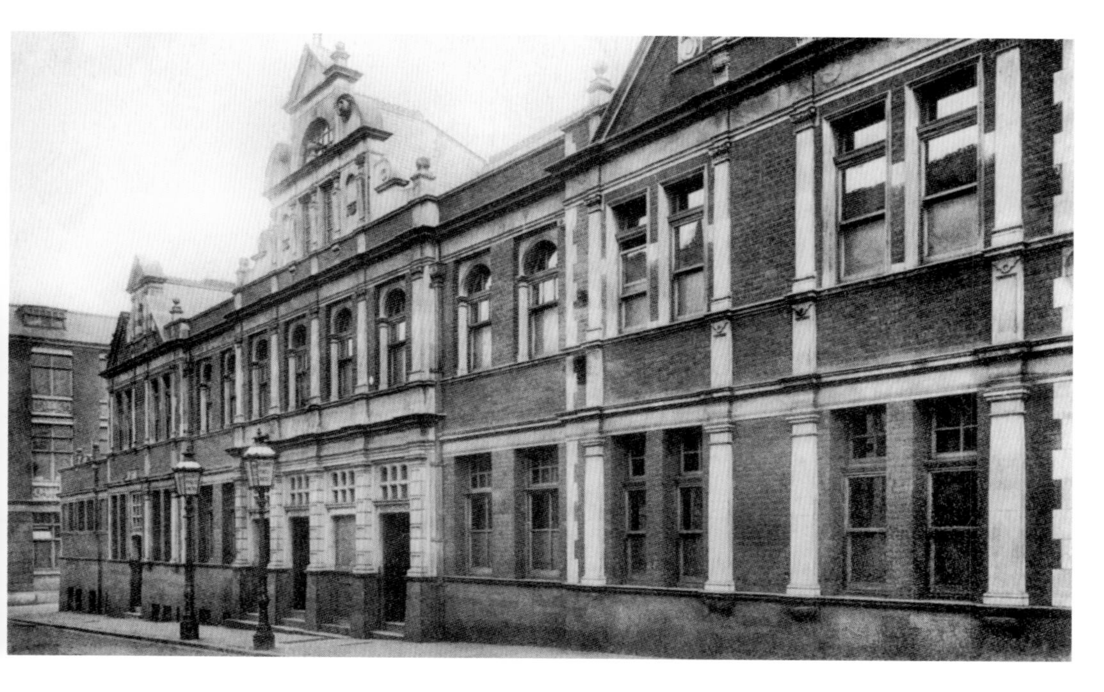

Public Baths, Woolwich, *c.* 1915

The construction of Woolwich's public baths in 1893/94 marked the first noteworthy municipal development outside the original market area, on what is now Bathway, directly south of Calderwood. Like the public library and Woolwich Polytechnic, the baths were designed by H. H. Church, whose consistent favouring of Renaissance decorative features adorning red-brick edifices brings a stylistic cohesion to Woolwich's civic district. It had baths for men and women, and first- and second-class swimming pools. Today, it functions as the students' union.

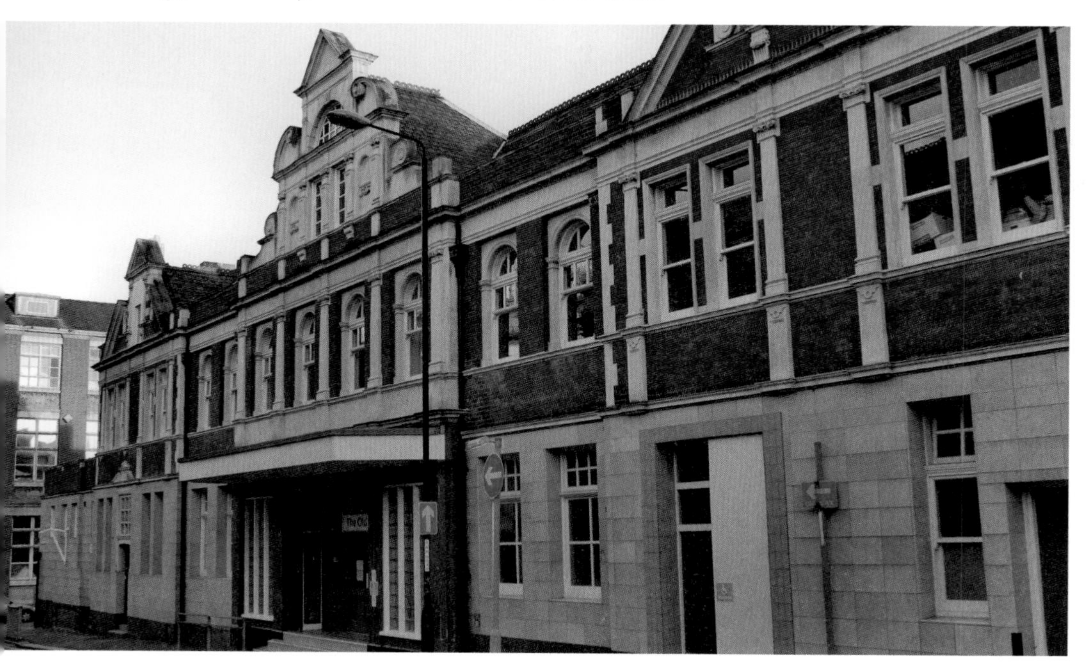

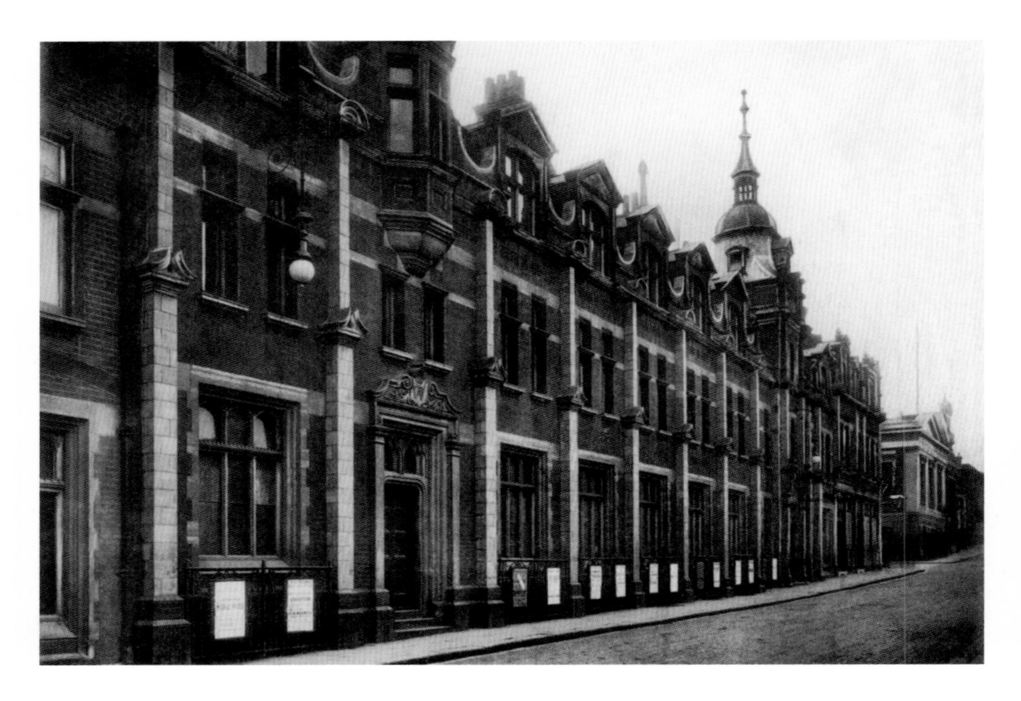

The Polytechnic, Woolwich, *c.* 1915
Situated east of the library, on the corner of William and Thomas Streets (named for the Powis brothers, leaseholders of the estate encompassing this area), Woolwich Polytechnic was established in 1891. Rapid expansion saw a science and art school open opposite the public baths in 1905. Merging with other local colleges, Woolwich Polytechnic became Thames Polytechnic in 1970, and was granted university status as part of the University of Greenwich in 1992. Thomas Street is now known as Polytechnic Street.

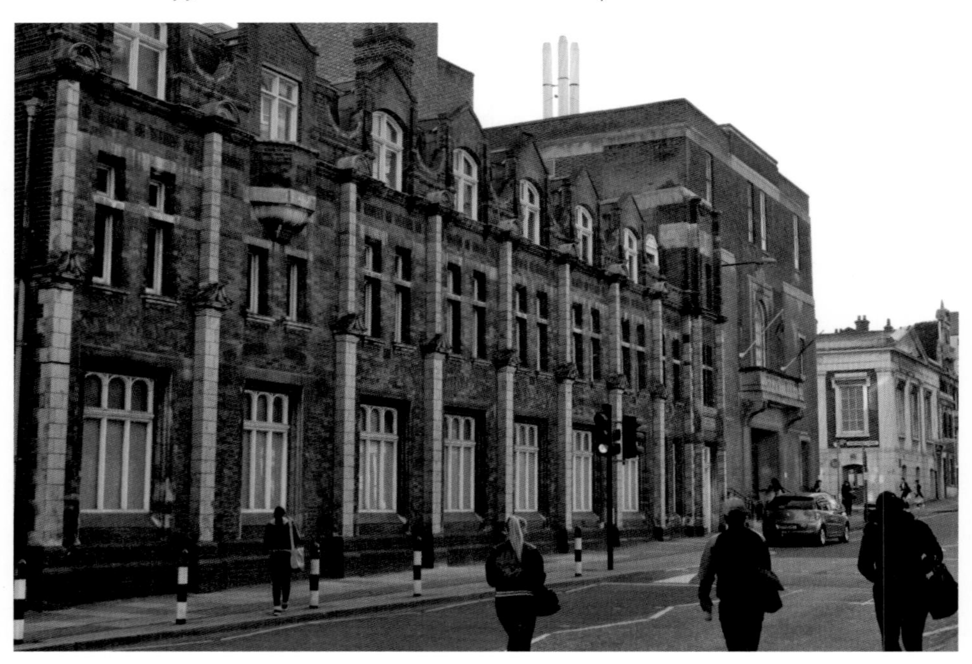

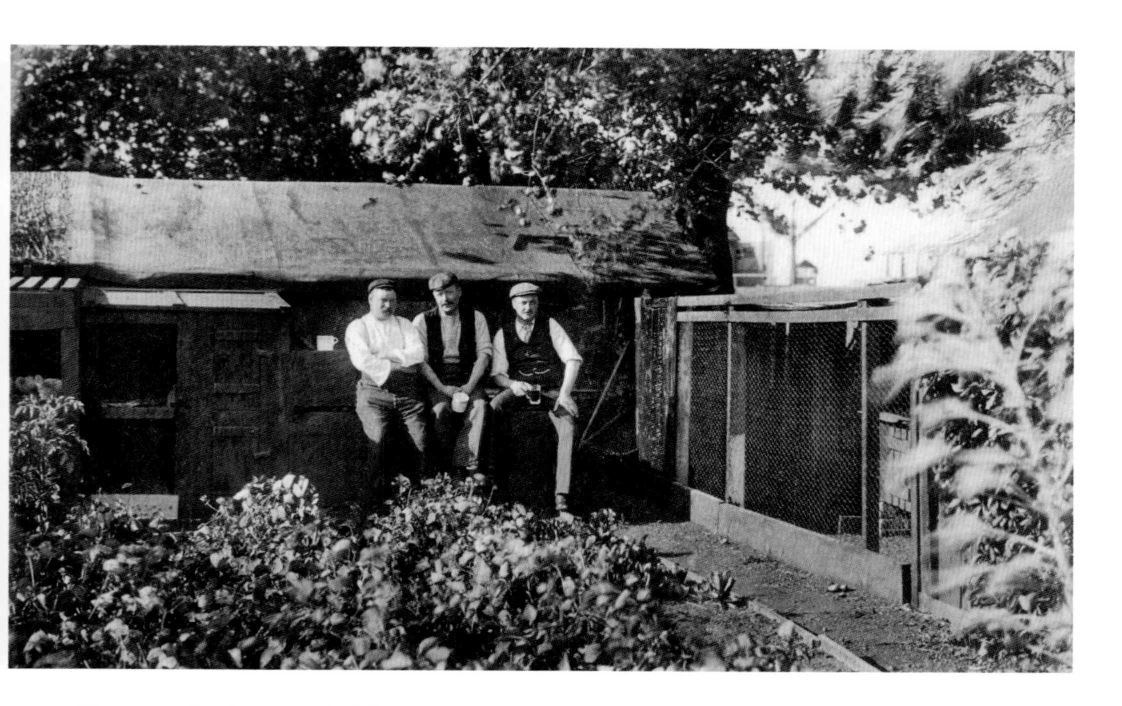

Allotment Garden, Woolwich, 1905

Although allotment gardening may date to Anglo-Saxon times, the system familiar today was a nineteenth-century development; the labouring poor were provided with land for food production, to offset the country's industrialisation. Three years after the above photograph was taken, the Small Holdings and Allotments Act – with allocation based on demand – was passed. At the end of the First World War land was made available to all. Today, the allotment gardens nearest to urbanised Woolwich may be found in Plumstead, Charlton, and Eltham (the site of the modern photograph).

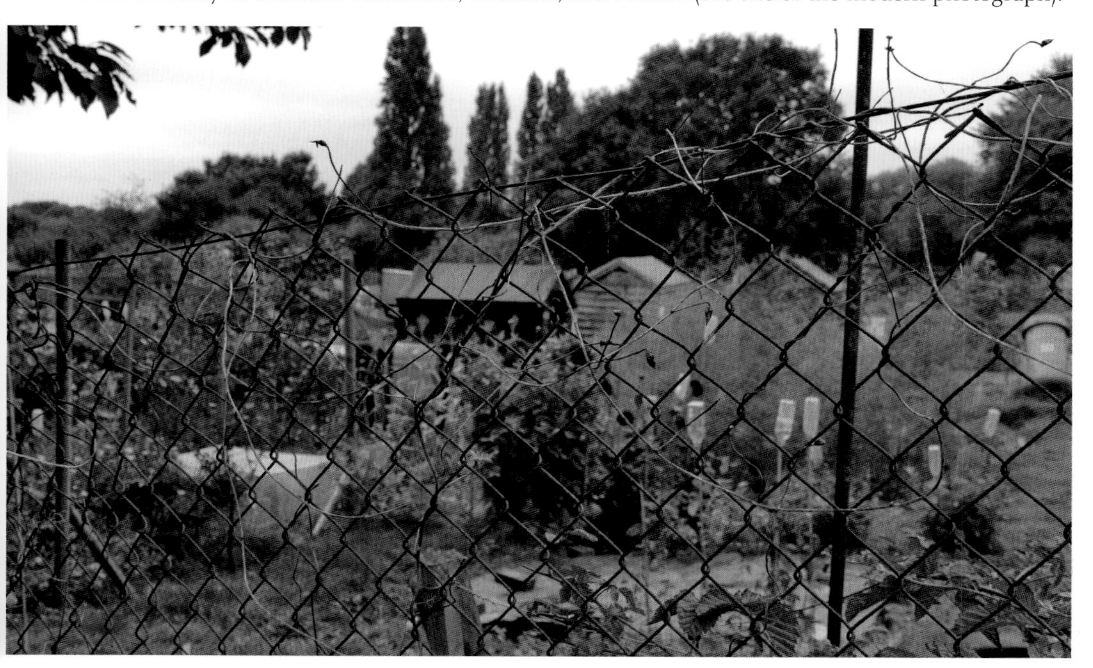

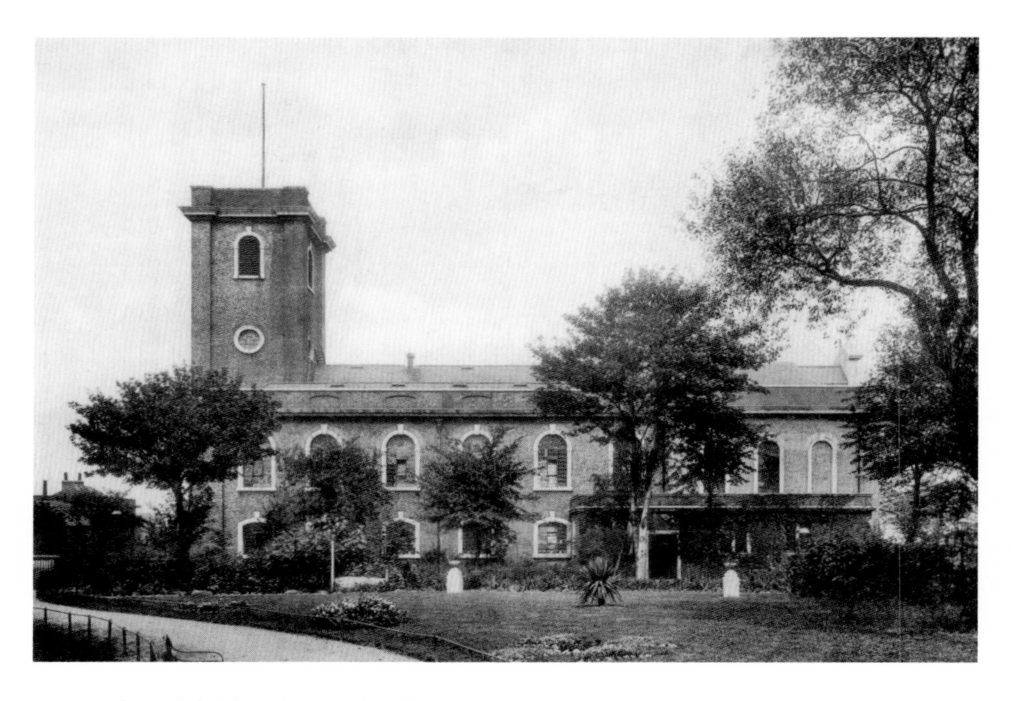

St Mary's Parish Church, Woolwich, *c.* 1915
The present Woolwich St Mary Magdalene was built between 1733 and 1740 by Matthew Spray on high ground near the river, hard by the church's mediaeval site, following the collapse of its Elizabethan spire. It was dedicated on 9 May 1740. The churchyard is now a public garden, one highlight being the tomb of bare-knuckle boxer Tom Cribb (1781–1848), under whose proud stone lion, with head upraised and right paw laid upon a stone urn, is inscribed 'Respect the Ashes of the Dead'.

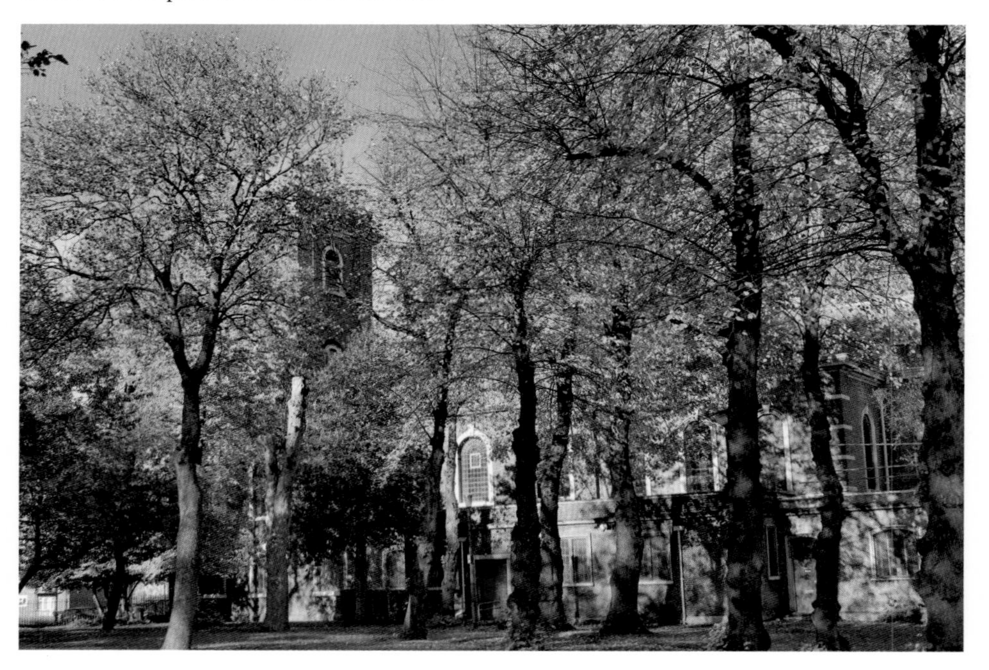

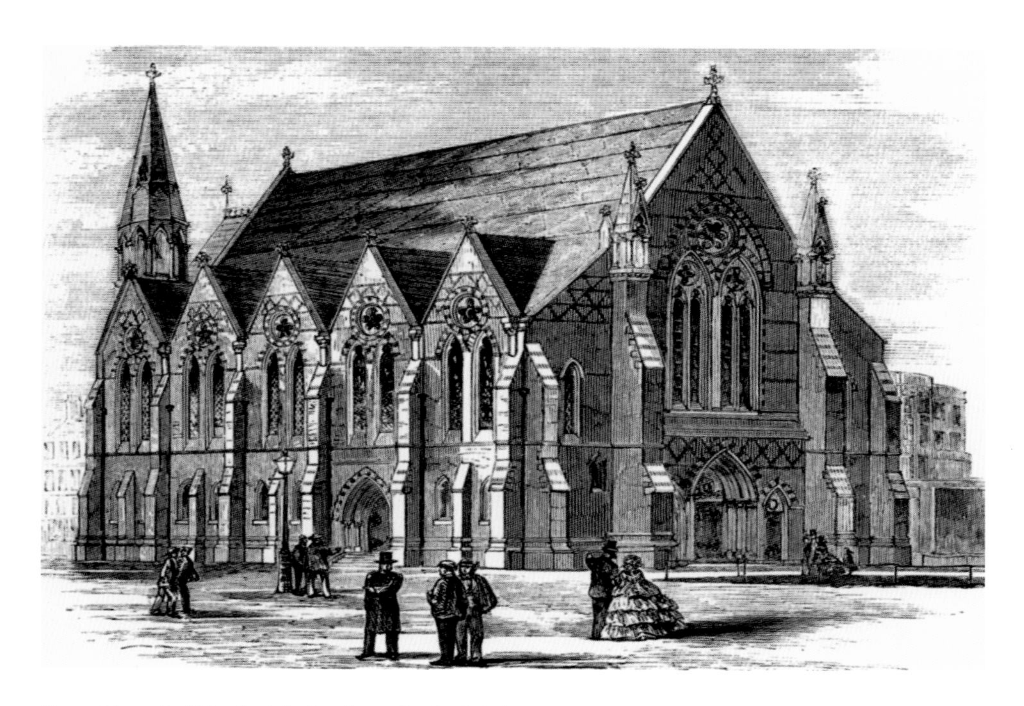

New Church, Woolwich Dockyard, 1858 Print
Designed by Sir George Gilbert Scott, the Naval Dockyard church was built between 1857 and 1859 at Woolwich Dockyard, becoming redundant after the latter's closure in 1869. In 1932/33, the distinctive red-brick edifice was reconstructed at Eltham, modified to fit its new site west of Well Hall roundabout. The rechristened St Barnabas church ministered to an expanding population of Arsenal workers residing in Eltham. Gutted by fire during the Second World War, it was restored in 1956 with a new roof and interior.

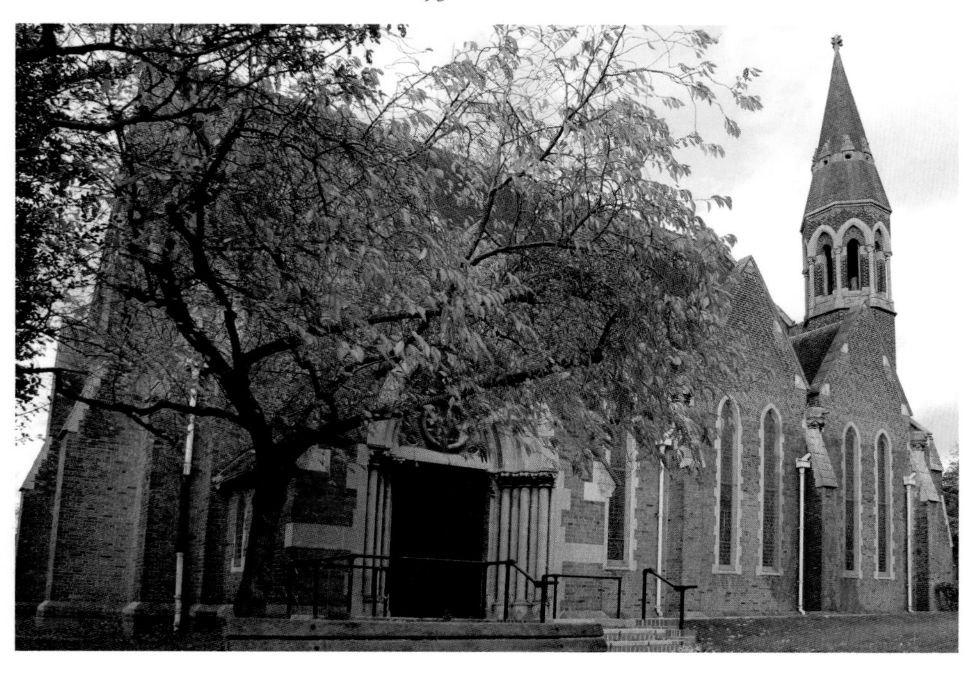

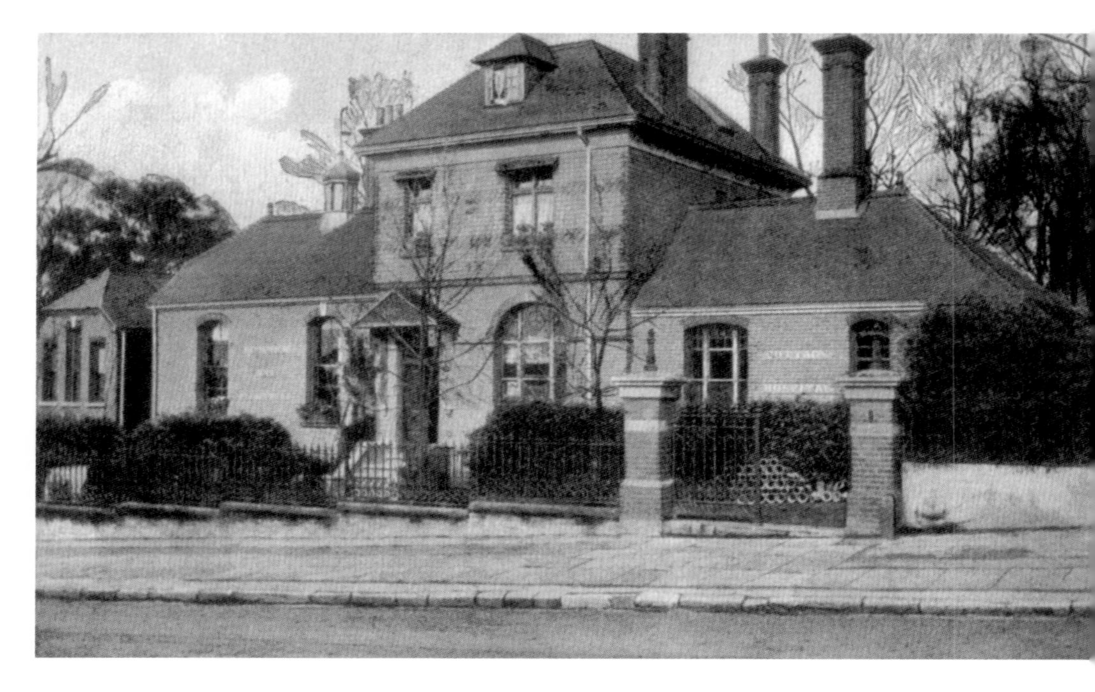

Cottage Hospital, Woolwich, 1906

Occupying half an acre at No. 25 Shooter's Hill, the three-storey Woolwich and Plumstead Cottage Hospital opened in 1890, containing twelve beds. By 1912, there were concerns it was too small to be economically viable and in 1920 a site was acquired for Woolwich Memorial Hospital. It opened in 1927 and patients from the Cottage Hospital were transferred in March 1928. Operating as Castlewood Day Hospital after the Second World War, it was closed in 2004 and was sold for redevelopment as residential housing in May 2007.

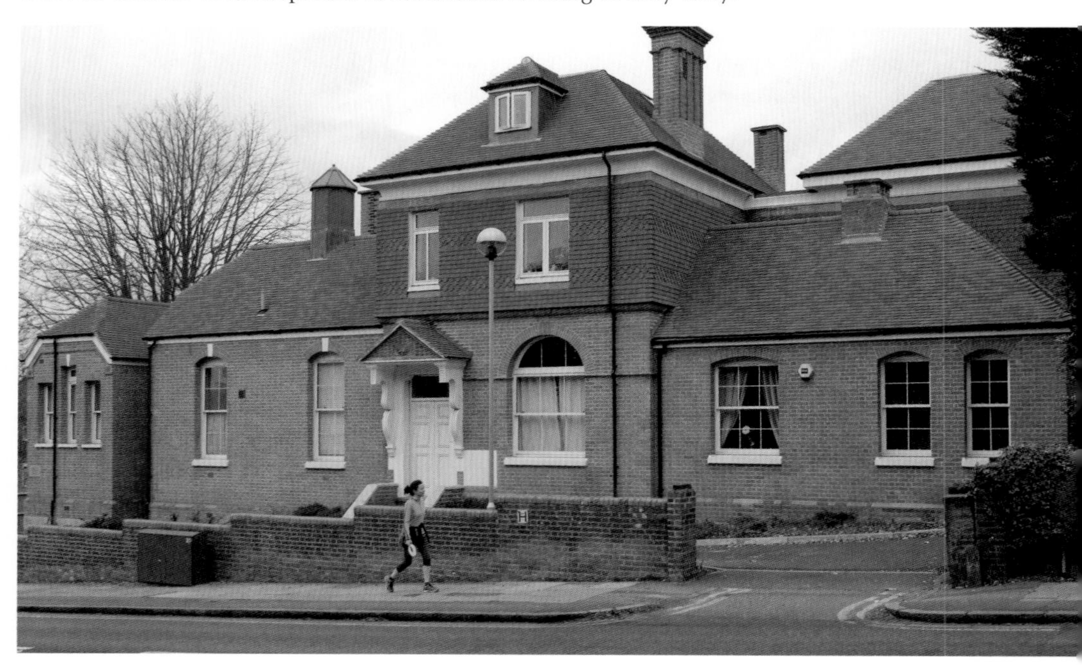

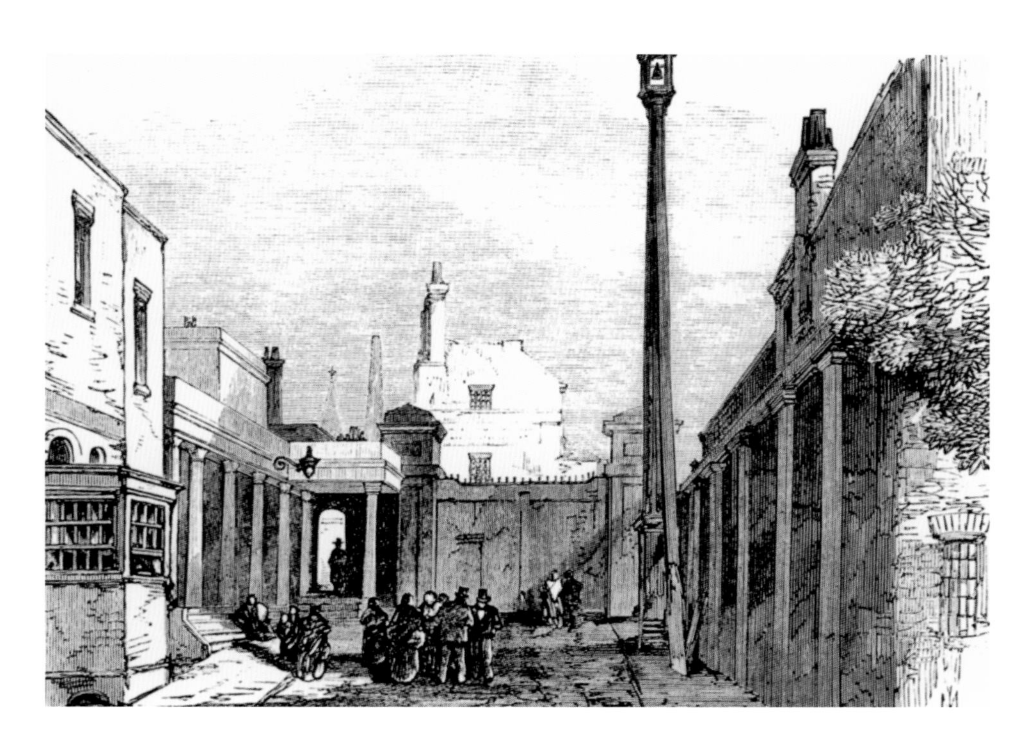

Main Entrance, Woolwich Dockyard, 1869 Print
King Henry VIII's foundation of its dockyard in 1512 transformed Woolwich from a small riverside fishing village to an important naval town. Its position, like that of Deptford, was chosen for its proximity to the Tower of London's armouries. It expanded to become one of Europe's foremost shipbuilding yards, but as ships grew larger and the Thames silted up, the site became unfit for purpose. Woolwich Dockyard closed in 1869 and was used for military storage by the Royal Arsenal before it was sold for residential redevelopment.

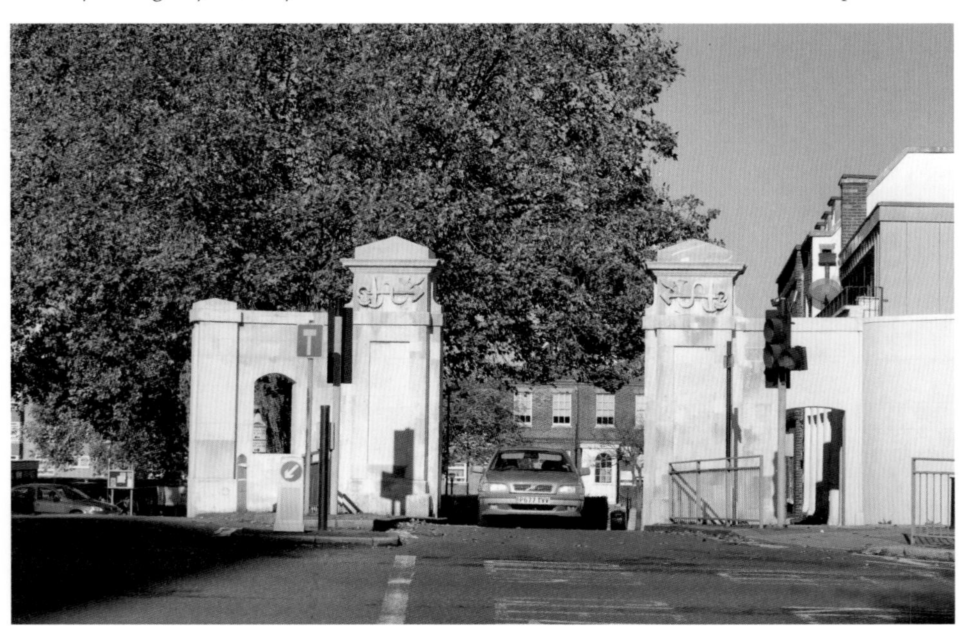

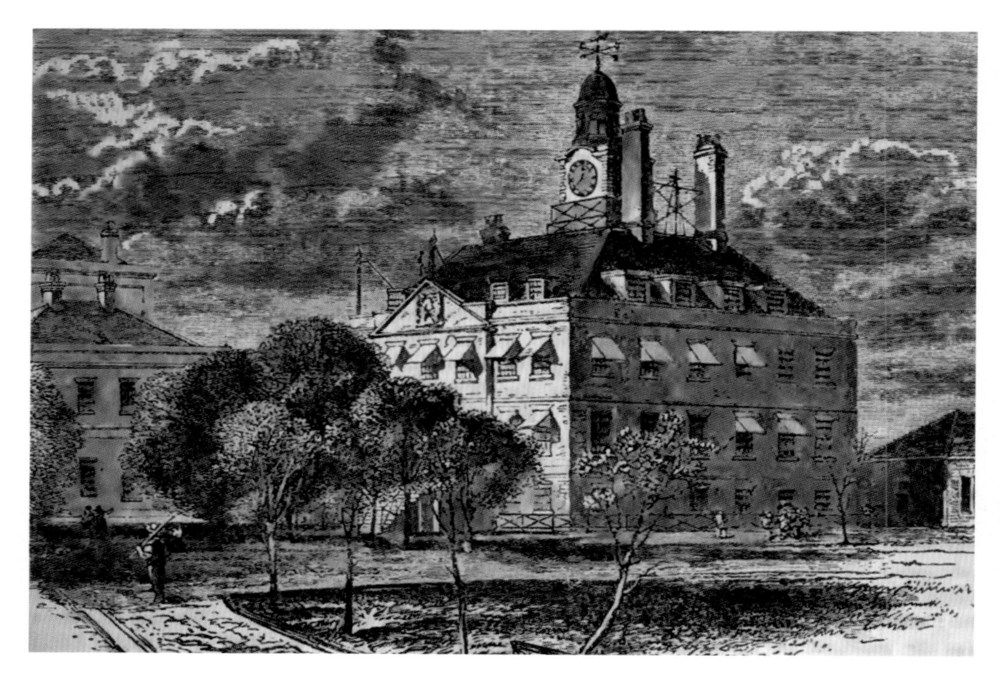

The Admiral-Superintendent's Office, 1869 Woodcut
Built between 1770 and 1779, Woolwich Dockyard's former superintendent's house and office, originally known as the Clockhouse, survives as a Grade II-listed building, still accessed via the Woolwich Dockyard's main entrance gates. It now operates as the Clockhouse Community Centre, as well as a conference venue for hire. Alice Frederica (Edmonstone) Keppel (1868–1947), mistress to King Edward VII, was born at Woolwich Dockyard, the daughter of Naval Commodore William Edmonstone, its superintendent, who was promoted to Rear Admiral in the year this woodcut was published.

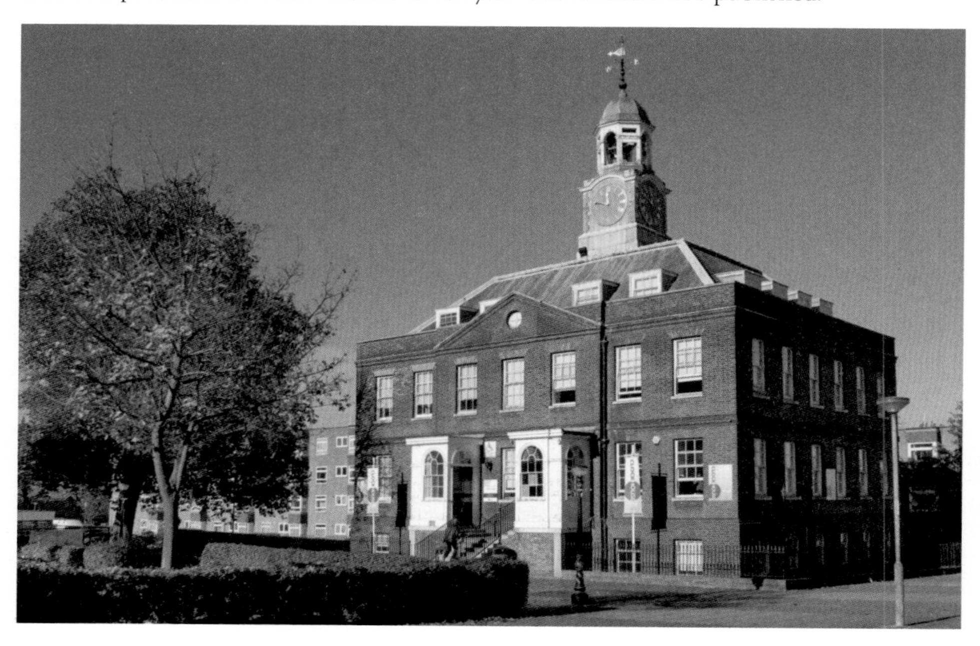

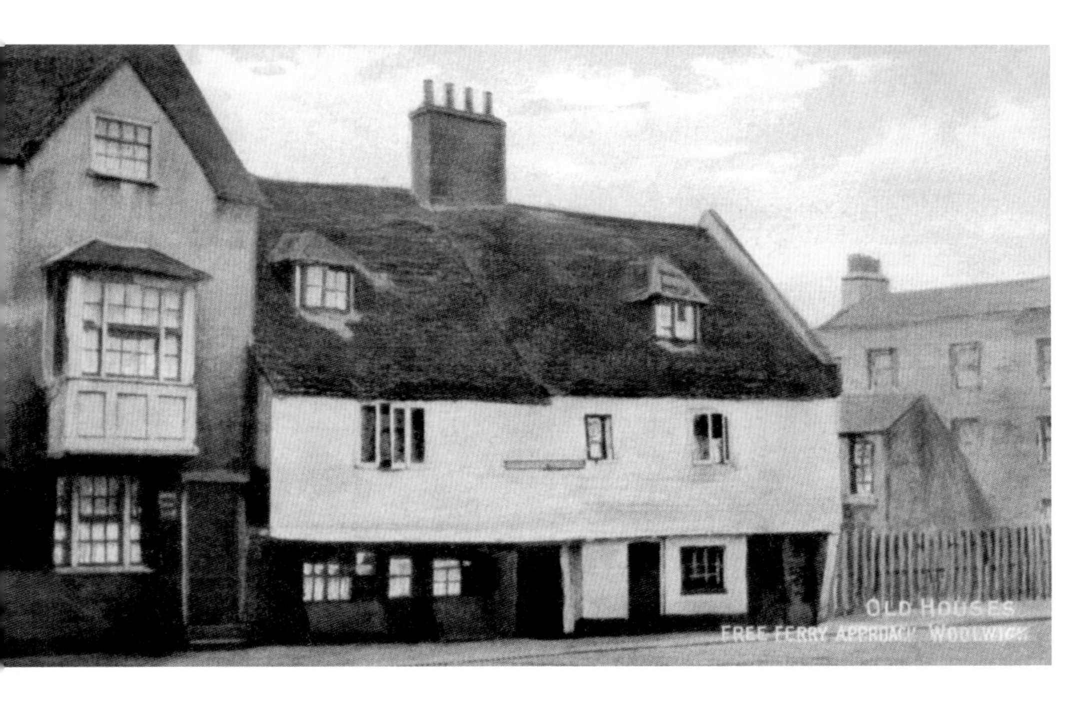

Old Houses, Free Ferry Approach, *c.* 1907

Situated on Hog Lane (later Nile Street), this timber-framed building of fifteenth- and sixteenth-century origin had deteriorated into a rough lodging house by the time its northern half was cleared for the Free Ferry Approach during the late 1880s. Its southern half survived until 1905, when it was condemned. Calls for its preservation delayed but did not prevent demolition. The adjacent building was probably of seventeenth-century origin, ending as the Ferry Eel & Pie House before demolition in the mid-twentieth century.

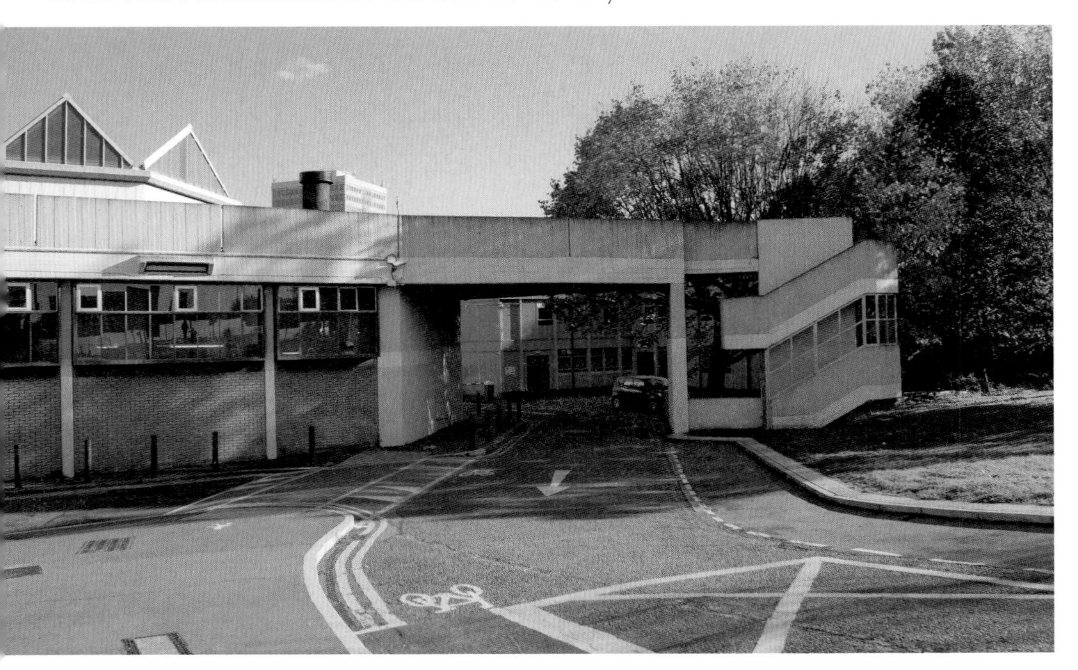

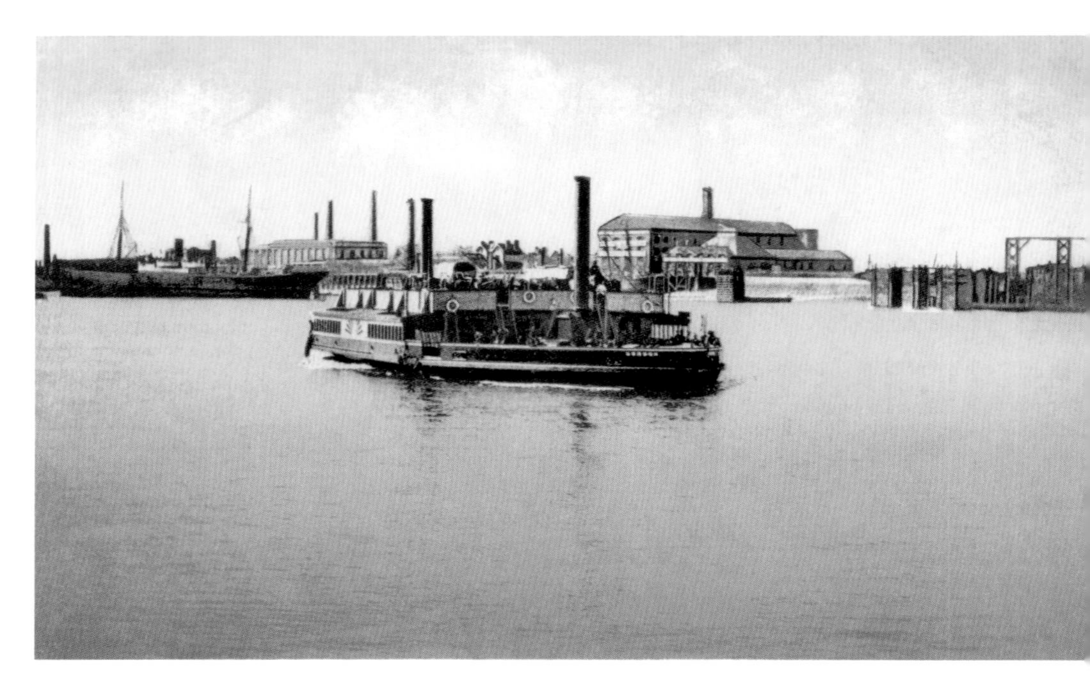

Gordon Free Ferry, Woolwich, 1907, and the John Burns Ferry, 2013

London County Council chairman Lord Roseberry opened the Woolwich Free Ferry on 23 March 1889, though ferry services had been in operation at Woolwich since 1308, when William Atte Halle purchased a small boat from William de Wicton for £10 to provide transport across the Thames. Competition between watermen grew so fierce that in 1330 the people of Woolwich petitioned Parliament to suppress rivals at Greenwich and Erith, arguing that theirs was a 'Royal Ferry' and was therefore favoured by the King.

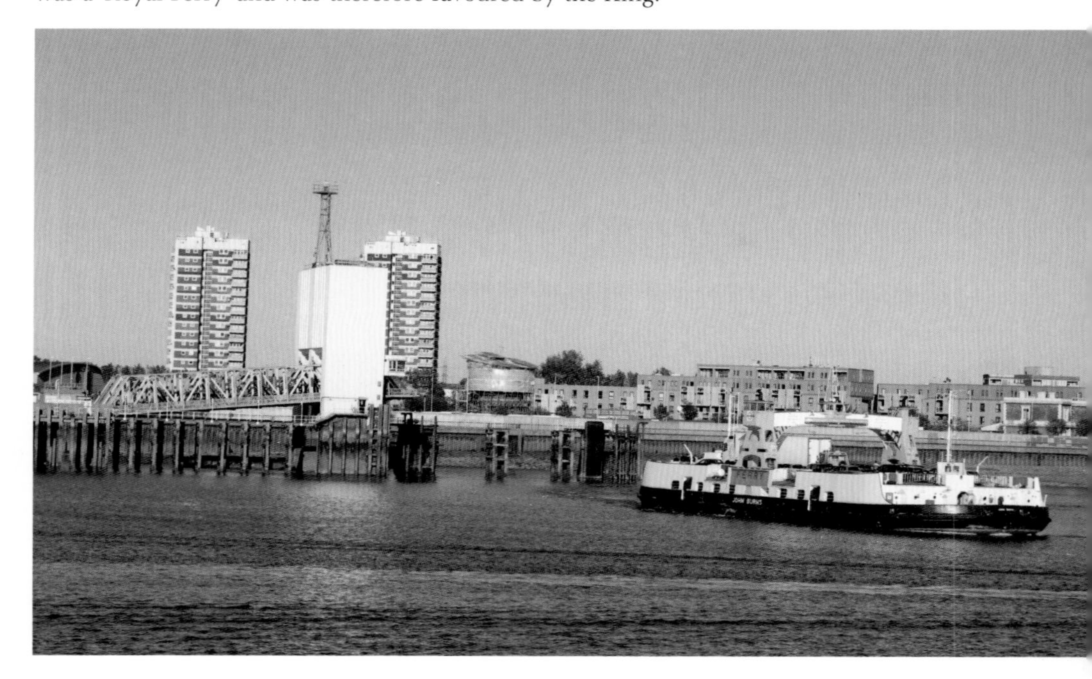

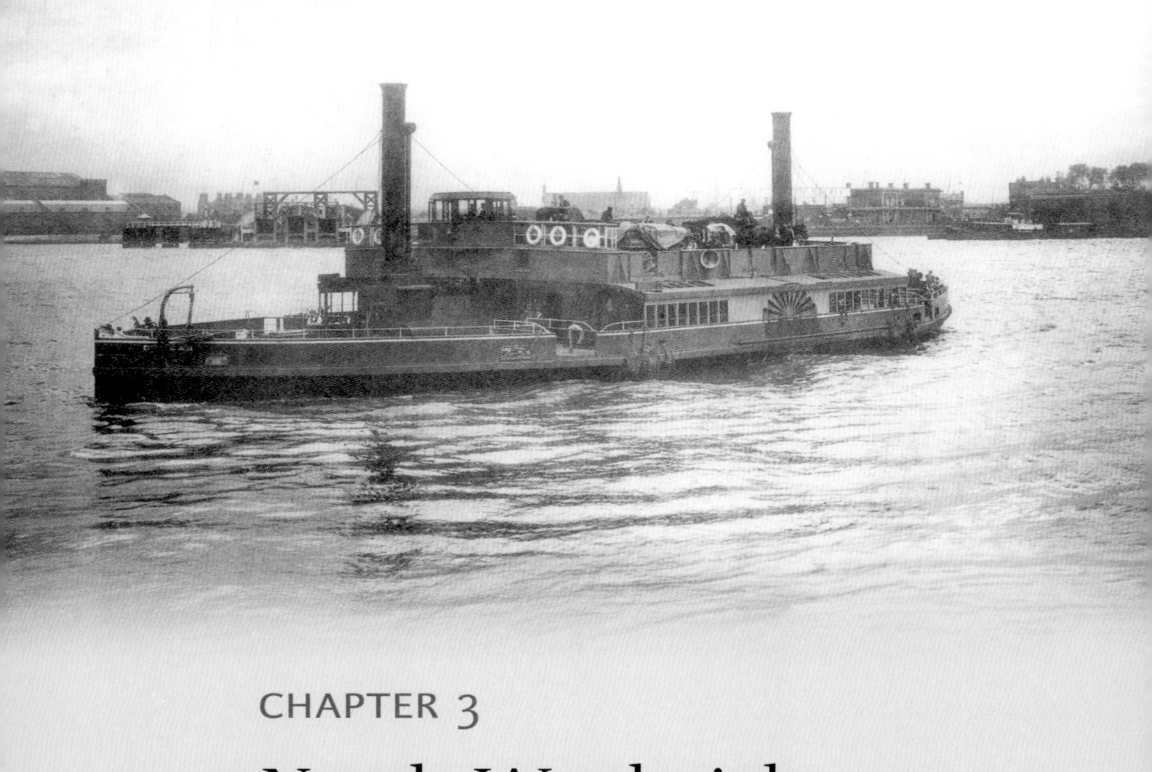

CHAPTER 3

North Woolwich

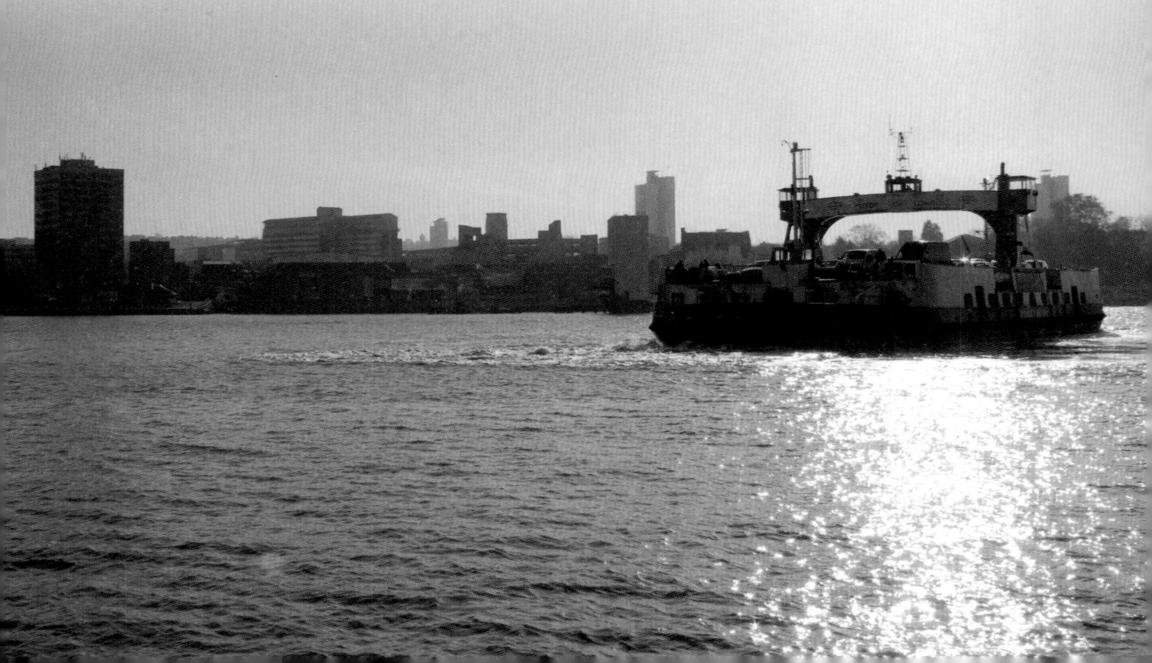

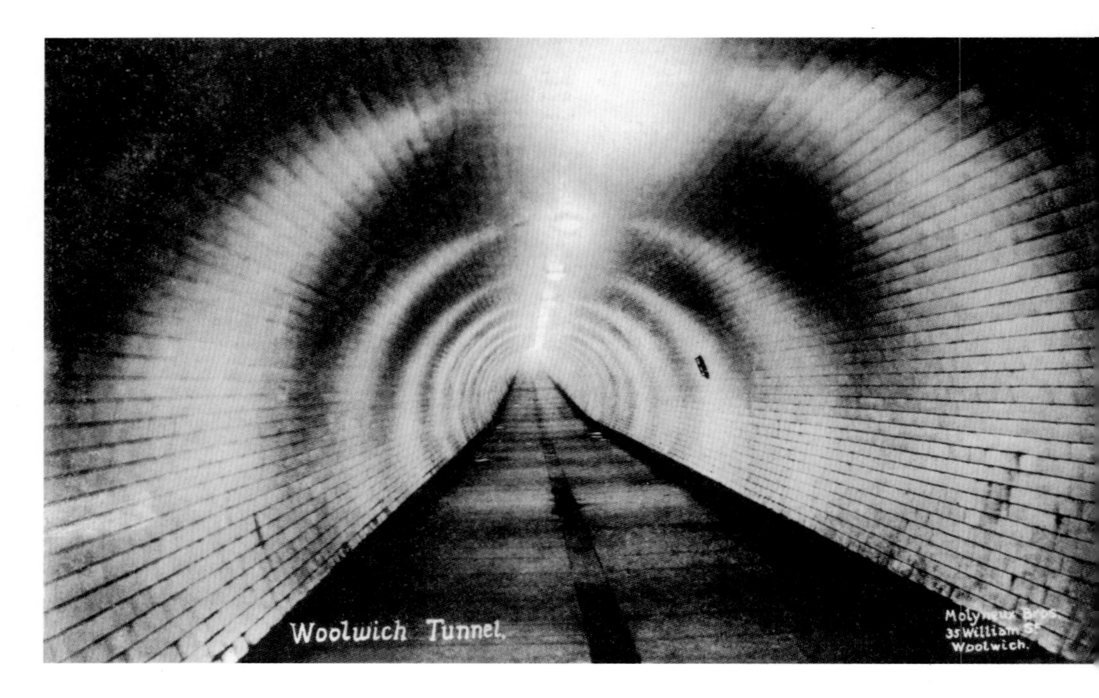

Woolwich Foot Tunnel, *c.* 1916

Designed by Sir Maurice Fitzmaurice for London County Council, and built by Walter Scott and Middleton, the Woolwich Foot Tunnel opened on 26 October 1912, offering a free 24/7 alternative to the ferry crossing, which was periodically suspended during bad weather. Entered via a rotunda on both banks, the shaft at North Woolwich is 64 feet deep, housing a steep spiral staircase. Its length runs nearly a third of a mile and has a York stone-paved footway measuring 9-feet 2-inches wide.

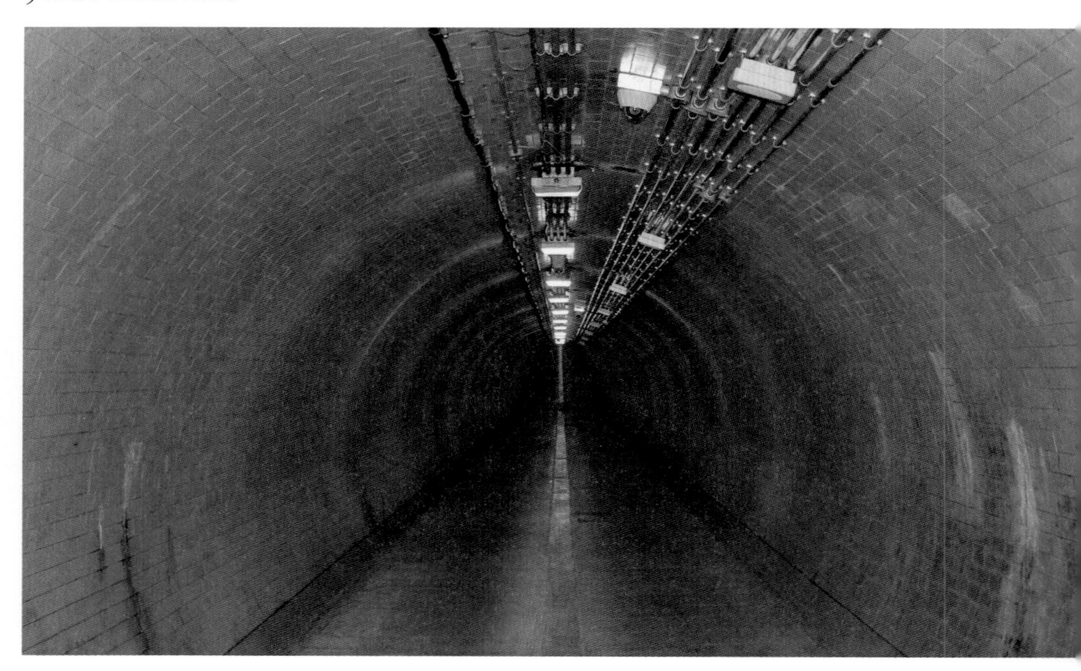

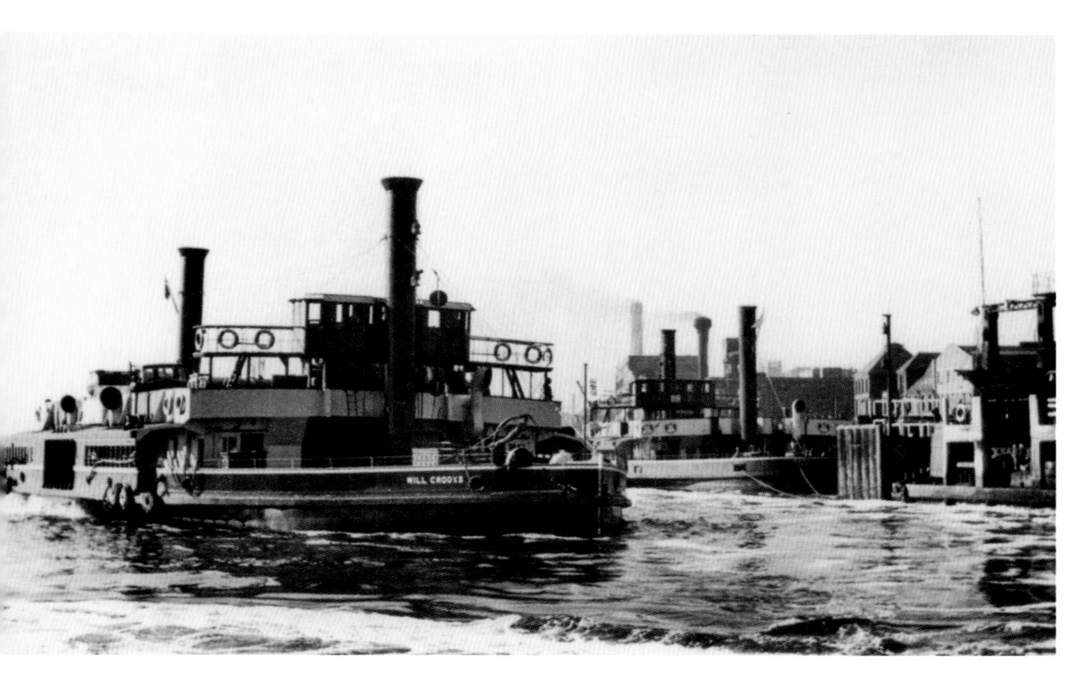

Woolwich Free Ferry – the *Will Crooks* and the *Ernest Bevin*
Future MP Will Crooks, who had himself worked as a casual labourer at East India Docks, acted as Chairman of the LCC Bridges Committee in 1898, supporting construction of the Woolwich Foot Tunnel. The ferry *Will Crooks* was built in 1930 by Samuel White & Co. Ltd and remained in service until paddle steamers were replaced by diesel-powered boats in 1963. Built in that year in Dundee, the *Ernest Bevin* commemorates the trade unionist who also served as MP for Woolwich.

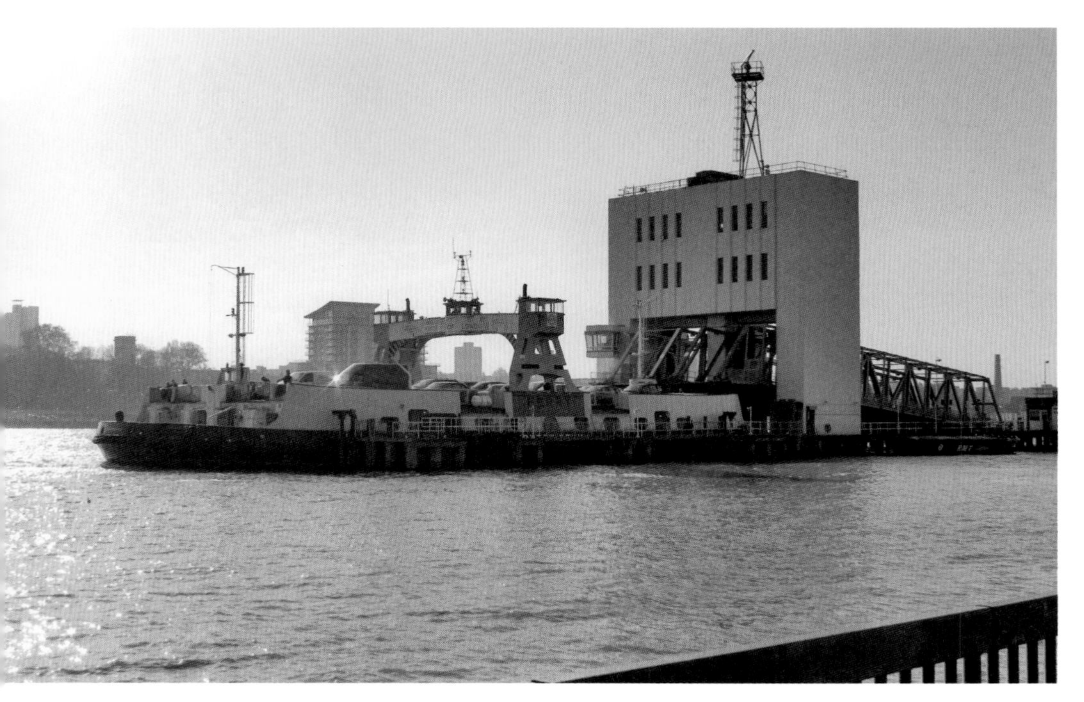

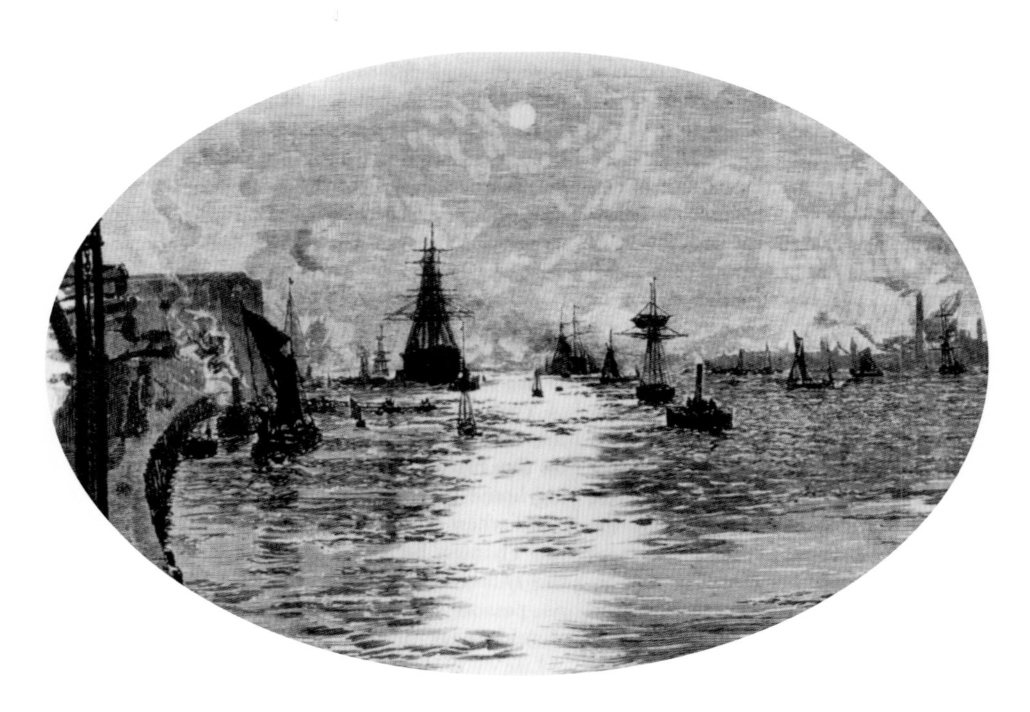

The Thames, Woolwich Reach, 1885 Woodcut Print
Woolwich Reach denotes that section of the Thames that divides its two banks, across which the ferry makes its passage. One Victorian writer observed that 'At Woolwich the water becomes brackish at spring tides', while another observed that the marshes protected by the north bank were 'not less than four feet three inches below the level of the high water in spring tides'. The river flows on, but the vista is nearly unrecognisable as residential high-rises stand in place of factory stacks across the Reach.

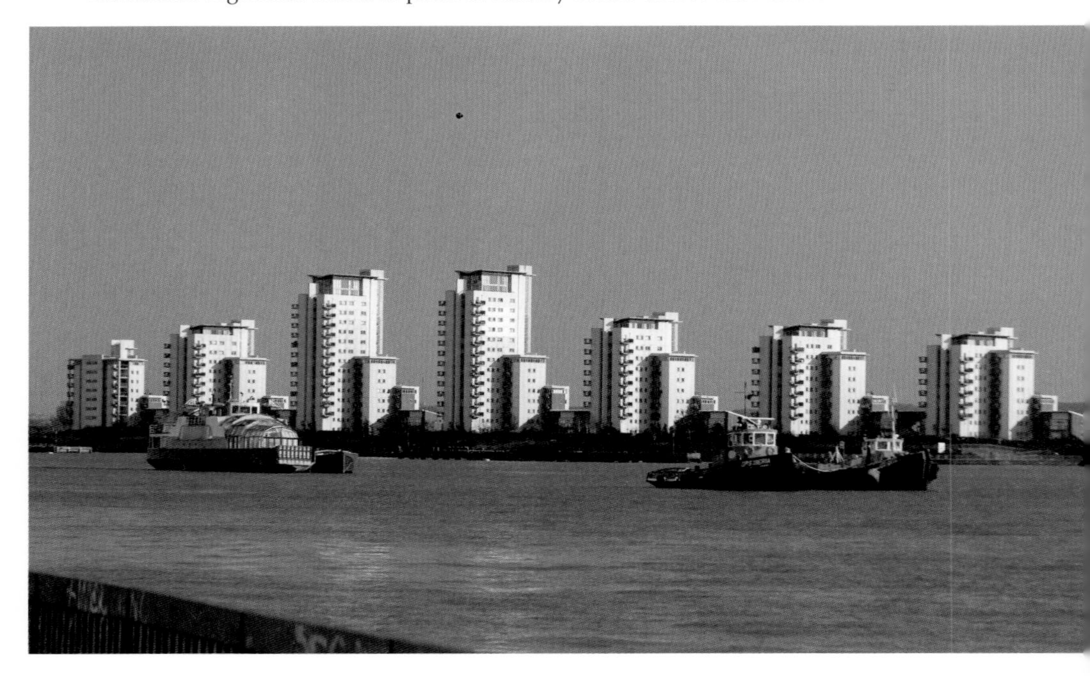

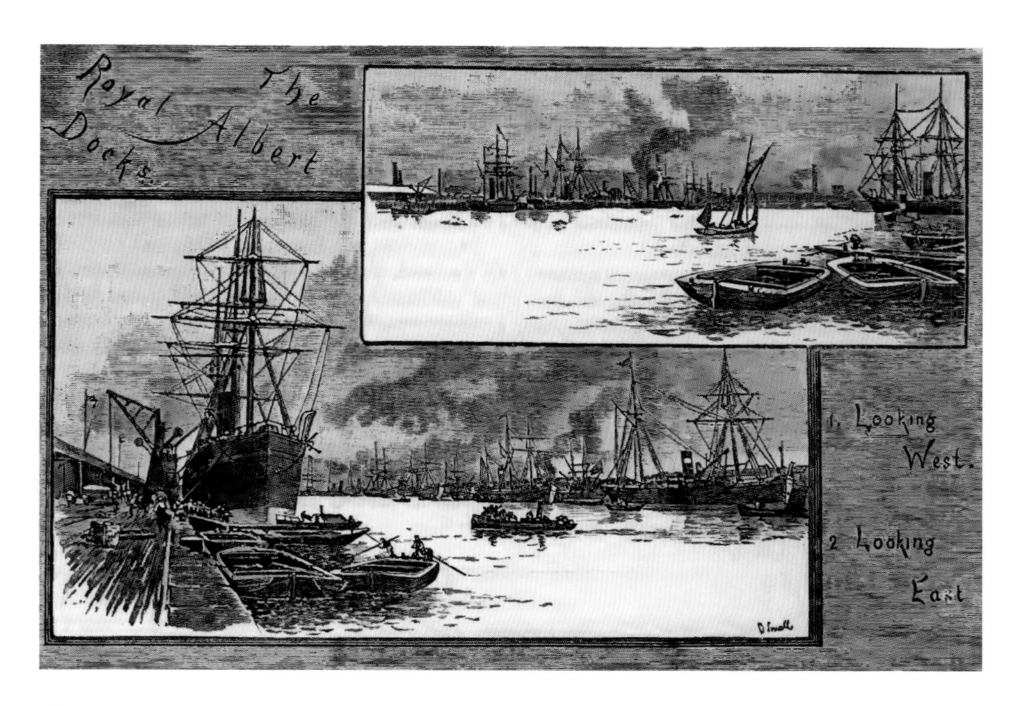

The Royal Albert Docks, 1888 Woodcut Print
Opened in 1880 by the Duke of Connaught, the Royal Albert Dock was constructed in accordance with an Act of Parliament passed five years earlier. It was the first London dock to be lit by electricity, equipped with steam winches and hydraulic cranes, allowing it to cope with ships weighing up to 12,000 tons. Following Britain's 1973 adhesion to the European Economic Community (EEC), alterations to trade policies and changes in technology, London's Royal Docks fell into decline, closing to cargo in 1981.

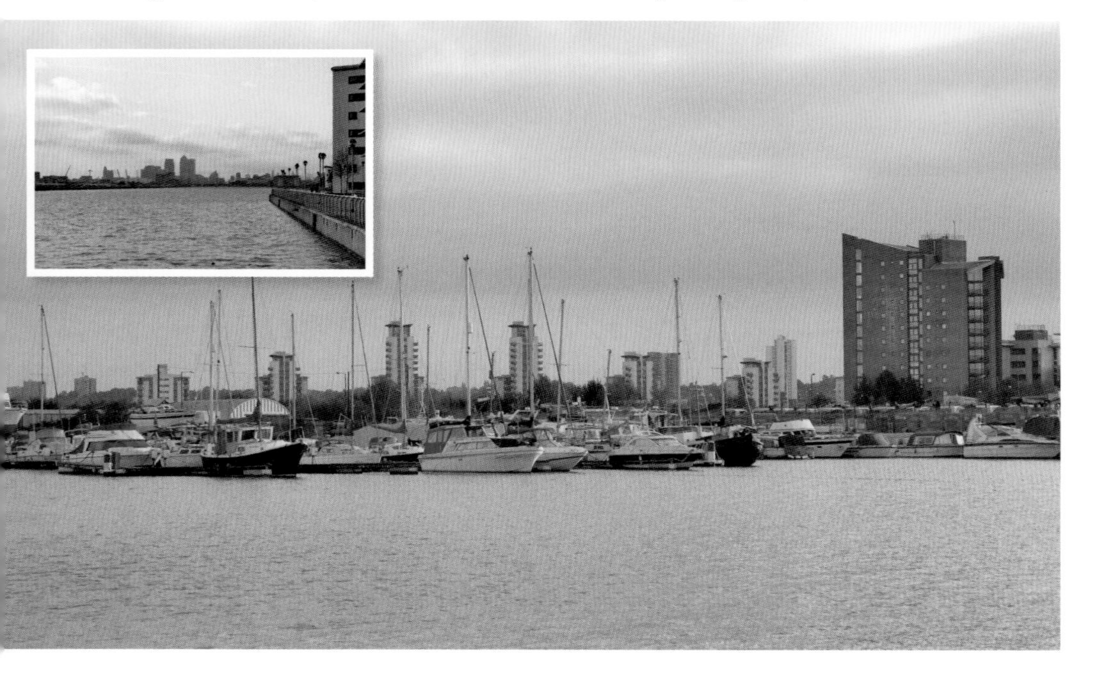

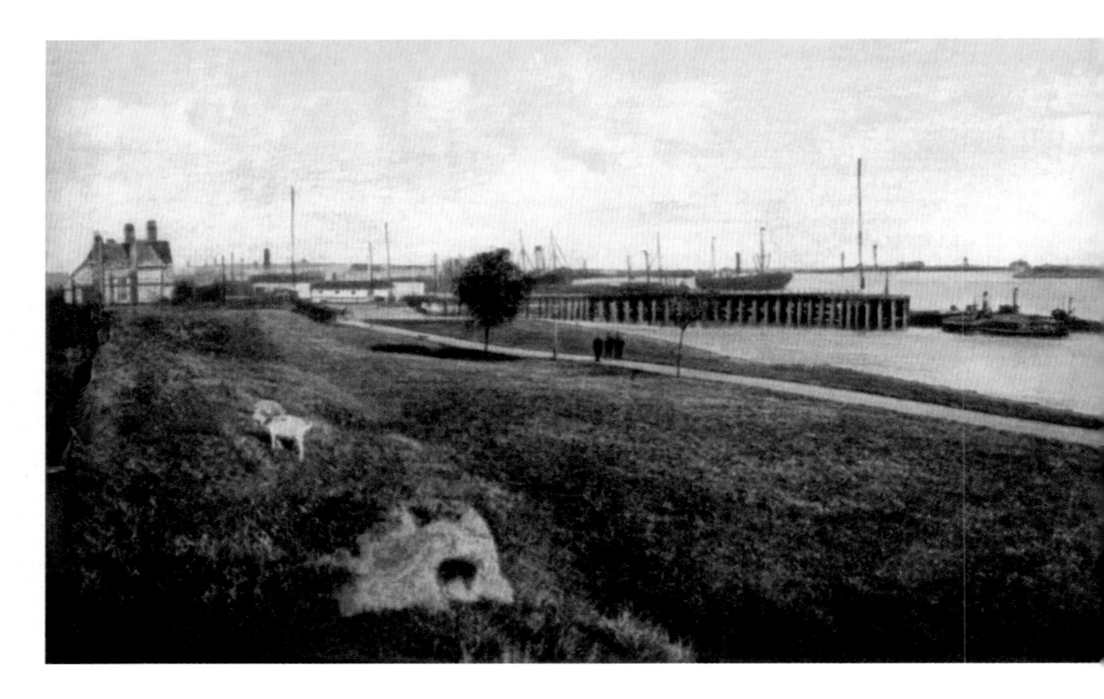

Dock Entrance, North Woolwich, 1907

Water access to the Royal Docks ceased by the end of 1982, London Docklands Development Corporation (LDDC) having been established in mid-1981 to strategise means of regenerating the area. The corporation acquired Royal Victoria Dock from the Port of London Authority in 1983, the Royal Albert and King George V Docks in 1986, and then the Thames Barrier site (1990–94). The recession of the late 1980s/early 1990s delayed redevelopment, as LDDC's successors struggled to realise their plans, but transformation is now well underway.

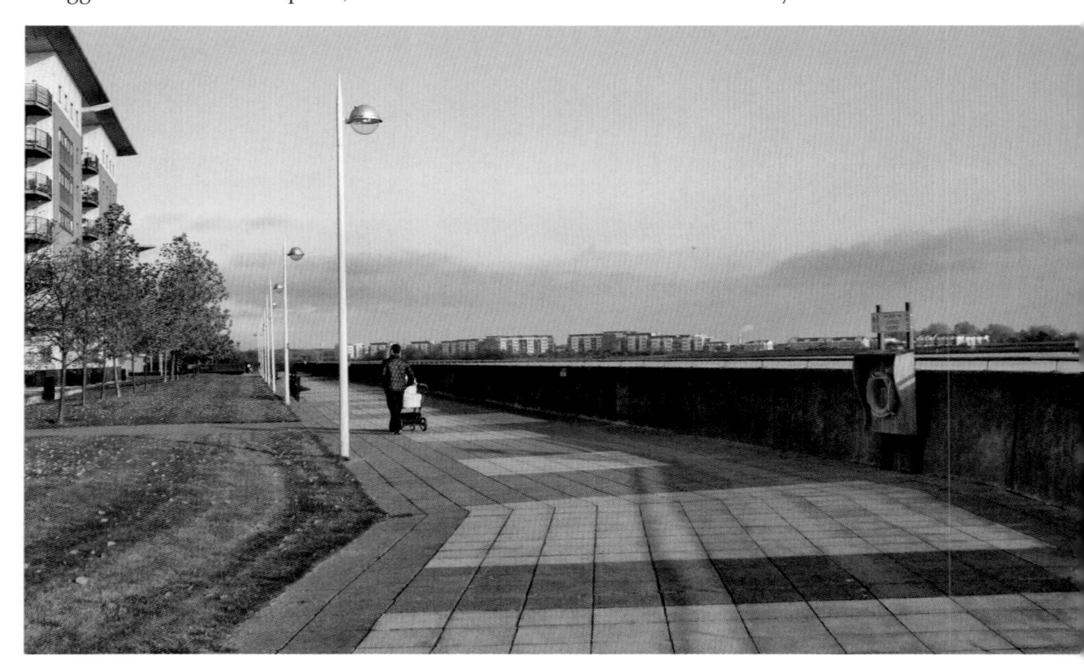

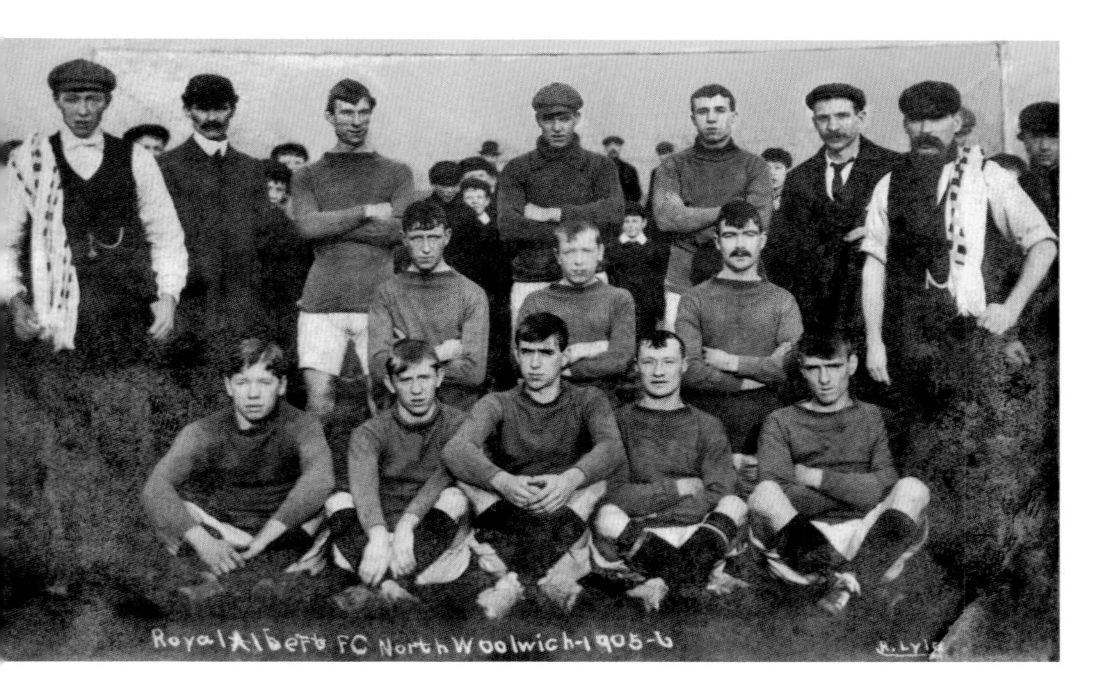

Royal Albert FC, North Woolwich, 1905/06, and Woolwich Spartans FC, 2013
Royal Albert FC – no doubt originally formed by workers from the Dockyard – would have played in one of the many local amateur football leagues that flourished in London and the surrounding counties during the late nineteenth and early twentieth centuries. This amateur tradition has continued in the area to the present day, with over fifty clubs participating in the Woolwich & Eltham Sunday Football Alliance. At the time of writing (November 2013), Woolwich Spartans lie third in the First Division.

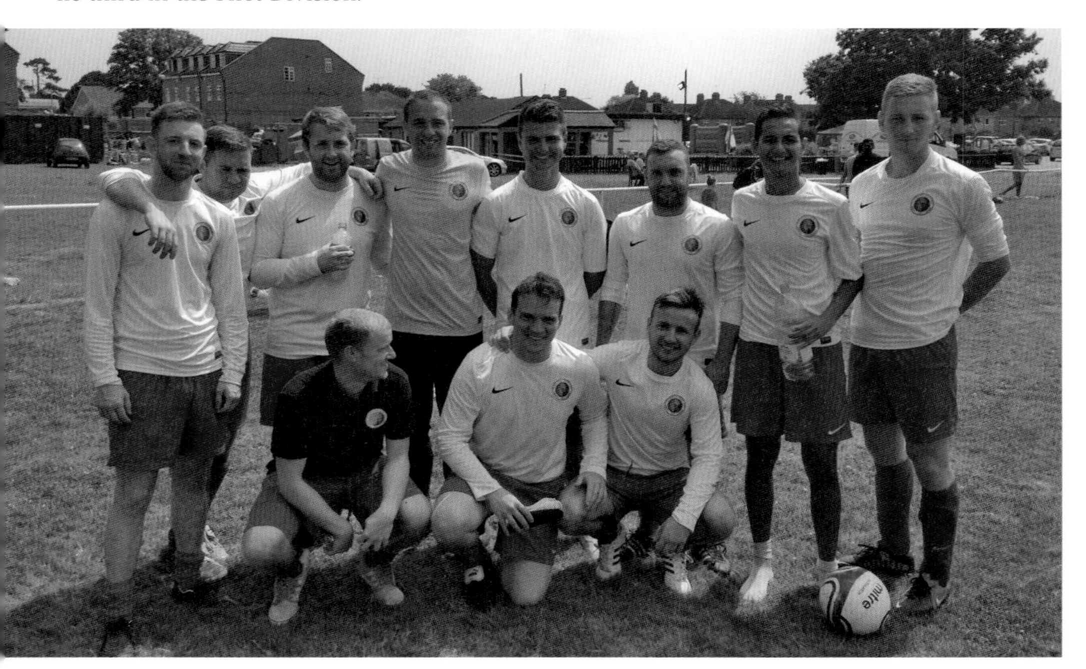

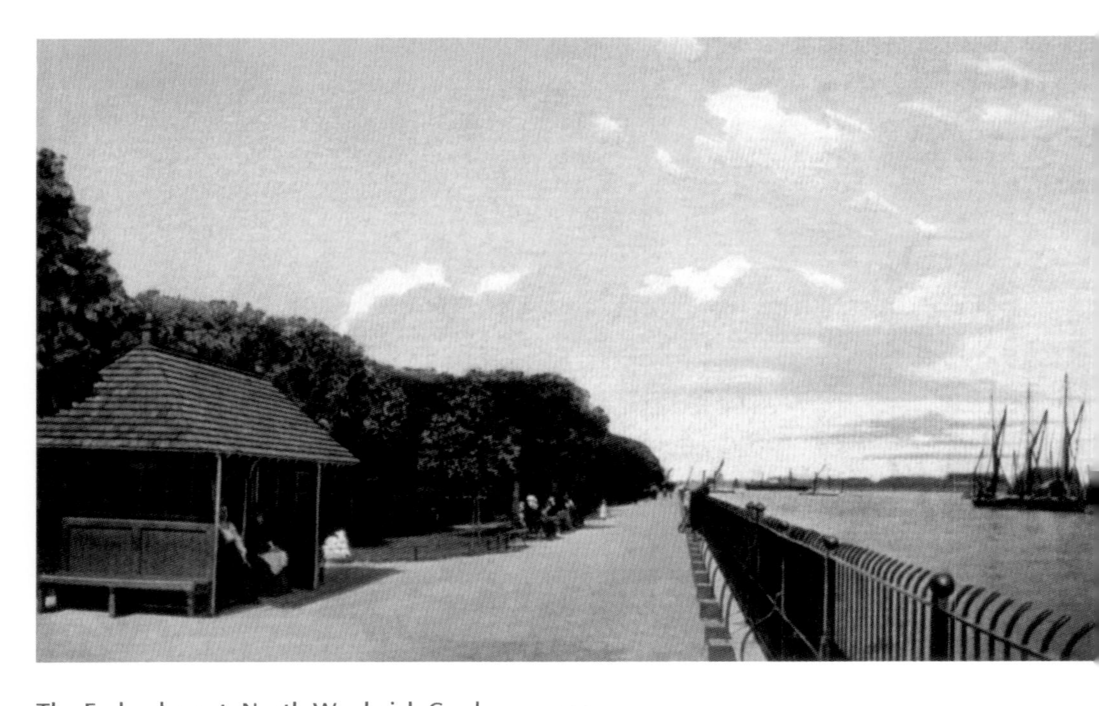

The Embankment, North Woolwich Gardens, *c.* 1907
Before the coming of the railway to North Woolwich in 1847, the area had largely been marshland. It was part of the Manor of Hammarsh, held by Westminster Abbey, and was predominantly used for grazing from mediaeval times. Railway engineer and owner of the North Woolwich Land Co. George Parker Bidder purchased it from the Abbey for industrial development. The Royal Pavilion Pleasure Gardens were opened by proprietor of the Pavilion Hotel William Holland in 1851, seeking to attract visitors from the Great Exhibition.

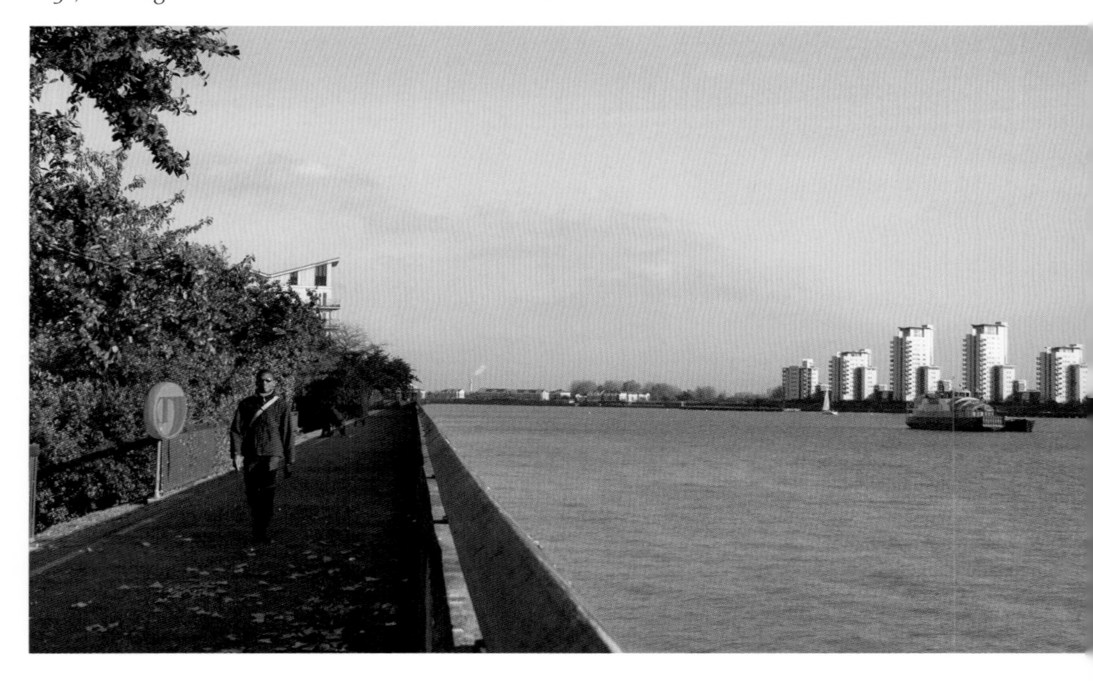

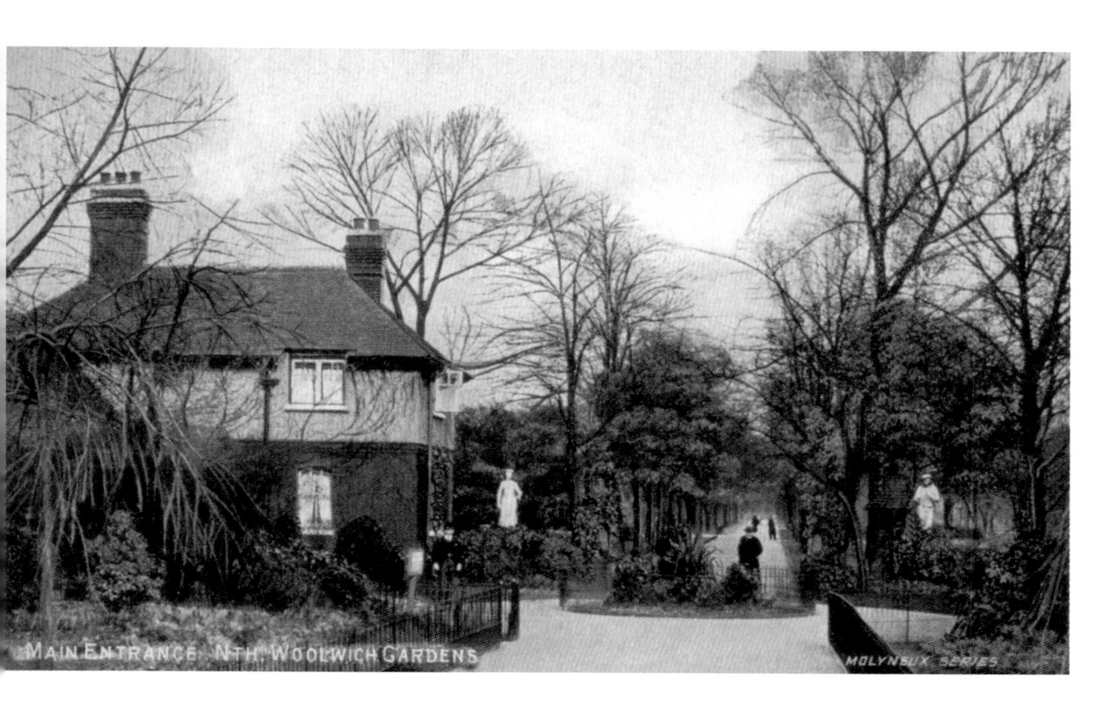

Main Entrance, North Woolwich Gardens, ***c.*** **1910**
Holland's Pleasure Gardens were a popular success, offering entertainment such as fireworks, open-air dancing, trapeze acts, and hot-air balloons (he is reputed to have escaped his creditors in one). Within two years, they boasted a bowling green, rose gardens, an esplanade and a maze. Despite the area's growing industrialisation, which caused a rise in pollution, impacting the Thames itself, visitor numbers remained strong through the 1870s, with the gardens becoming the sole survivor of their type by the end of the decade.

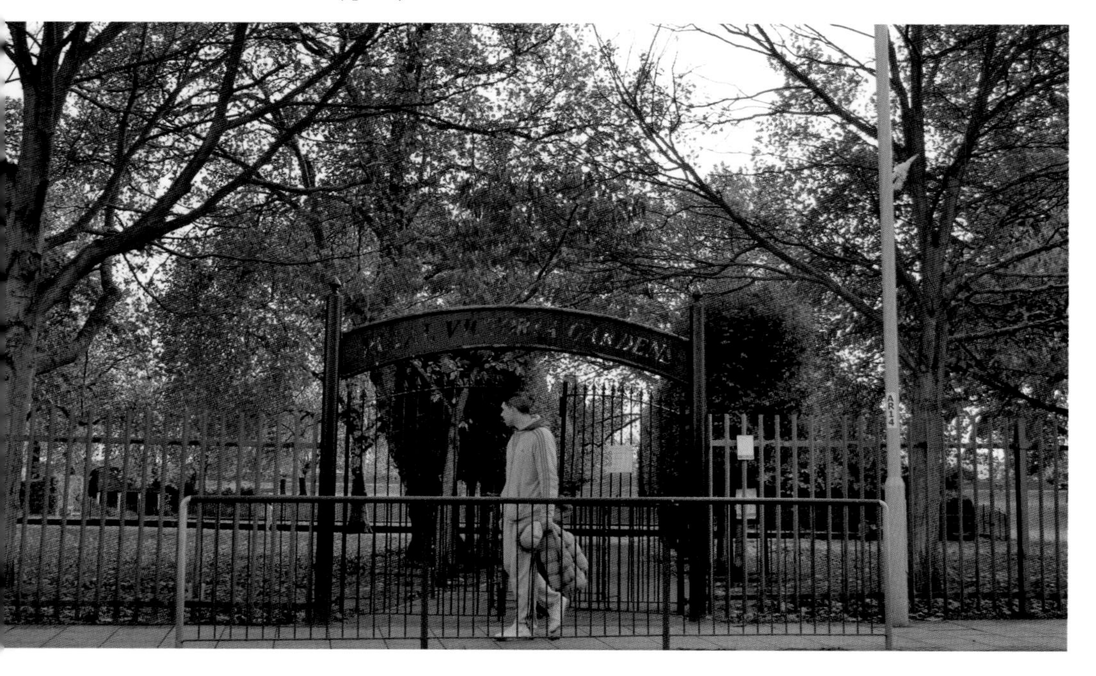

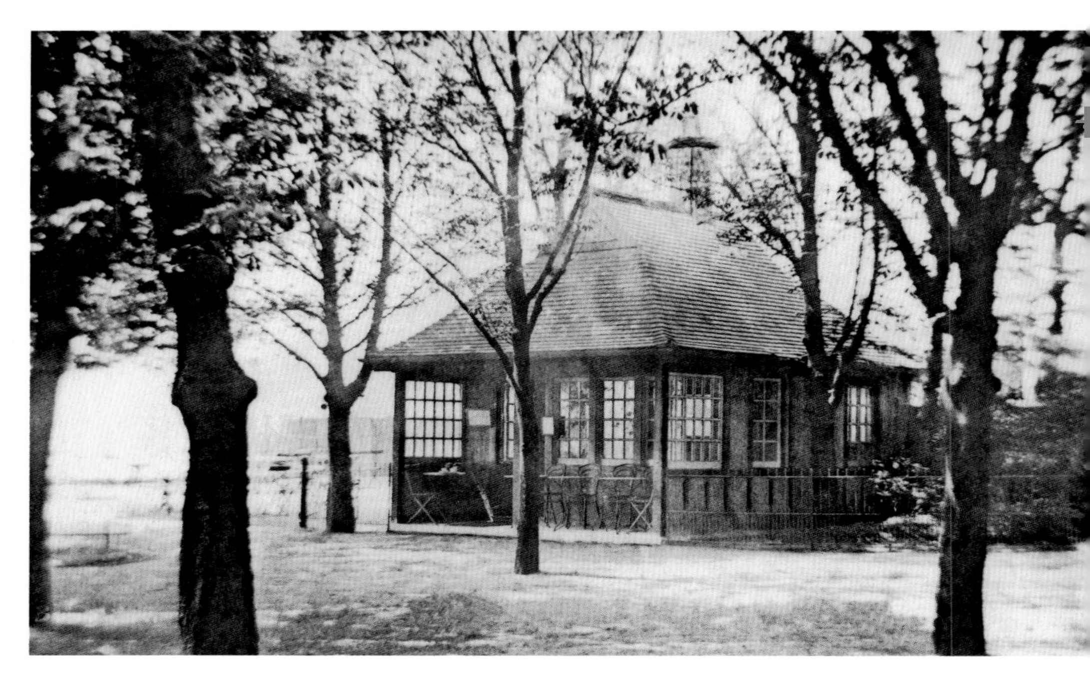

The Bungalow, Royal Victoria Gardens, North Woolwich, *c.* 1907
The gardens deteriorated during the 1880s, prompting the North Woolwich Land Co. to propose building over part of the site. This was countered by pressure for its acquisition as a 'breathing space for the occupants of these very dreary localities which are without anything of the sort'. The North Woolwich Acquisition Fund was established, with the Duke of Westminster as chairman. The balance of £2,300 demanded by the Land Co. was finally raised in 1889, including a £50 donation from Queen Victoria.

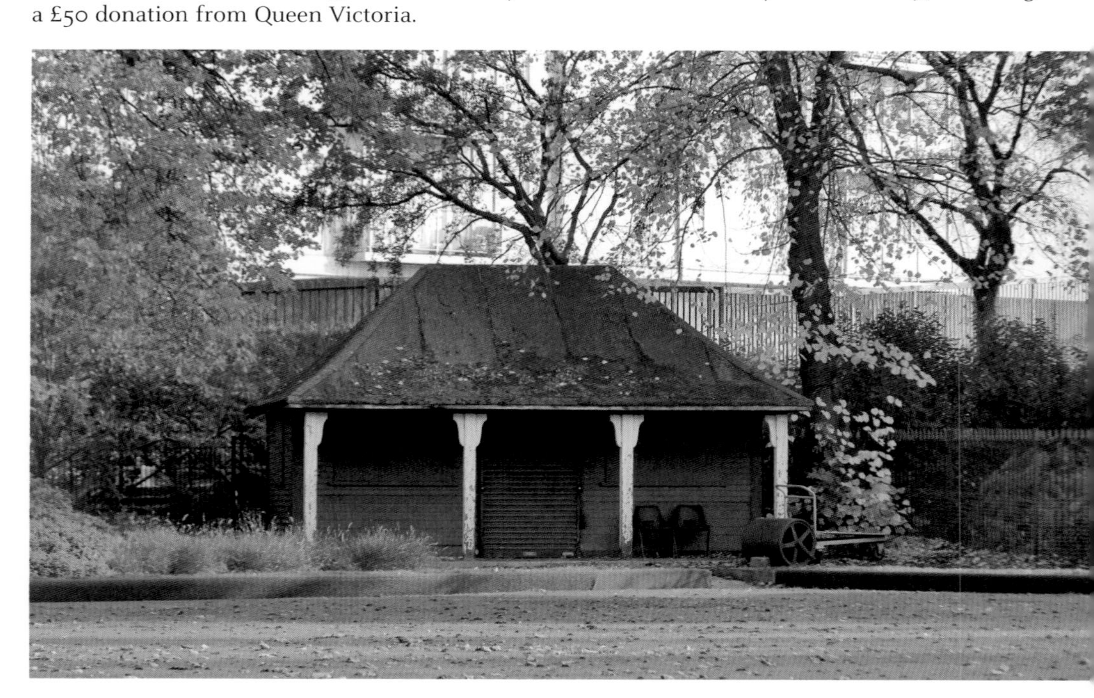

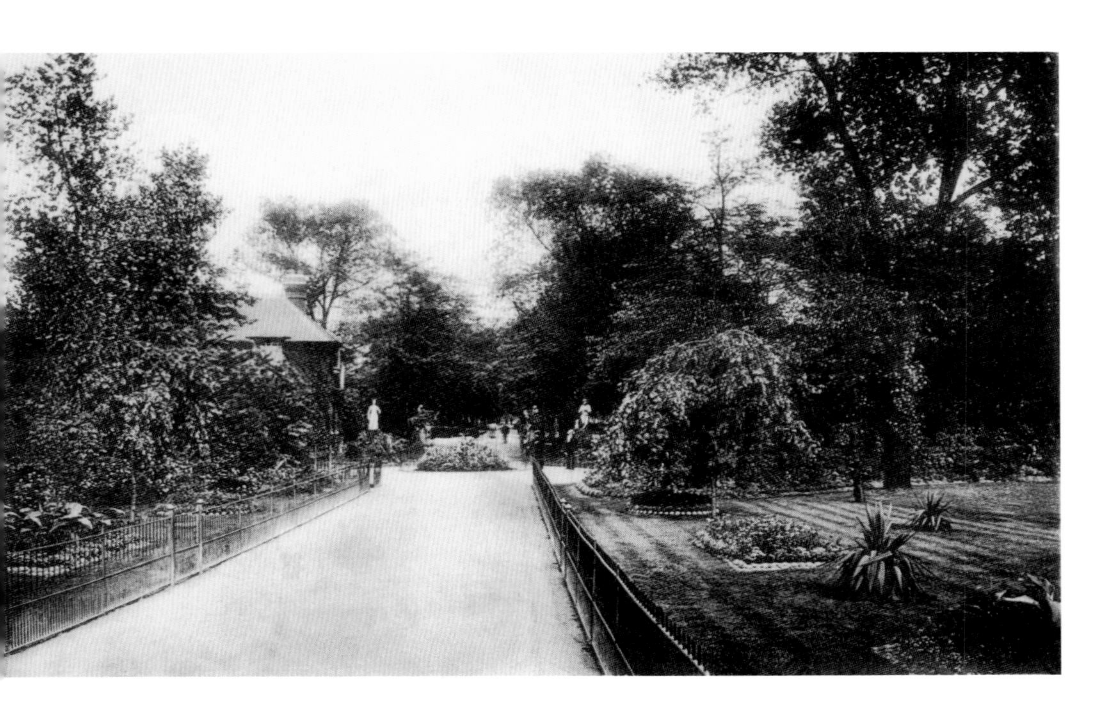

Victoria Gardens, North Woolwich, ***c.*** **1915**

The gardens, now called the Royal Victoria Gardens by royal permission, were redesigned and reopened in 1890, retaining few of their original aspects, aside from the central walk and riverside situation. Having suffered bomb damage during the 1940s, little survives from their 1890s incarnation, except for the bowling green, and a tree- and shrub-lined enclosure to the west. Deteriorating again during the later twentieth century, they have recently been re-renovated, boasting a new entrance, and welcoming community events and sports tournaments.

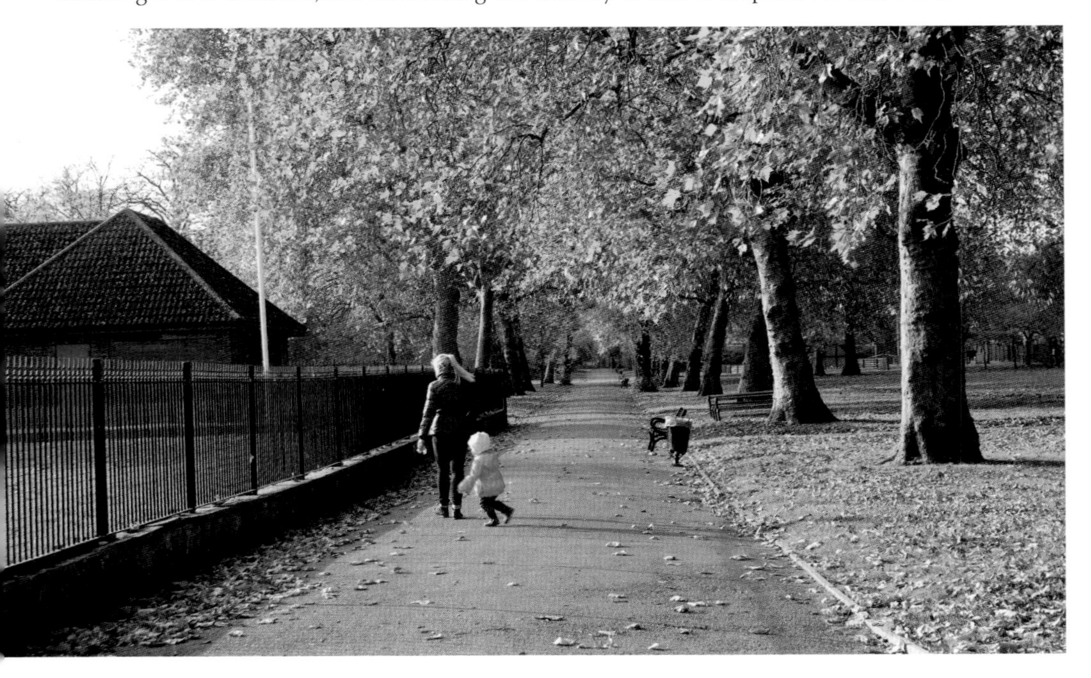

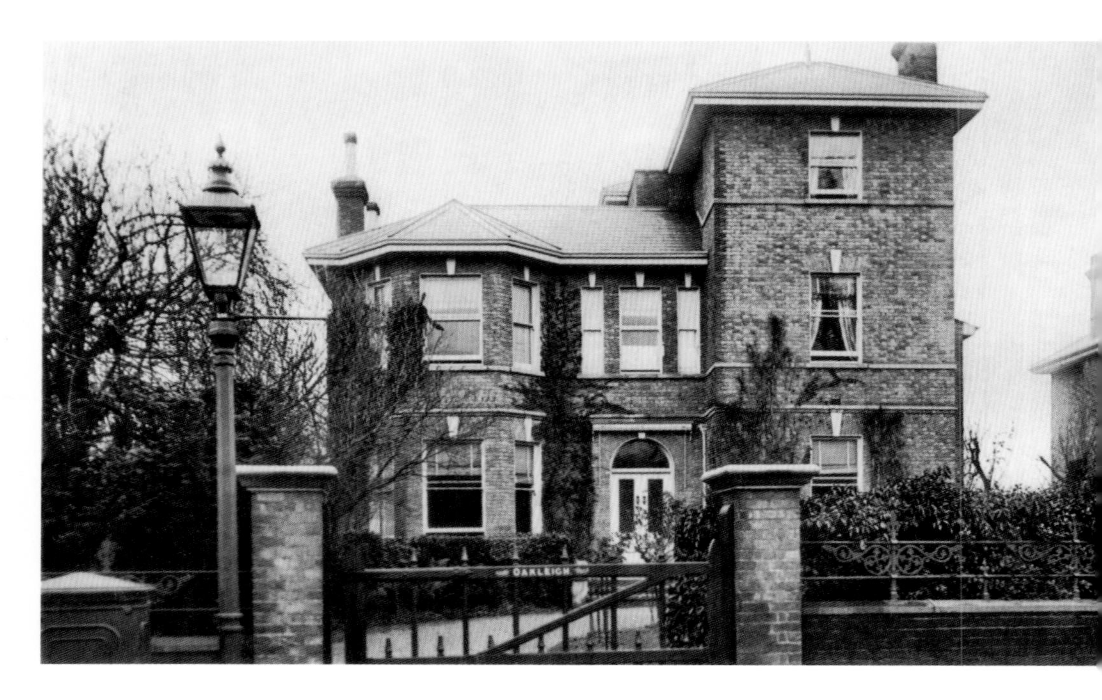

Oakleigh, North Woolwich, and The Royal Oak

At the time this photograph was taken, Oakleigh stood at No. 220 Elizabeth Street, between the Embankment and the Royal Albert Dock. Later rechristened Woodman Street, none of its original residences survive, North Woolwich having suffered substantial bomb damage during the Blitz. The Royal Oak – reputed to be the first meeting place in 1886 of the club that would become the Arsenal – represents one of its oldest buildings, but is currently boarded up and listed for sale by auction, with a guide price of between £140,000 and £150,000.

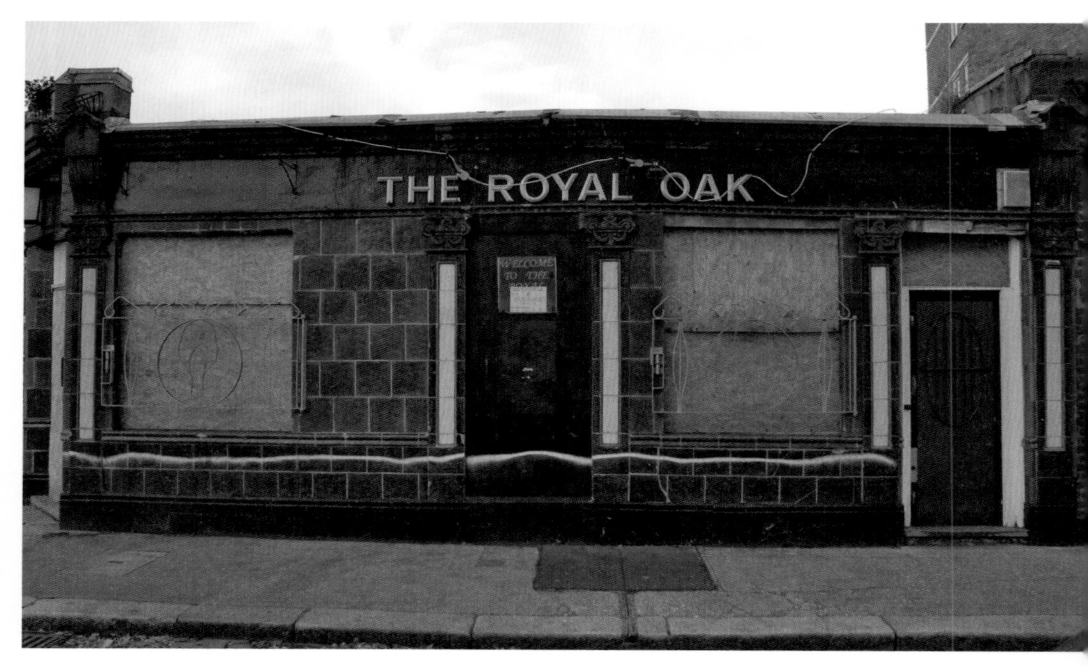

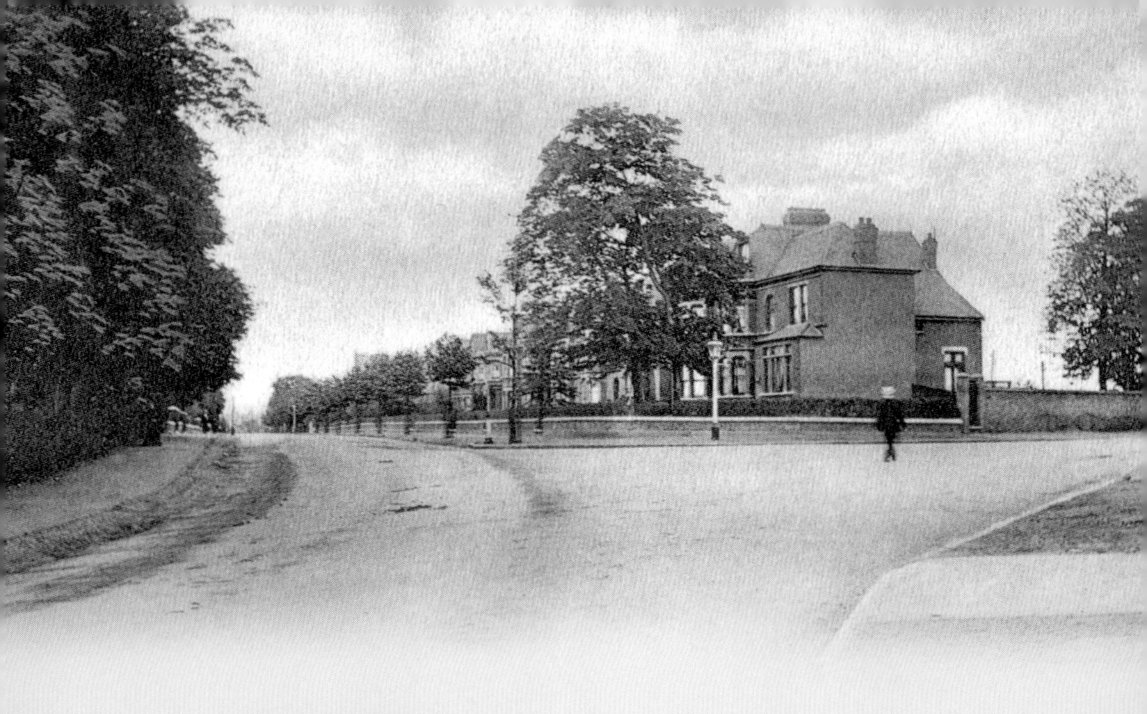

CHAPTER 4

'Next-Woolwich'

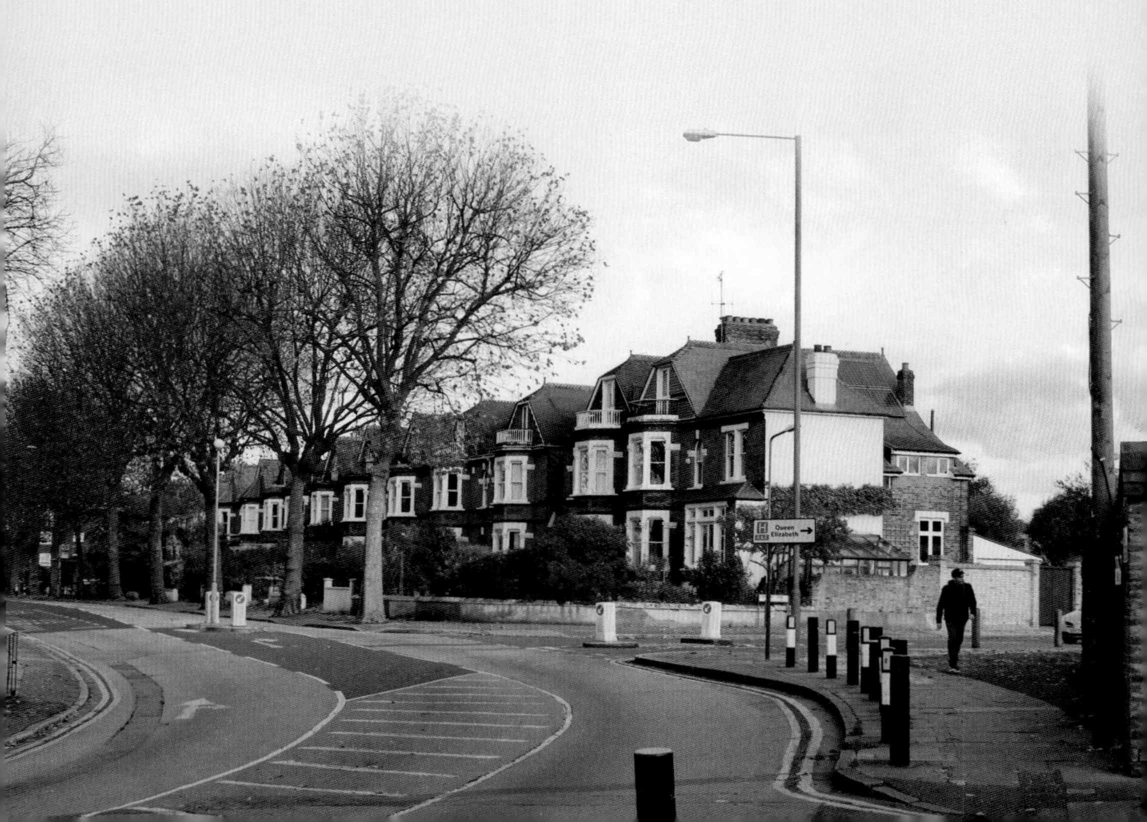

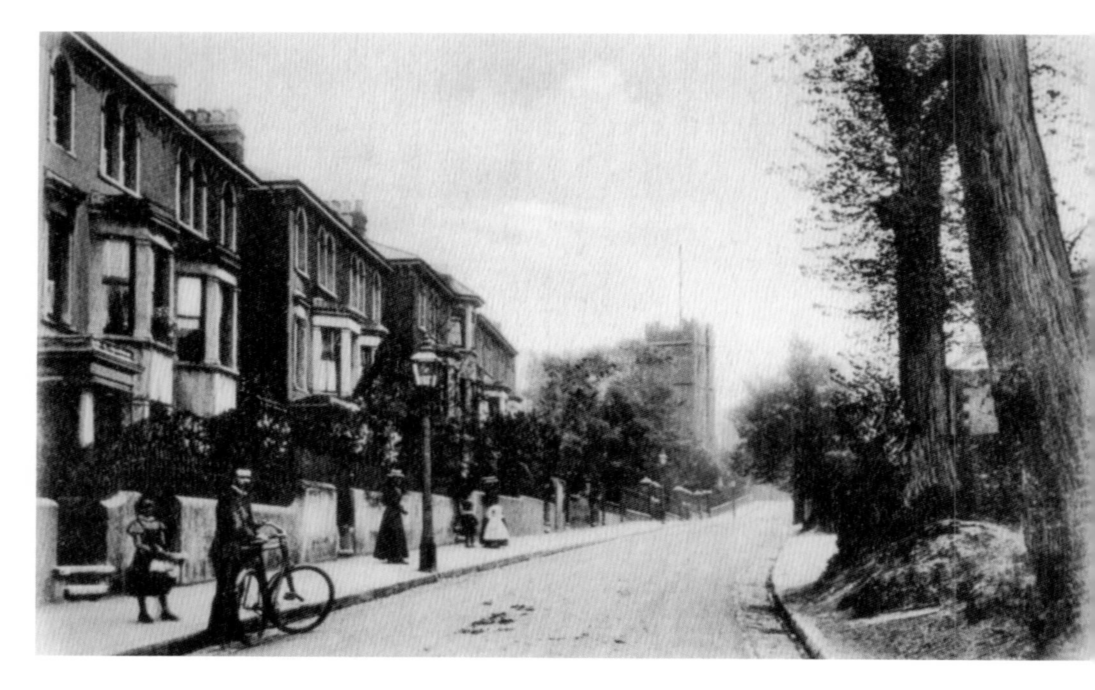

Church Lane, Old Charlton, ***c.*** **1904**
'Charlton-iuxta-Woolwich', or Charlton-next-Woolwich, was so-called to distinguish it from a second Kentish village of the same name, similarly known as Charlton-by-Dover. Written as 'Cerletone' in Domesday, meaning 'town of the churl' (i.e. husbandman), it was held, like Woolwich, of Bishop Odo. Before the Conquest, brothers Goduin and Alward held it of Edward the Confessor for two manors. The original village included Charlton Church Lane, which runs down a steep hillside, overlooking the Thames, with St Luke's perched at its top.

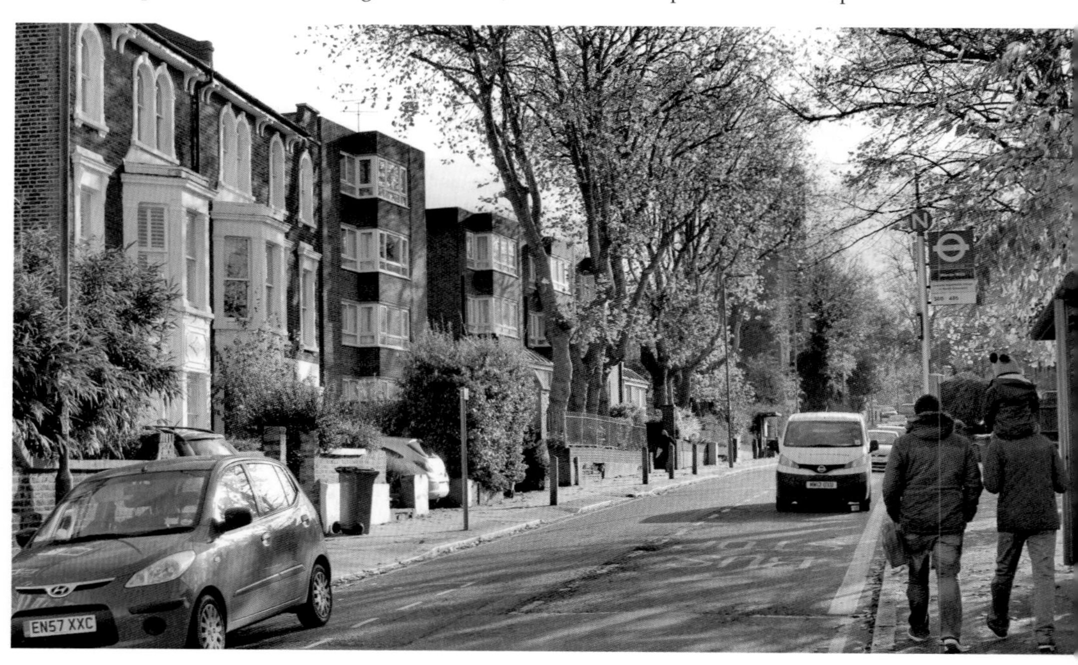

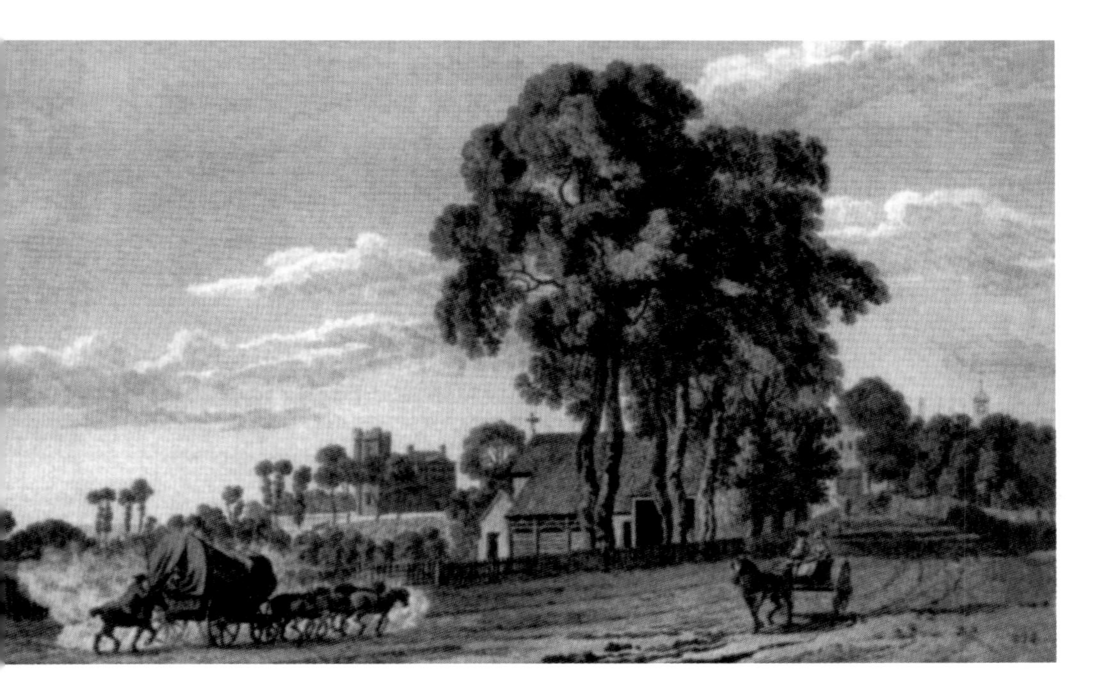

A View of Charlton near Woolwich in Kent, 1775 Watercolour
The above scene is viewed from Horn Fair Road, whose name commemorates the fair held yearly on 18 October, the feast day of St Luke, granted by King Henry III to the priory of Bermondsey, along with Charlton's weekly Monday market, both of which were later discontinued. Horn Fair references both the goods sold there, predominantly made of horn, and the cuckold's horns worn on the heads of the boisterous revellers who attended. It was revived in 1973 as a respectable family-friendly event.

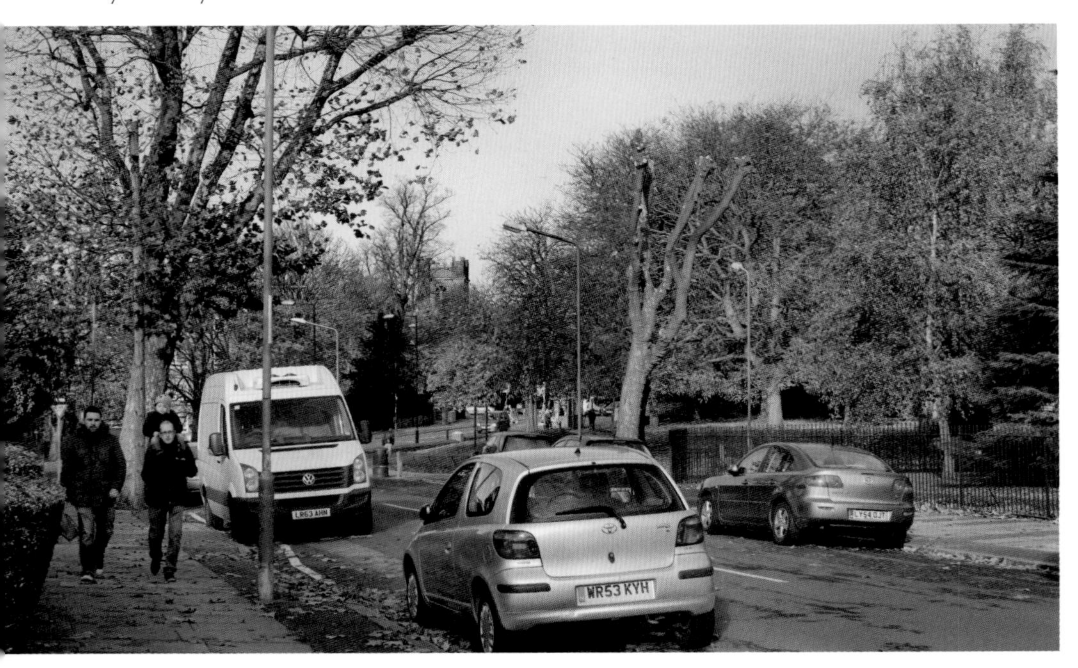

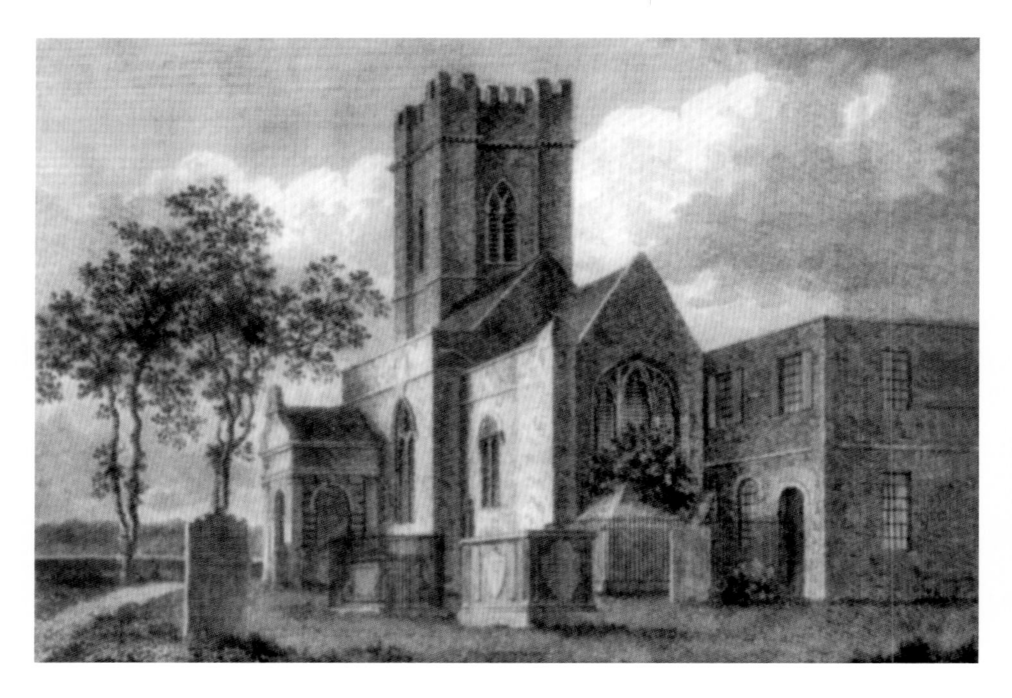

St Luke's, Old Charlton, *c.* 1775 Watercolour

The church at Old Charlton is dedicated to St Luke, and was allegedly surrendered to the crown, along with the Manor of Charlton, as part of the possessions of the Monastery of St Saviour's of Bermondsey at its dissolution in 1536. It was granted by King James I and VI to Sir Adam Newton, Dean of Durham and tutor to his eldest son Prince Henry, who died before he could realise his designs for remodelling the church.

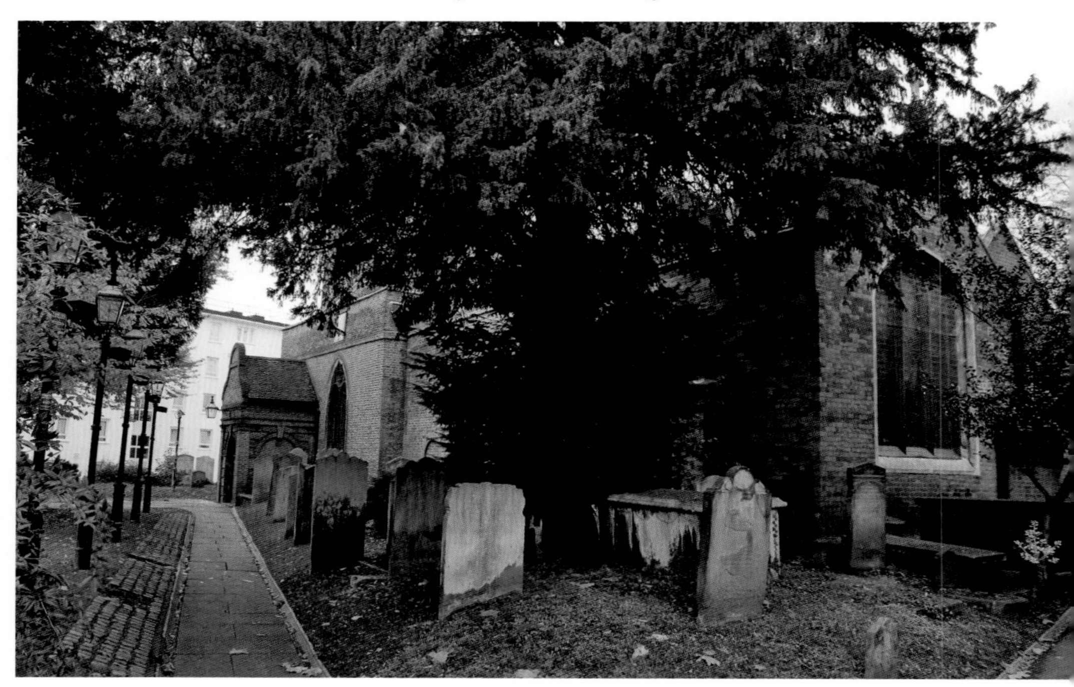

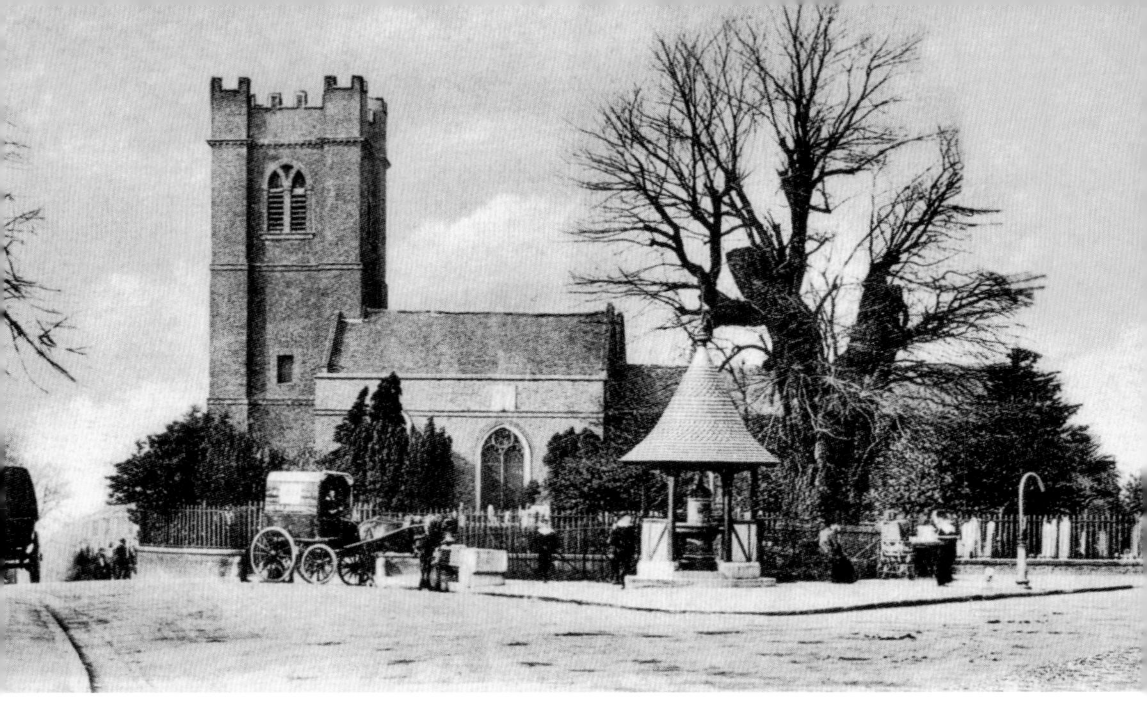

St Luke's Church & Fountain, Charlton, 1910

Sir Adam Newton's trustees rebuilt the church in 1630, replacing its previous chalk and flint incarnation. Little is known of the original building, although one early record dates it back to 1077. Sir Spencer Percival (1762–1812), the only British Prime Minister to be assassinated, is buried in the crypt and commemorated by a plaque and bust in the church, having married Jane Wilson of Charlton House. Charles Edward Drummond, assassinated in error for Sir Robert Peel, is also buried here.

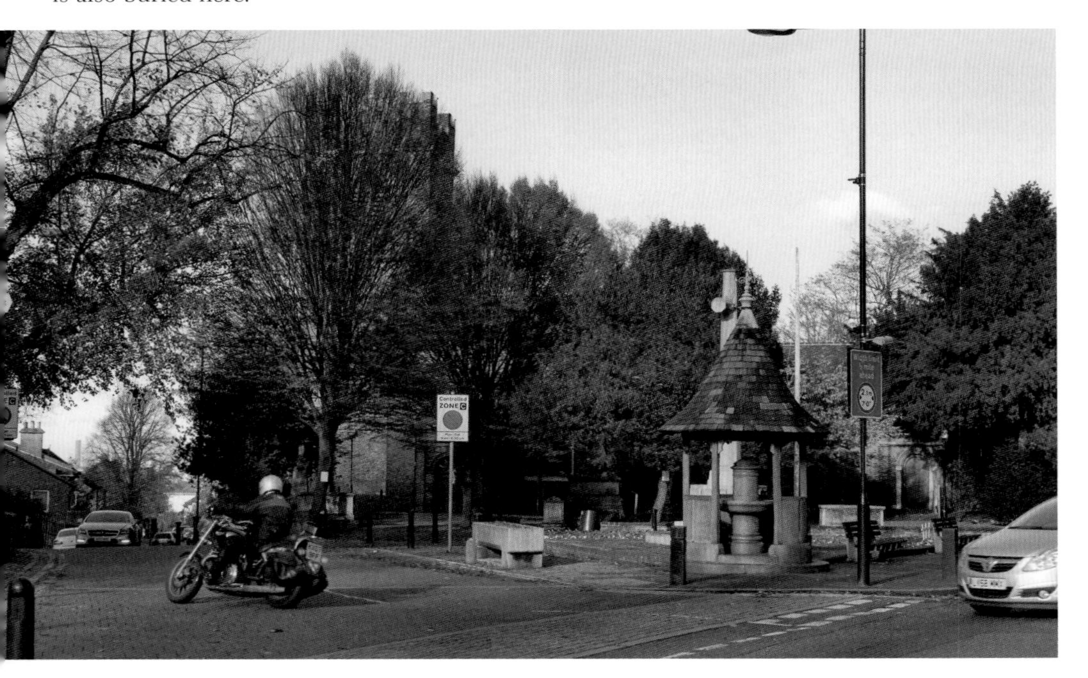

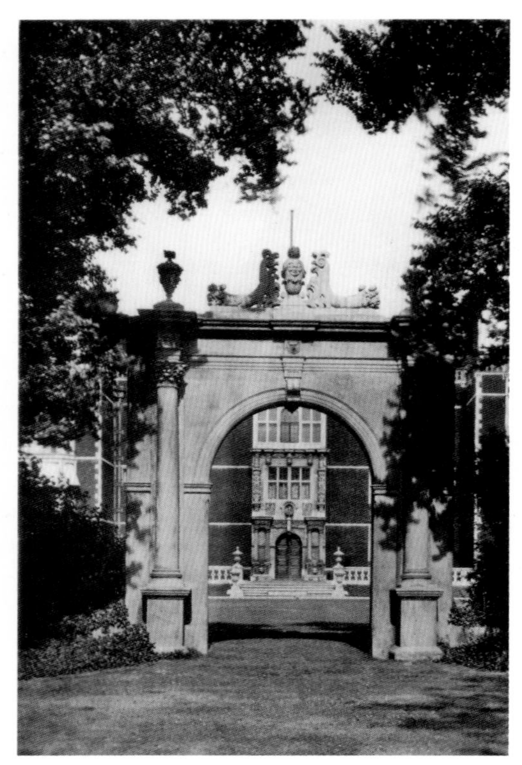

Old Archway, Charlton House, *c.* 1915
Built between 1607 and 1612 for Sir Adam Newton, Charlton House stands at the west entrance of the Village. Its Gothic design, with decorative Royalist flourishes, is attributed to John Thorpe (1560–1620). The Horn Fair was held on the green in front, before the area was enclosed by the Maryon-Wilson family in 1829. The fair was then moved to a field in Fairfield Grove, until its suppression for lewdness in 1874. It now takes place on the green behind Charlton House.

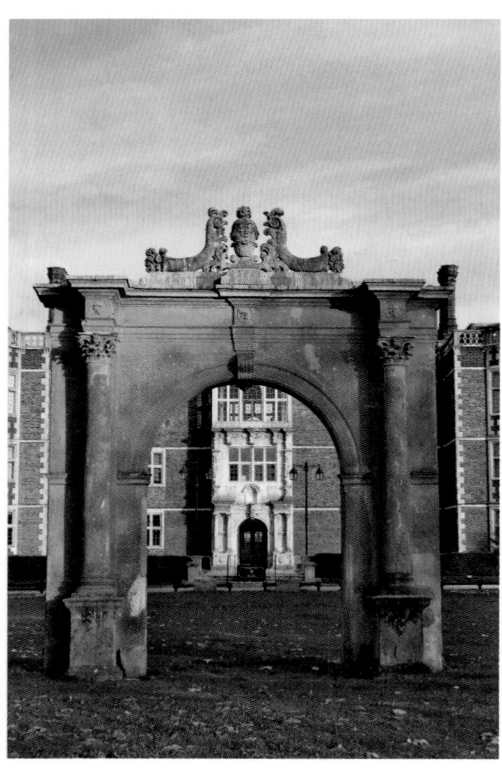

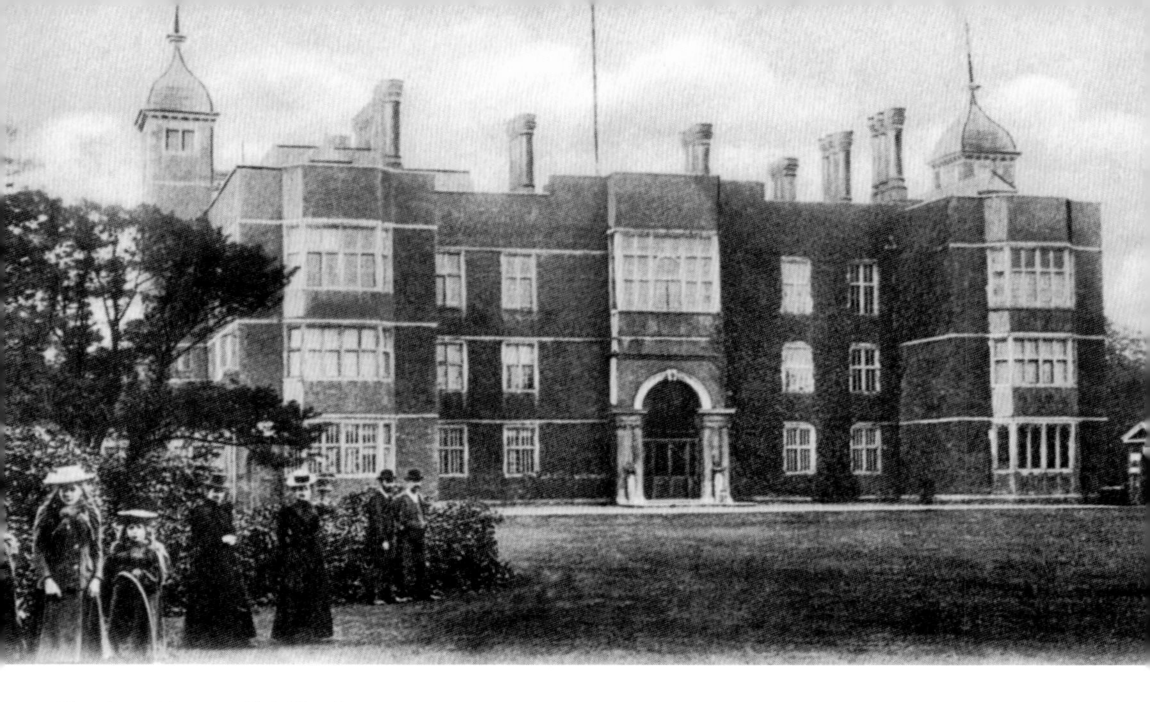

Charlton House, Old Charlton, 1907

Here viewed from the back green, Charlton House is judged the best preserved Jacobean mansion in London. Its formal gardens were separated from neighbouring pasture lands by a ha-ha (sunken ditch) in 1847, as protection from grazing cattle; that pasture is now a park adjoining Woolwich Common. Having had numerous owners since Sir Adam Newton's son Sir Henry was forced to leave Charlton during the Civil War, it was held by the Maryon-Wilson family between 1767 and 1923 before passing to the Borough of Greenwich in 1925.

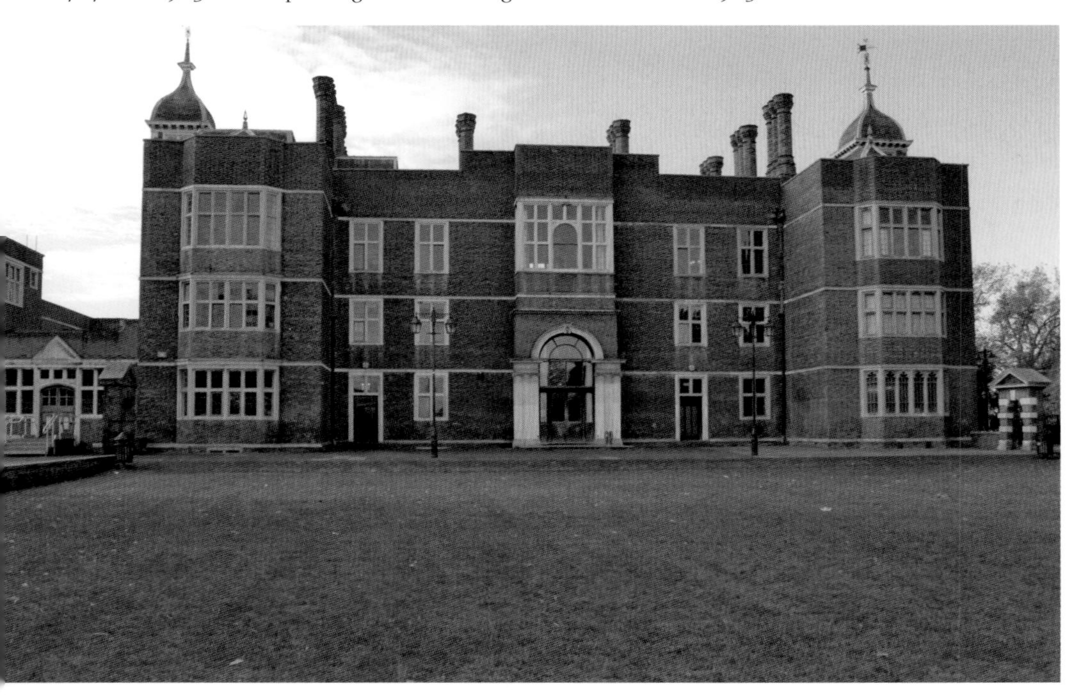

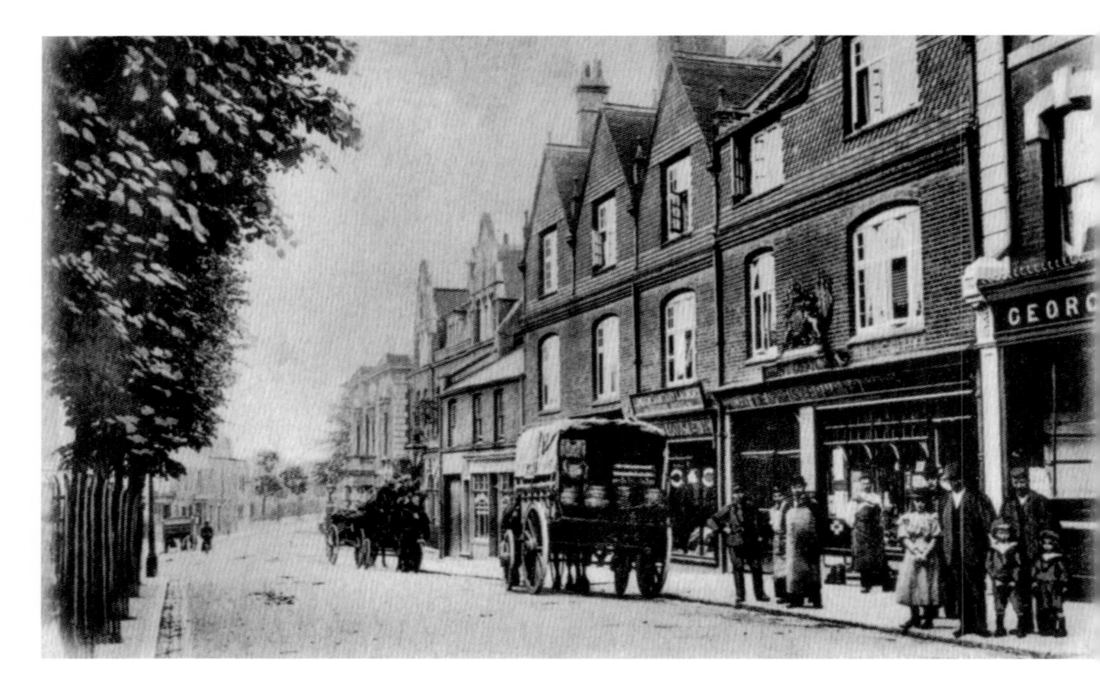

The Village, Old Charlton, 1904

Old Charlton has managed to preserve its historic identity as a village, despite having been subsumed into Greater London as a residential suburb. Its main components are Charlton House, the church and the village street. Beginning at the junction of Charlton Church Lane, the traffic island in front houses a war memorial (erected in 1920) and a drinking fountain and horse trough commemorating King Edward VII's coronation in 1902 (see page 79). Lining the street are compact Victorian shops, which are still recognisable today despite modern frontages.

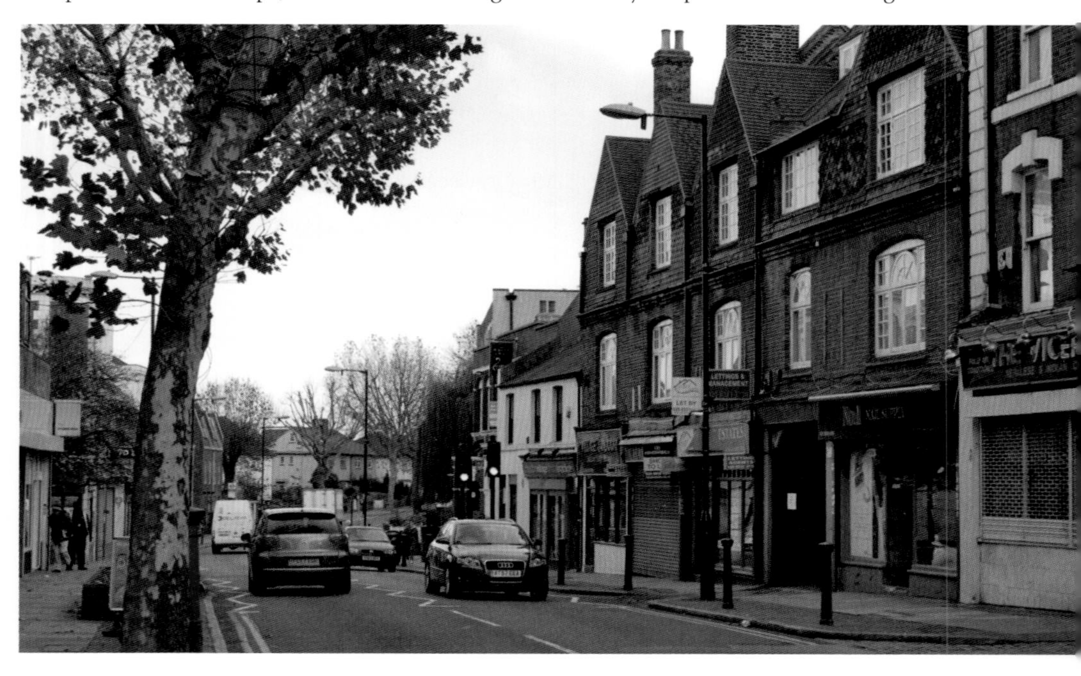

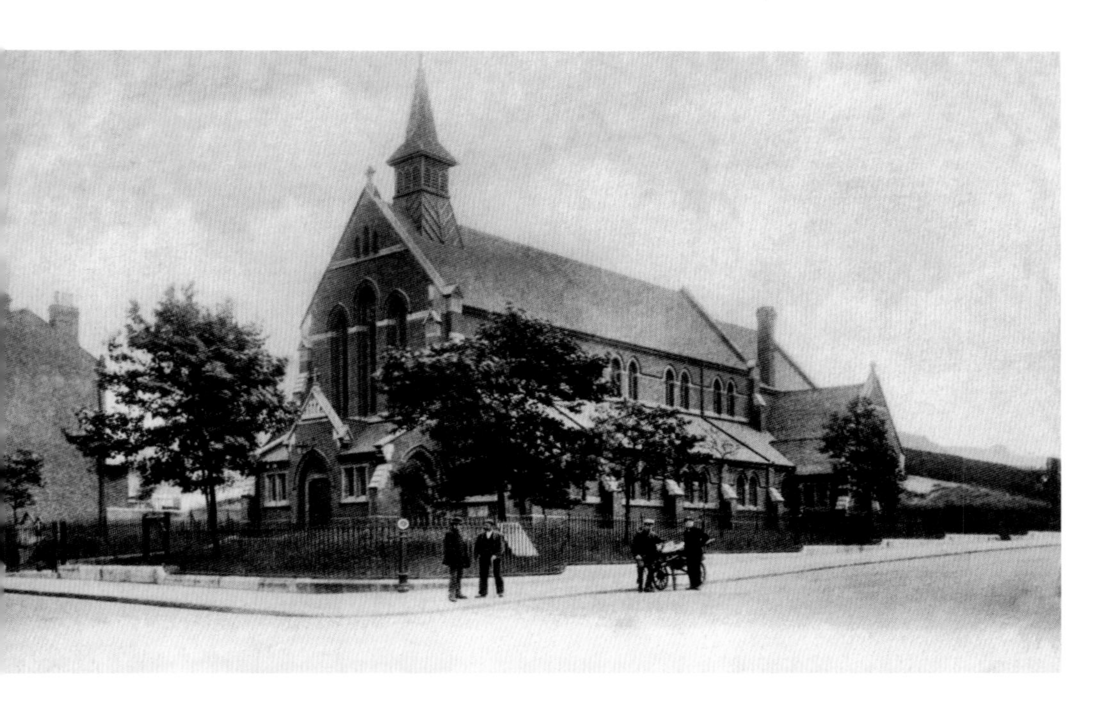

Holy Trinity Church, New Charlton, 1909

Designed by local architect John Rowland, New Charlton Holy Trinity was built in 1894, taking the place of a temporary church dating to 1887. Cruciform in shape, in the early English transitional style, with cusped lancets and a red-brick fabric with stone dressings, it seated 420 congregants. Although listed in 1973, it was declared redundant the following year and demolished in 1975. The parish was merged with Old Charlton St Luke and residential housing now occupies the Holy Trinity site.

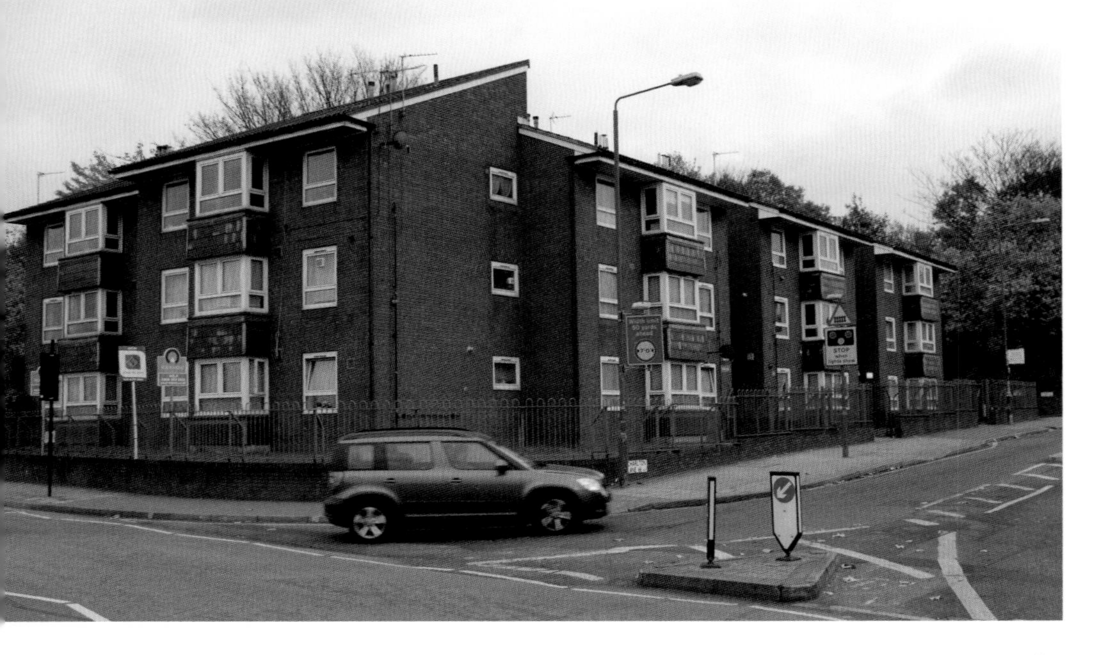

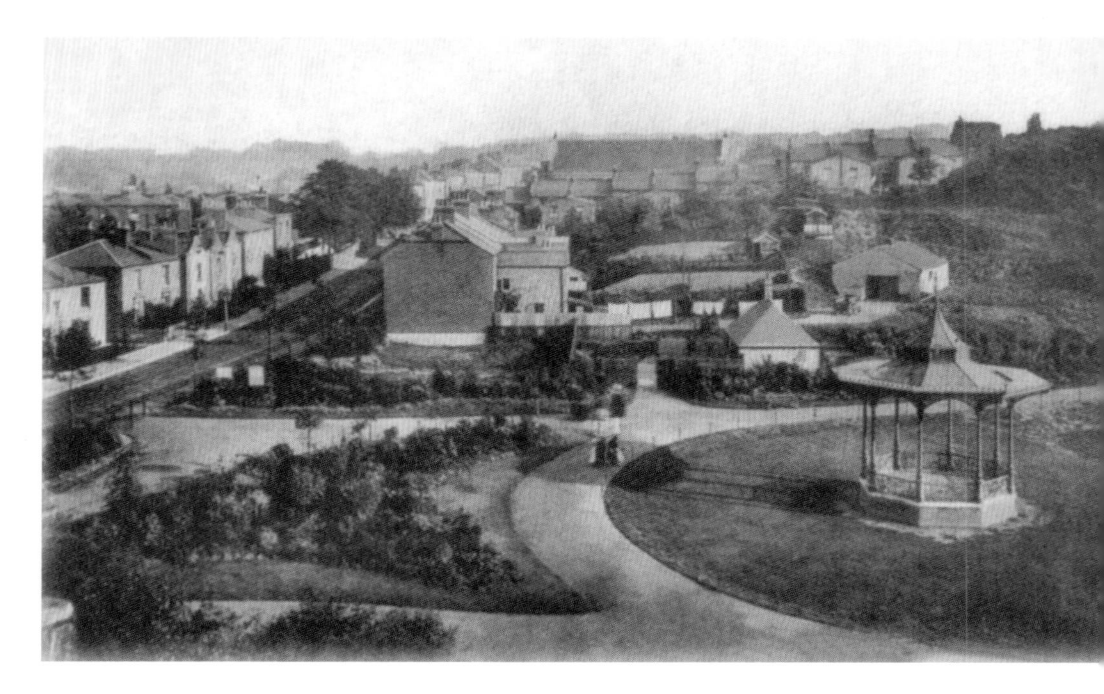

Maryon Park, Charlton, 1905

Together with what is now Maryon Wilson Park, Maryon Park formed part of the Charlton Sandpits, which were presented by the Maryon-Wilson family to London County Council in 1921. A third pit was redeveloped into The Valley, home to Charlton Athletic FC. The Sandpits were themselves part of the 'Hanging Wood', so called as the favoured retreat of highwaymen who roamed Shooter's Hill and Blackheath, and who were hanged there if caught. Maryon Park provided the location for Antonioni's film *Blow-Up* in 1966.

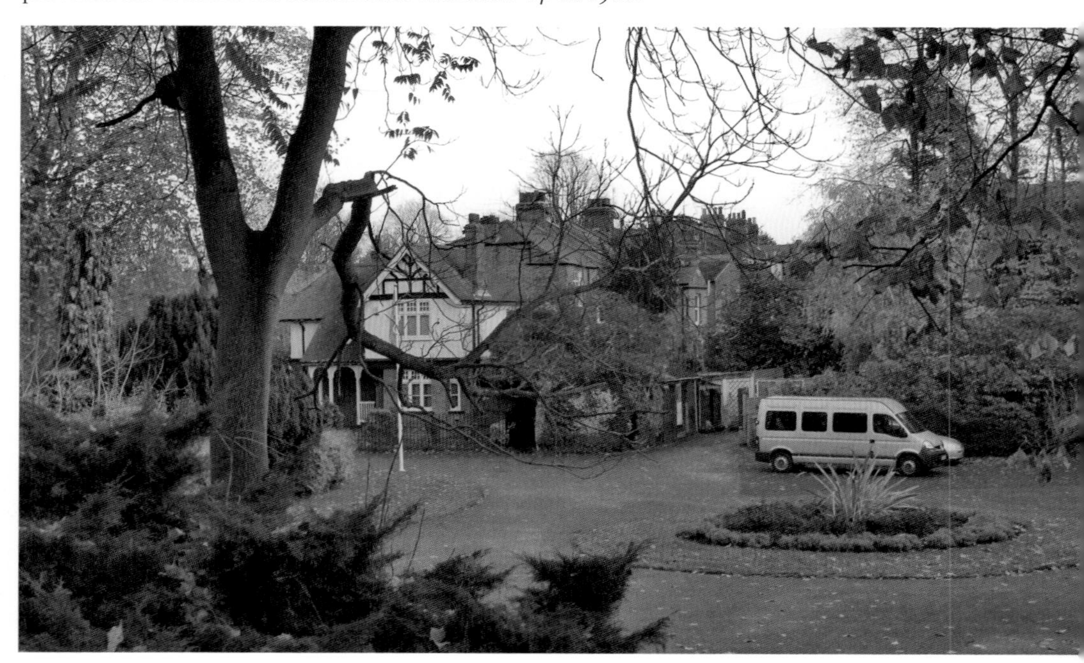

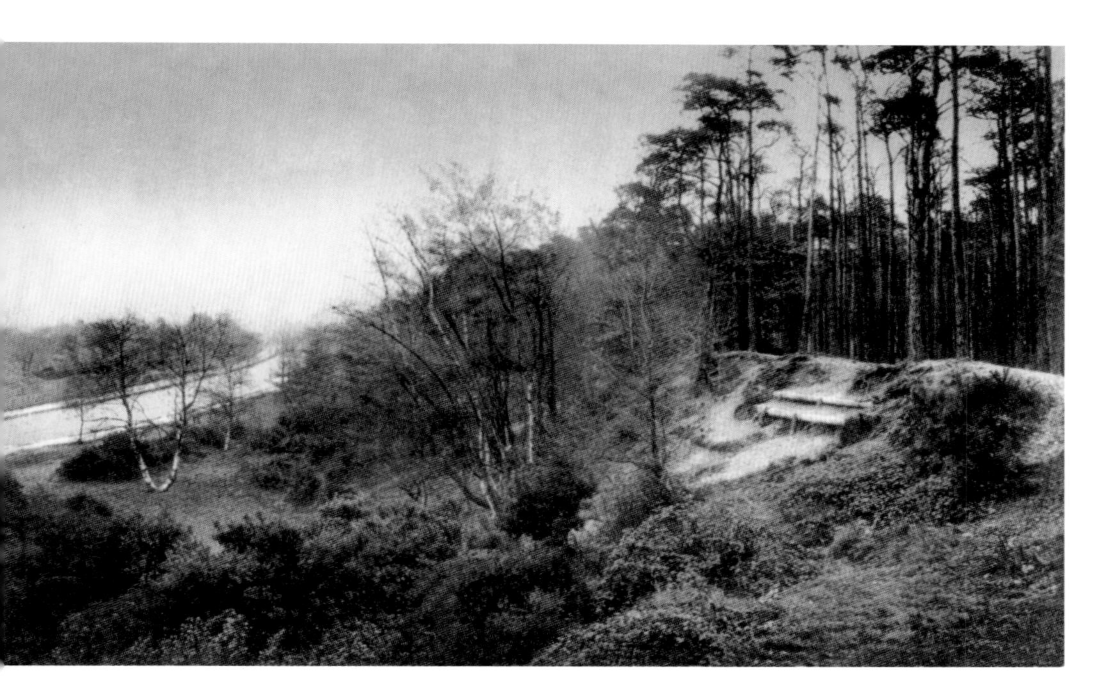

Bostall Woods, Near Woolwich, ***c.*** **1910**
Like Charlton's Hanging Wood, Plumstead's Bostall Woods were notoriously used as a refuge by highwaymen. According to legend, the most infamous brigand of all, Dick Turpin, hid in Bostall Woods while escaping from the King's troops. Dick Turpin's Cave, a hollow at the south end of the woods, celebrates the connection, although its original use is thought to have been as a tunnel leading to a nineteenth-century chalk pit. It has since been bricked up on health and safety grounds.

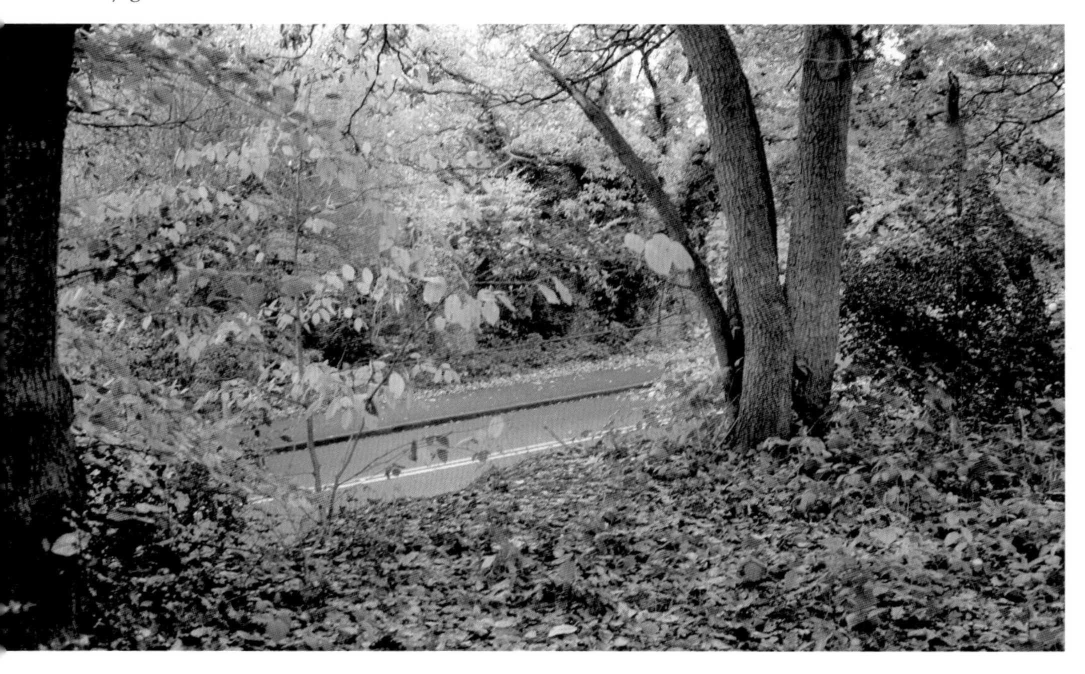

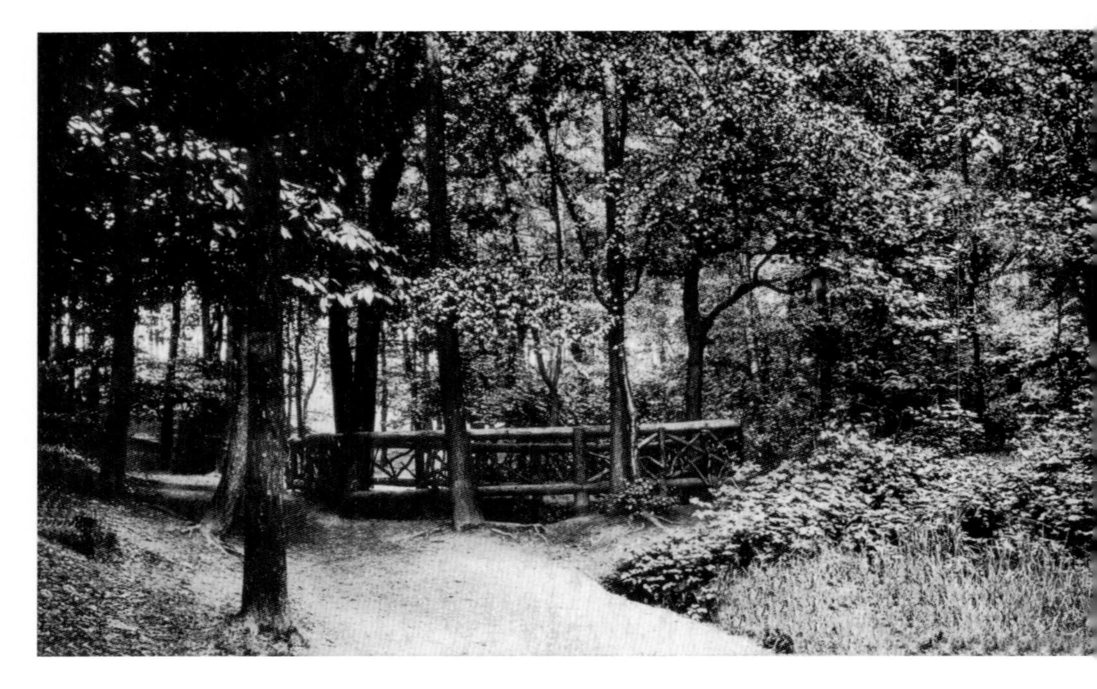

Bostall Woods, *c.* 1915

The meaning of Bostall is unclear, but may denote a road winding up a steep hill, which fits with local topography; in Old English, *boske/buske/busch* appropriately signifies woodland. During the Reformation, King Henry VIII acquired many properties in Plumstead; he granted Bostall Heath and Woods to his clerk and estate manager, Edward Boughton, within whose family it remained until 1656. Bostall Heath and Woods were acquired by the Metropolitan Board of Works in 1878, to safeguard them for open public access.

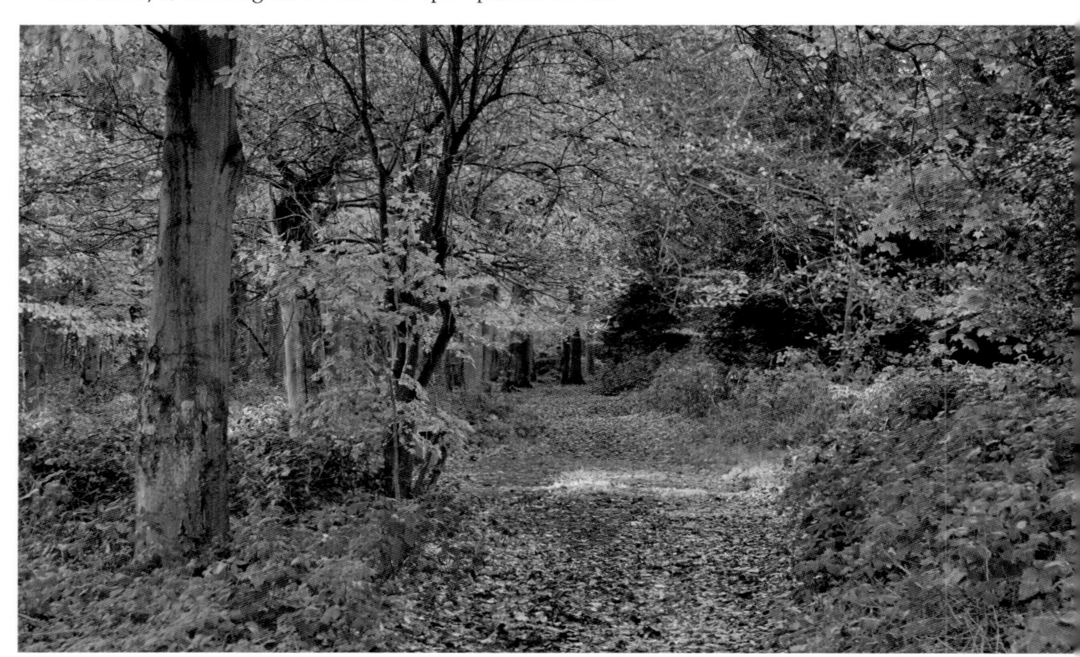

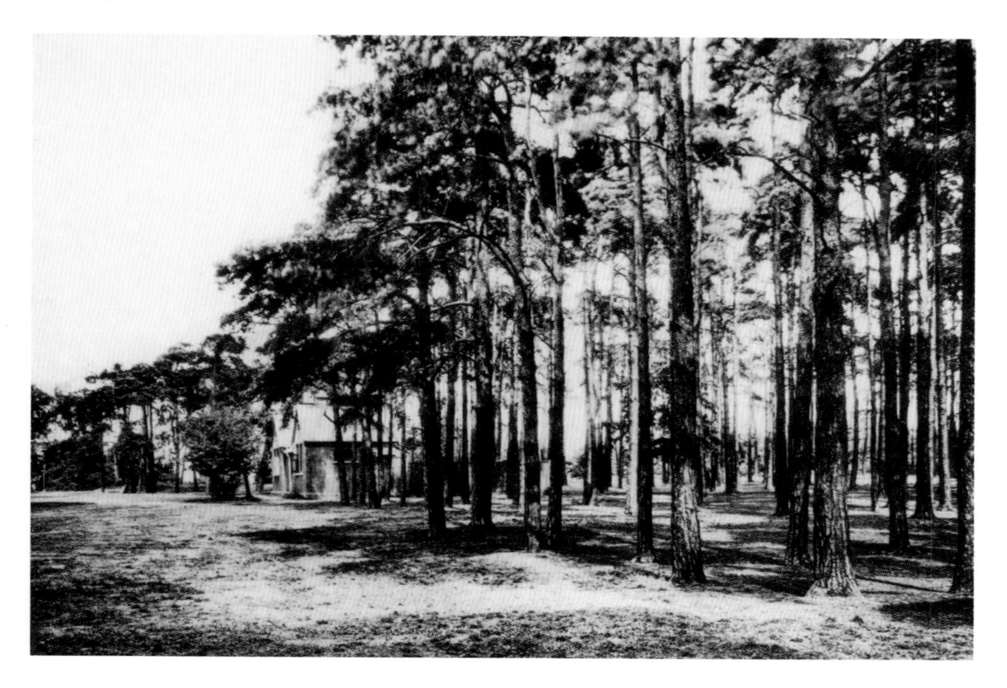

The Pines, Bostall Wood, Plumstead, ***c.*** **1915**
Bostall Woods today contain only a handful of the Scots pine with which they were once so densely planted, this species having been ravaged by beetle by 1939, with survivors lost to the Great Storm of 1987. However, they remain spectacular for an abundance of oak, birch, chestnut, sycamore, blackthorn, holly, rowan and a host of ground flora. As one of the most valuable areas of wildlife in Greater London, it boasts the status of a Site of Metropolitan Importance for Nature Conservation.

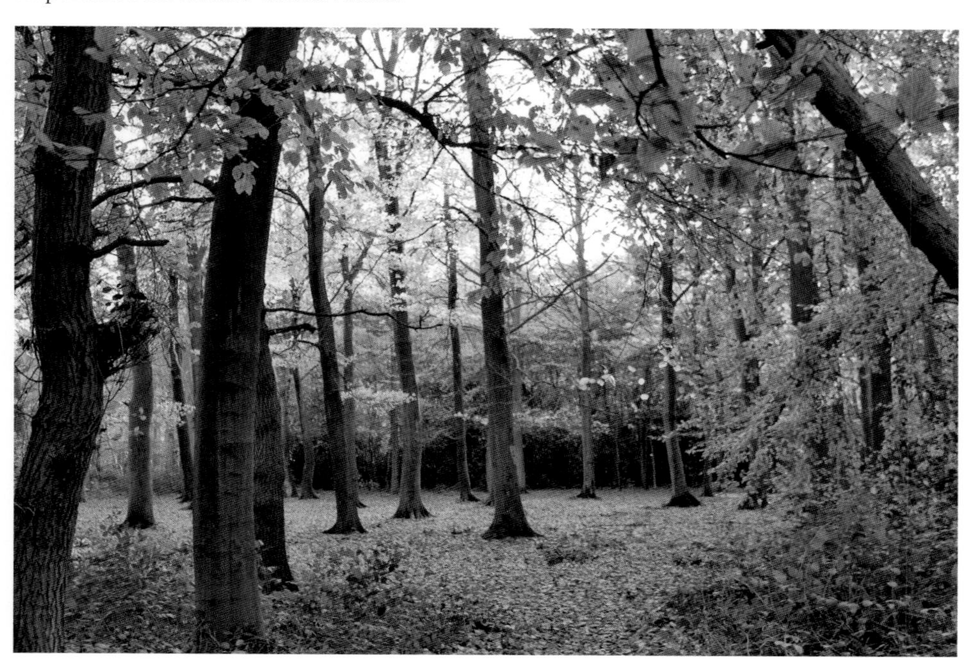

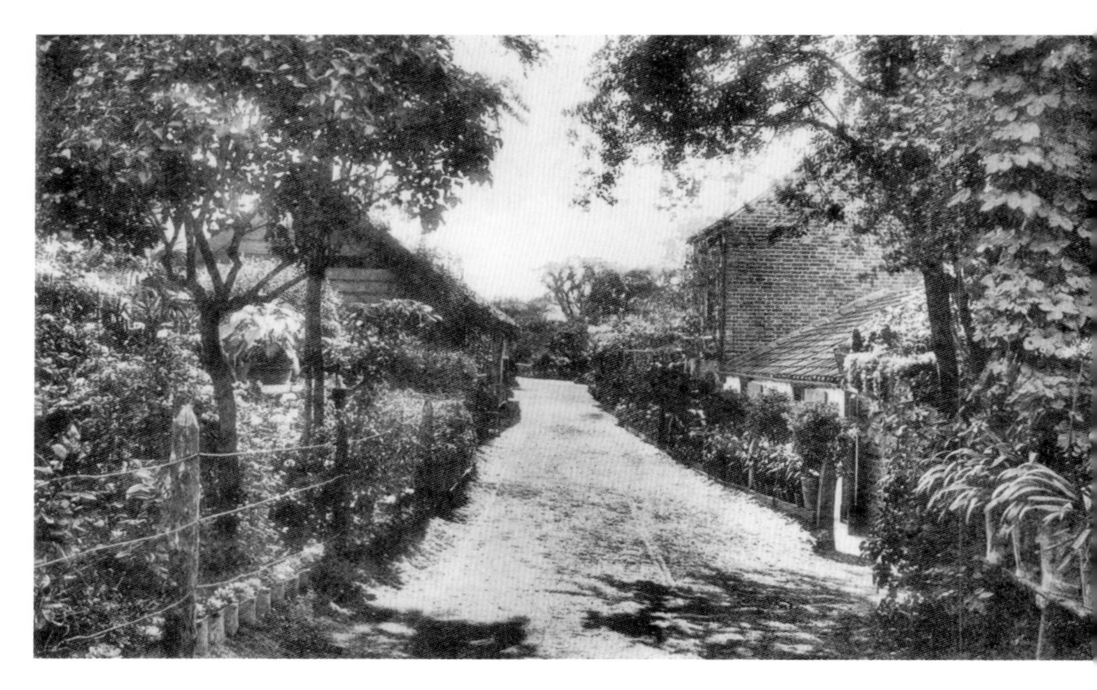

Cook's Orchard, Bostall Wood, Plumstead, *c.* 1915, and Bostall Heath, 2013
The Cook family, Walter, Aida, and their children, owned farmland situated off Old Park Road, Plumstead, near Wickham Lane, Bostall Heath and Woods, during the early decades of the twentieth century. Both they and their home feature in a number of published photographs dating from between 1919 and 1935. Sadly, Cook's Farm and Orchard were destroyed during the Second World War. Today, the view most closely resembling their aspect may be found on nearby Bostall Heath. The heath keeper's cottage was built in 1880.

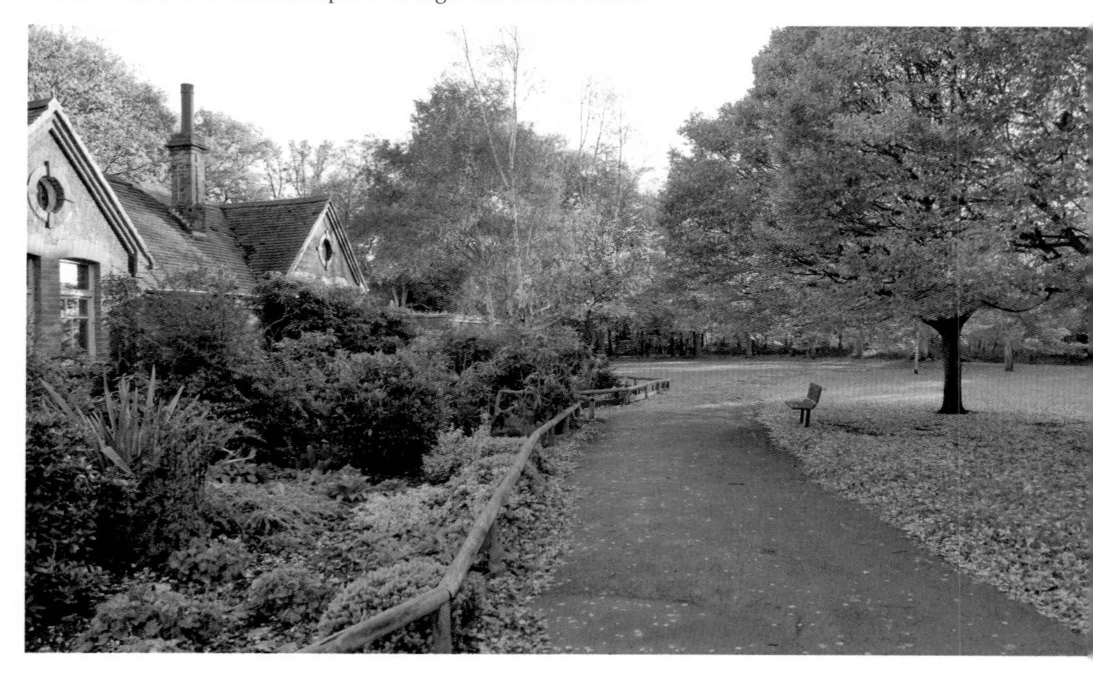

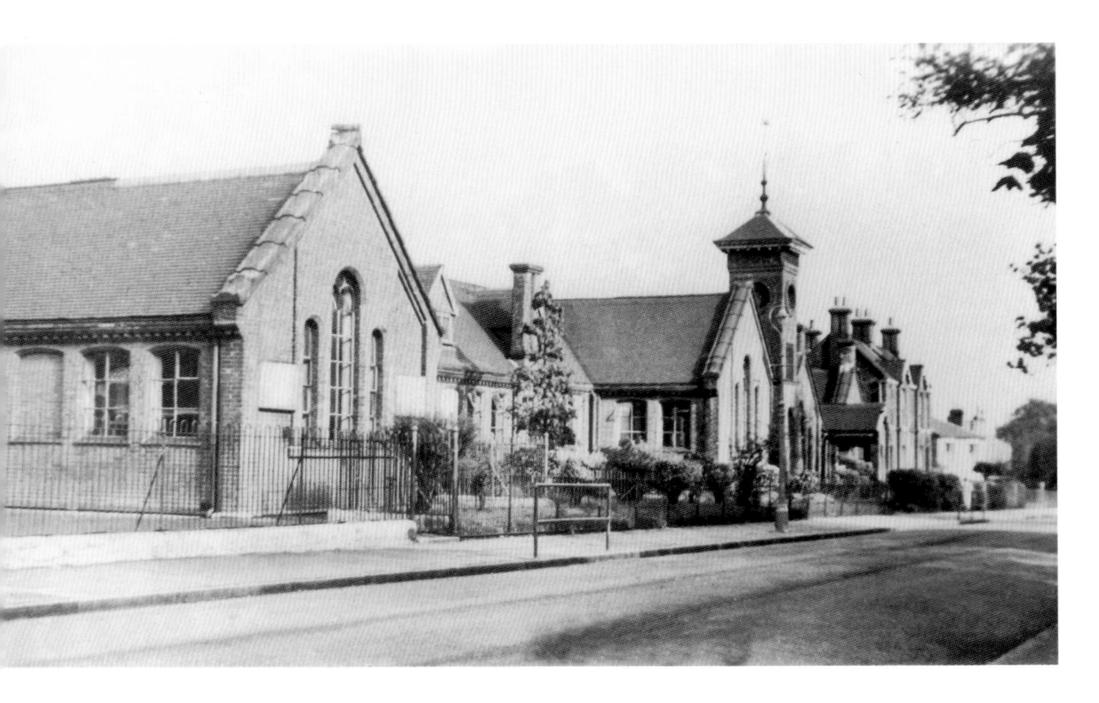

St Margaret's School, Plumstead Common

The original school building dates to 1856, overlapping with the construction of neighbouring St Margaret's church. Further classrooms and outbuildings were added during the 1970s. St Margaret's is a Church of England School, retaining strong ties with the 'replacement church' of St Mark with St Margaret (see page 90), where it celebrates major festivals. With around 300 children on roll, forty places are annually allocated to the reception class, whose students are of mixed ages and of diverse ethnic backgrounds.

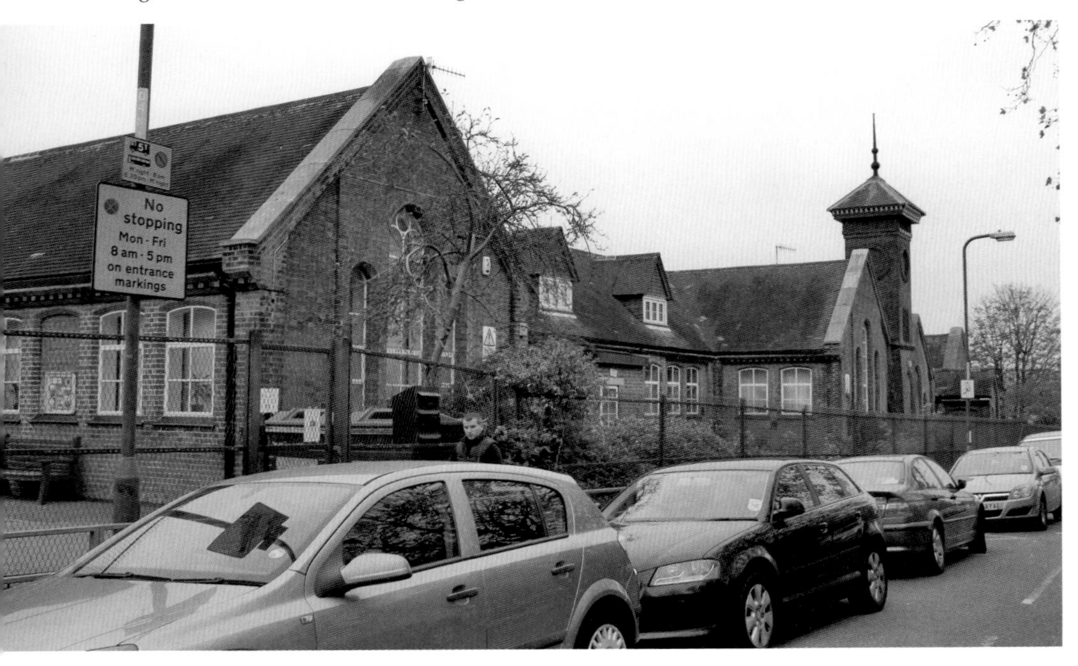

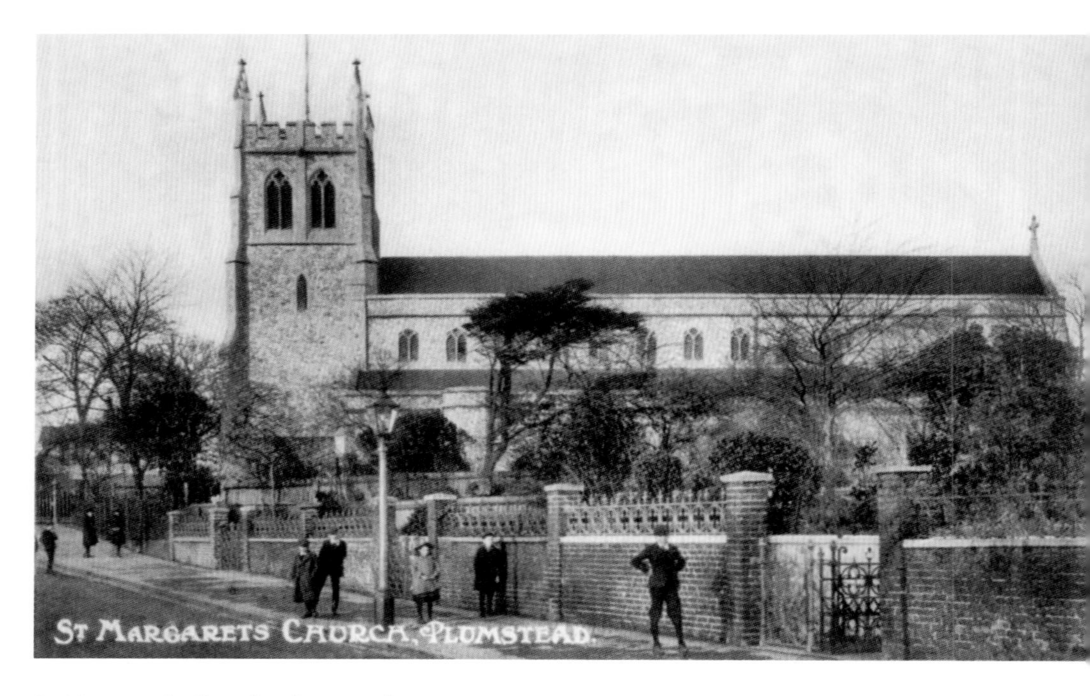

St Margaret's Church, Plumstead

Completed in 1859 to accommodate Plumstead's growing working-class population, St Margaret's filled the role of parish church, which has since been taken over by St Nicholas'. Its fabric fell into disrepair during the 1960s. With the outlay required for renovation deemed unjustifiable, the church was closed in 1968, its parish uniting with that of St Mark. St Margaret's was demolished in 1974, and a residential high-rise now occupies its site. Its principal fittings are housed in the church of St Mark with St Margaret.

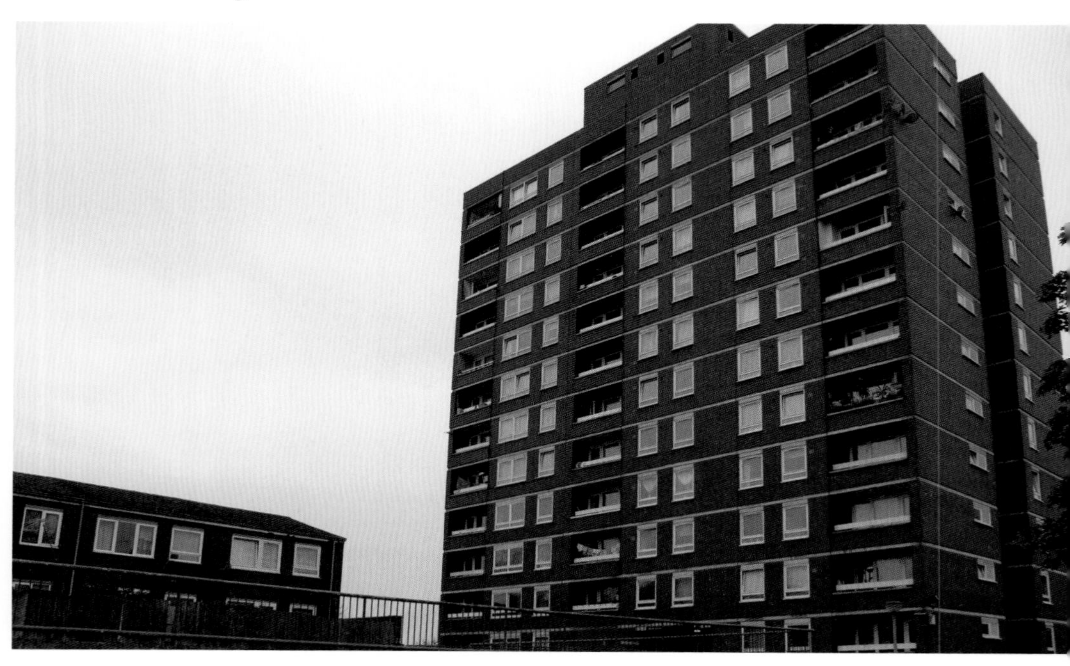

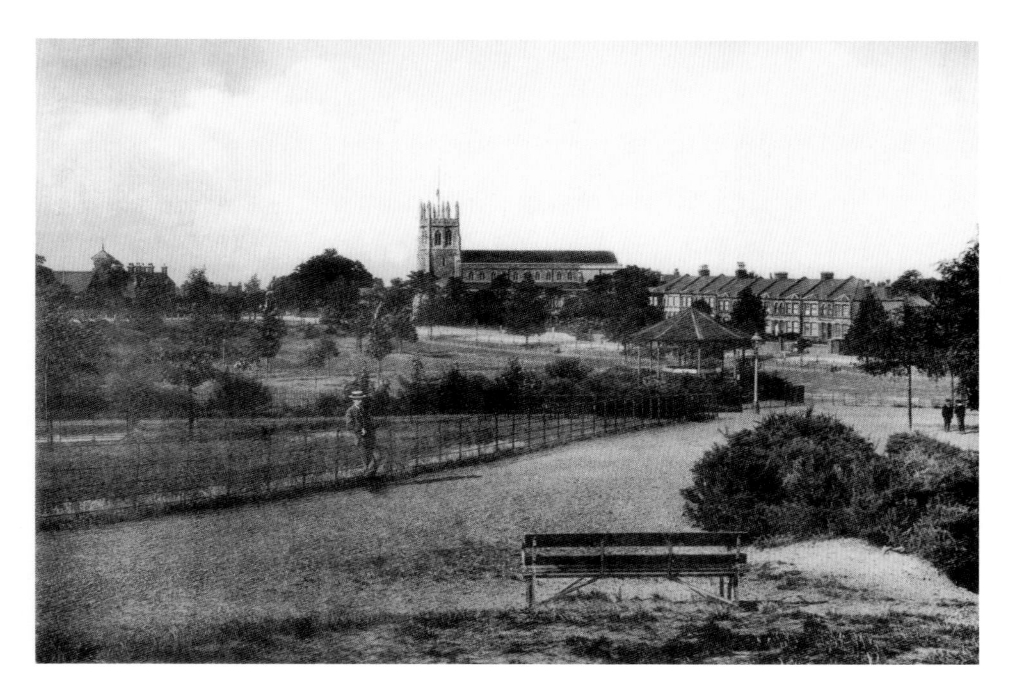

St Margaret's Church and Plumstead Common, ***c.*** **1915**

Between the early 1800s and 1860s, Plumstead's population trebled from 1,000 to 3,000, as it was transformed from a farming to suburban village by the growth of Woolwich Arsenal. Reacting to the acute need for workers' housing, Queen's College, Oxford, as the owners of Plumstead Common, began to sell plots of its land to property speculators, also permitting the Army to use it for exercises with horses and gun carriages. Local residents vehemently protested against the violation of their ancient grazing rights.

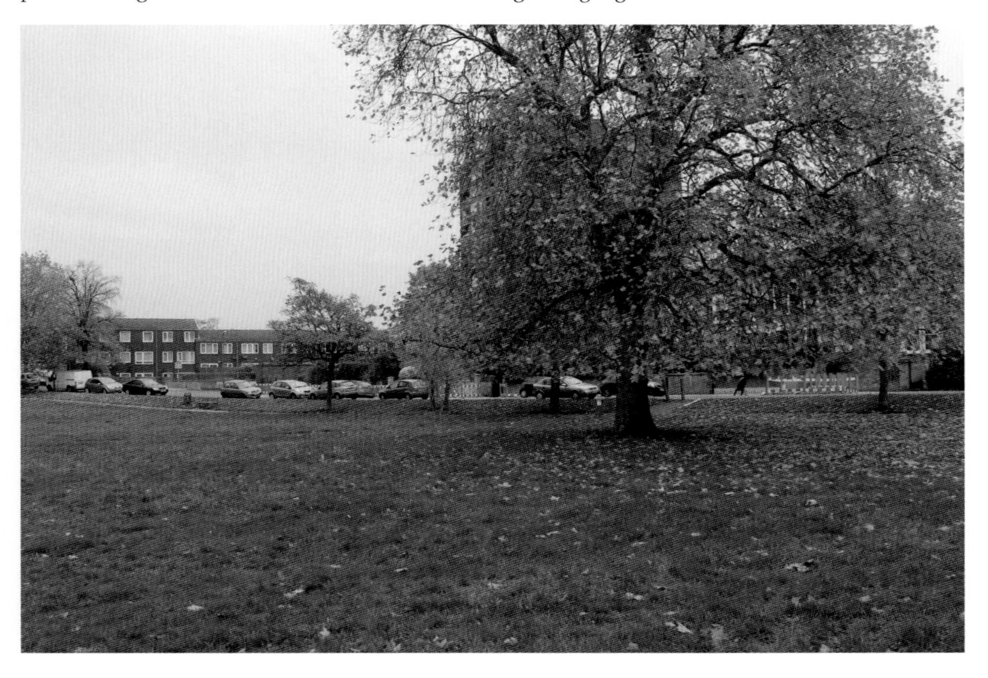

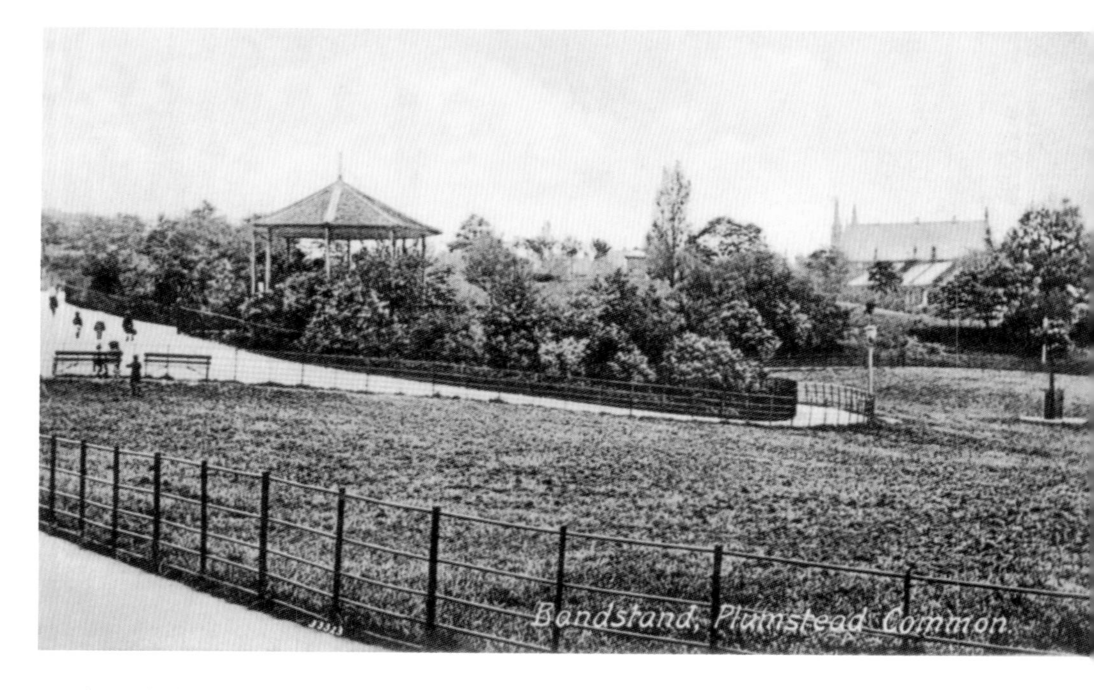

Bandstand, Plumstead Common

John de Morgan of the Commons Protection League led a demonstration on Plumstead Common on 1 July 1876, demolishing illegally erected fences. As they were replaced overnight, rioting broke out the following day. Purchase of the common by the Metropolitan Board of Works was enabled by an Act passed in 1877, with the 1878 Plumstead Common Act safeguarding its 1,000 acres as open public space. Plumstead expanded rapidly with the Arsenal during the 1880s, but the downsizing of the factory after the First World War brought decline.

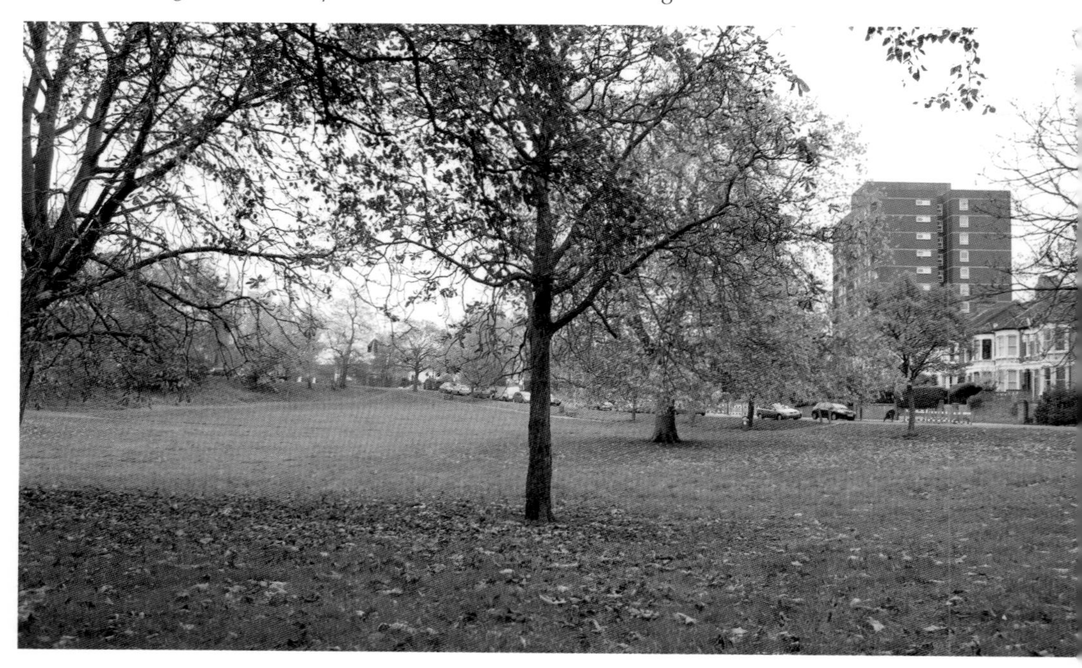

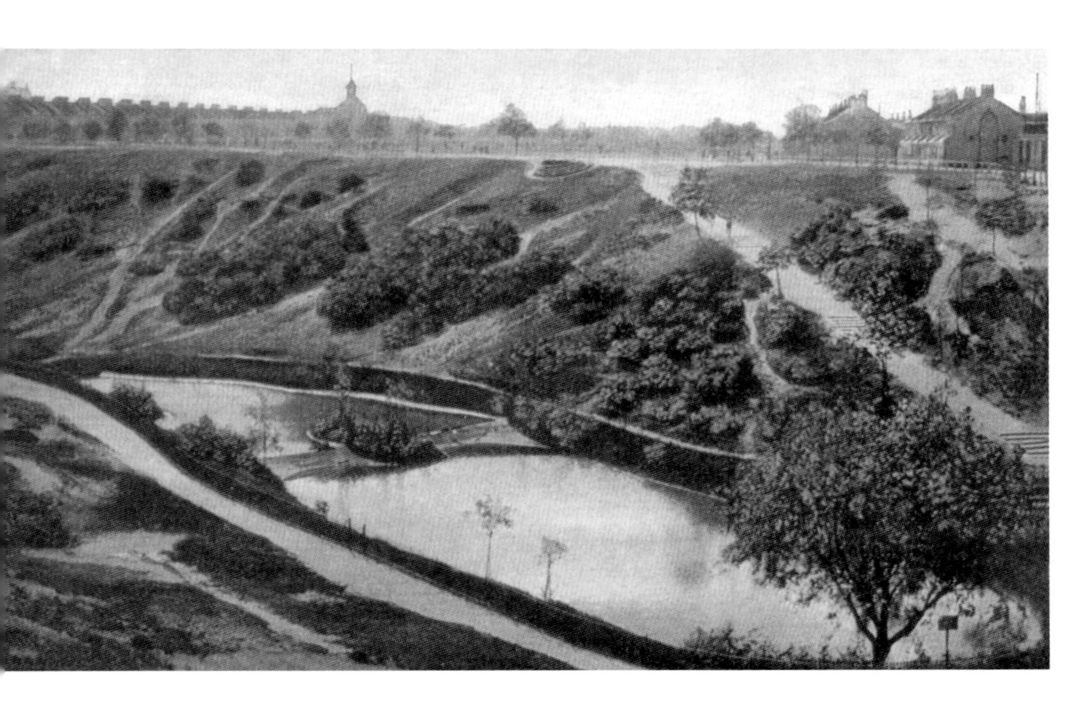

The Slade, Plumstead, 1908

First recorded around 970 as 'Plumstede', and appearing as such in Domesday (1086), Plumstead is clearly a place where plums grew. It has been suggested that occupying Romans planted orchards there. The landscape certainly retained a rural character into the early nineteenth century. 'Slade' denotes a valley or ravine, formed at Plumstead at the end of the last Ice Age, when melting glaciers eroded both soil and rock. The Slade's ponds still exist but are no longer visible from above.

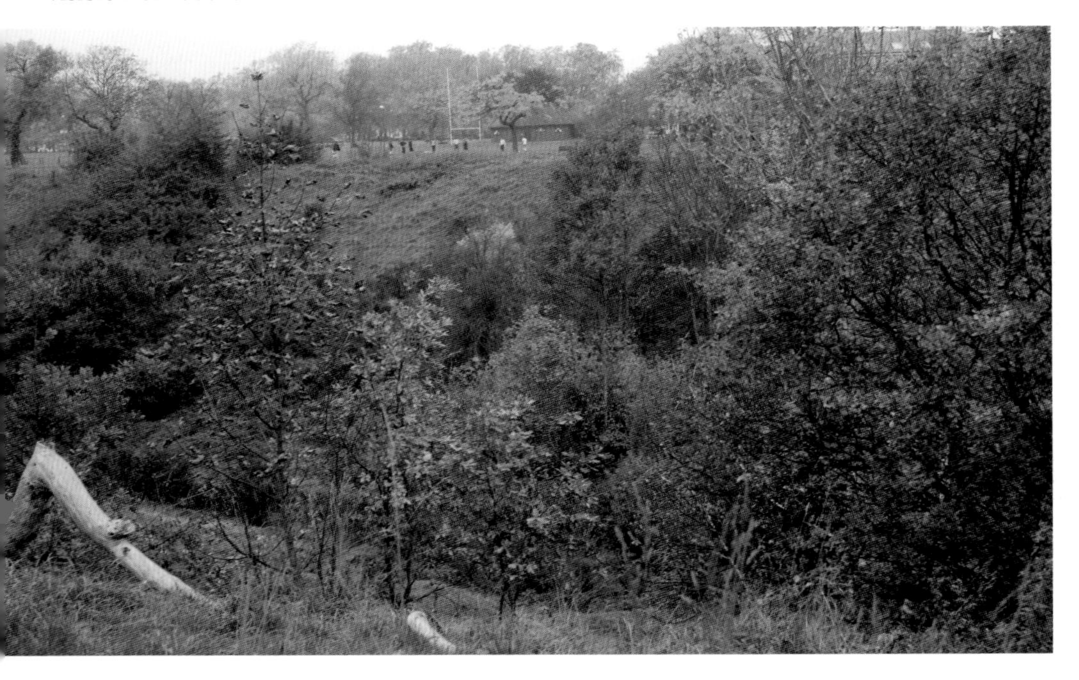

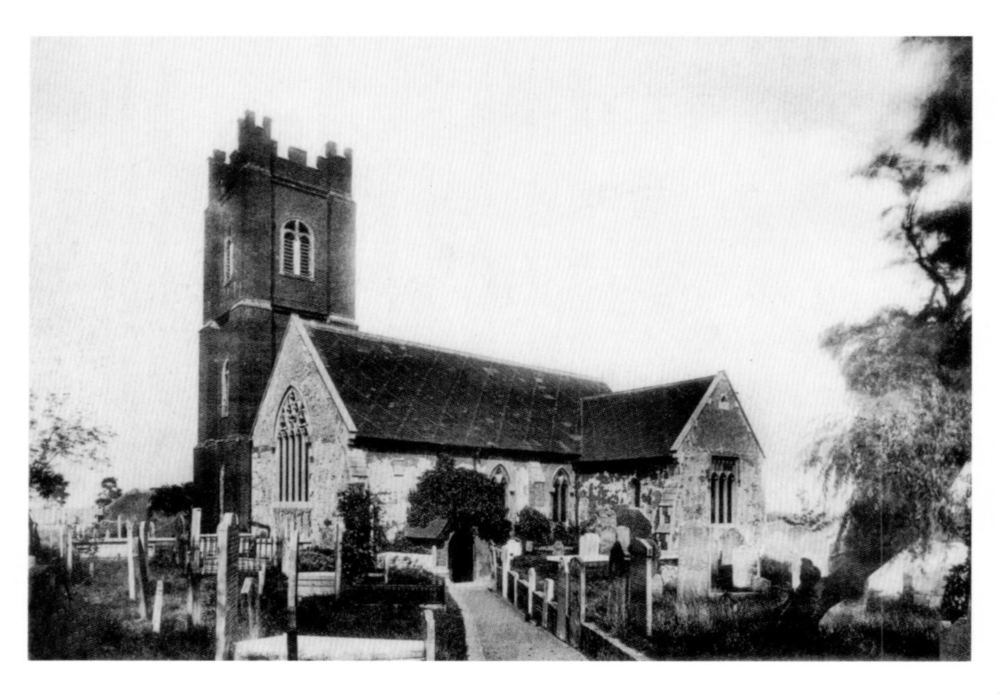

St Nicholas Church, Plumstead, ***c.*** **1915**
With foundations dating from 960, St Nicholas' church was largely built during the twelfth century, its west tower added in the early 1660s and extensive enlargements made in 1907/08. Its fabric suffered severe damage during the Second World War, but was repaired by T. F. Ford & Partners in 1959. St Nicholas' sits on a slope descending to the Thames on the north side of Plumstead high street, adjacent to a small open space on the south side. Parish registers survive from 1654.

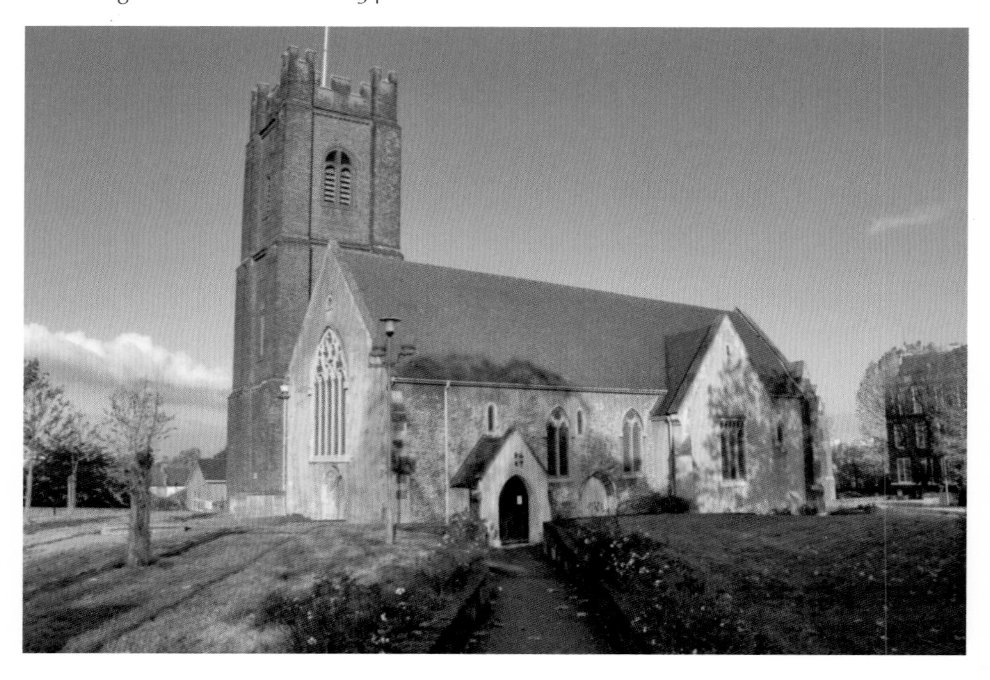

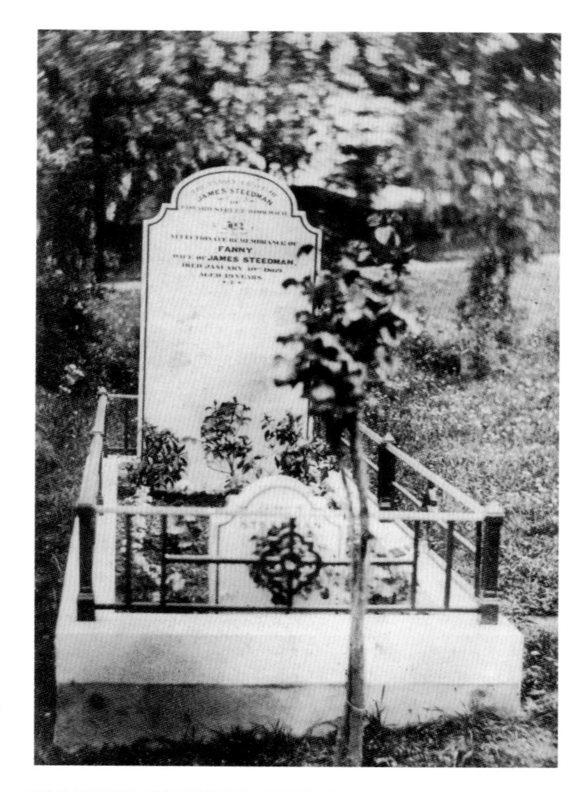

The Family Grave of James Steedman of Edward Street, Woolwich Cemetery, 1869 CDV

'In Affectionate Remembrance of Fanny, Wife of James Steedman, Died January 10th 1869, Aged 49 Years.' Fanny was buried on 15 January. The 1851 census records engineer James Steedman as born in Scotland. He married Fanny Joyce, born in Woolwich, at Deptford St Paul on 14 December 1840. James died on 15 July 1899, aged eighty-seven, and was buried without a memorial on 19 July. Edward Street was rechristened Powis Street (see pages 44–45). Tombstones were cleared during the 1960s to facilitate grounds maintenance.

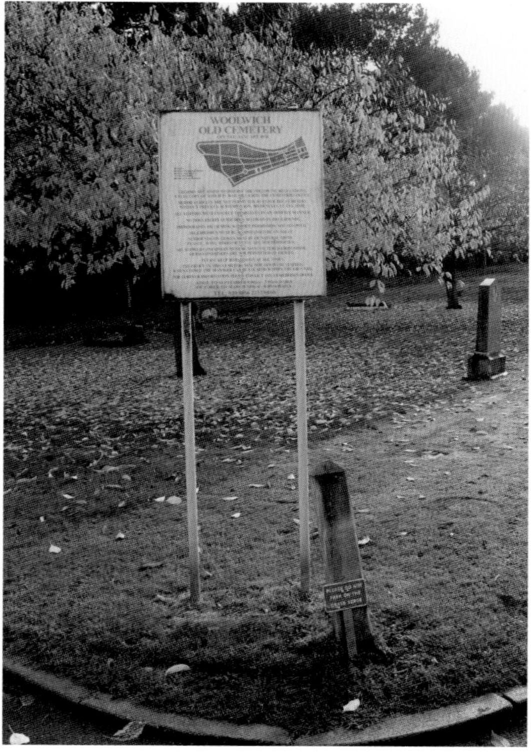

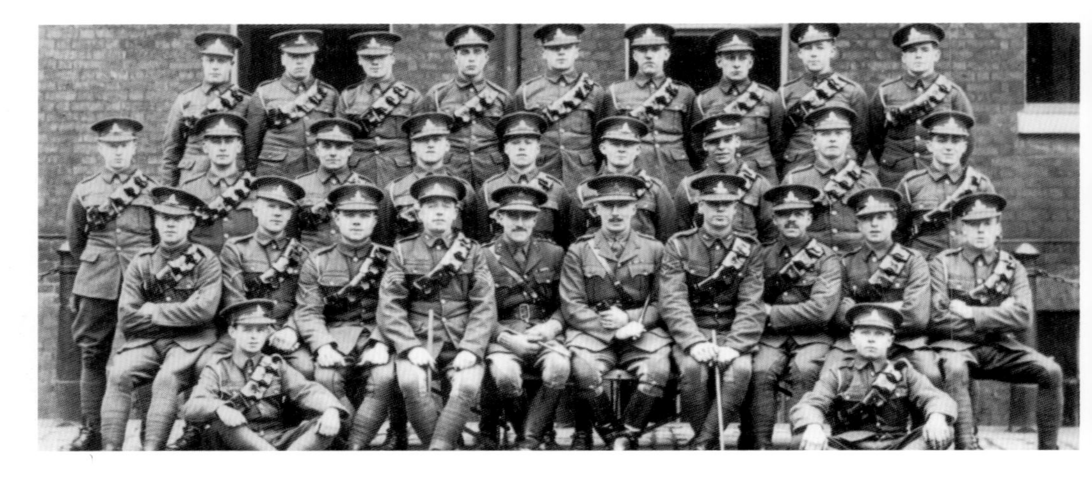

The 'U' Squad, Royal Artillery, Woolwich, 1925/26
From left to right, back row: Driver Crouch, Dvr Found, Dvr Richardson, Dvr Wayne, Dvr Watson, Dvr Brown, Dvr Warren, Dvr Jones, Dvr Francond. Middle row: Dvr Keane, Dvr Forde, Dvr Blair, Dvr McGarry, Dvr Cooper, Dvr Wilson, Dvr Ash, Dvr Bushill, Dvr Hare. Front row: Dvr Kelly, Lance Bombardier Powell, L/Bdr Kennedy, Sergeant Marr, Lieutenant Freeberker, Lt McClowo, Bdr Wright, L/Bdr –?–, Dvr T. H. Brown, Dvr Butts. Left front: Ingerson; Right front: Mears.

Acknowledgements

My warmest thanks go to Professor Antonette diPaolo Healey, Editor of *The Dictionary of Old English*, for confirming the etymology of 'Wull-wic'; to Maj. Les Carr, Stn Staff Officer at CVHQ RA & HQ Woolwich Station, who arranged access for photography on the Parade Ground of the Royal Artillery Baracks, and to the MGS CSO there who provided escort; to Mr Nick Raynsford, MP for Woolwich, who contributed his chapter on Will Crooks as published in *Men Who Made Labour* (Alan Haworth and Dianne Hayter, eds.; Routledge, 2006), in addition to a contemporary photograph; to Steve Scrivener and Dean Humphries of Woolwich Town Hall, who permitted interior photography of the council chamber and shared their extensive knowledge of the building; to Adrian Green, creative director of The Woolwich Grand Theatre, and Scott Cowling of the Woolwich Spartans, who respectively contributed the modern photographs that made it possible to represent both entertainers and footballers in action; and to the curator at Woolwich Cemetery for confirming the clearance of the Steedman Family tombstone and its cause.

I am, as ever, indebted to two websites in particular, which provide direct access to multiple sources for historical research: the Internet Archive, a digital Library of out-of-copyright materials, and the University of London's British History Online. I have also benefitted from the Draft Surveys of London featuring Woolwich drawn up by English Heritage and uploaded to the internet in 2012. My thanks to the numerous bookshops and auction sellers with whom I have enjoyed trading over the past year while searching for vintage photographs and postcards, and most of all to my family and friends for their support and patience throughout, especially during the reclusive phase of collating the collected images and research. Spending the last month in Woolwich has been a joy, one which fortunately will not end with the publication of this book, thanks to being a long-term neighbour in Charlton-next-Woolwich.